The Design of Urban Manufacturing

American cities are rediscovering the economic and social value of urban manufacturing. However, urban manufacturing is often invisible and poorly understood in terms of urban design, architecture, and policy. *The Design of Urban Manufacturing* brings a multidisciplinary approach to a new complex reality that urban manufacturing now sits squarely at the intersection of research, education, and neighborhood revitalization. Using cases studies from across North America and beyond, this book presents innovative approaches not only to the design of districts and buildings, but to the design of policy as well: the special roles that governments, local development corporations, and not-for-profit organizations all have to play in supporting manufacturing.

This book presents current models for working neighborhoods where factories enable fine-grained, mixed-use communities and face-to-face contact while creatively solving the very real problems of goods movement and functional buildings. Design guidelines and policy recommendations are calibrated to different types of production districts.

The Design of Urban Manufacturing is the essential resource for policy makers, designers, and students in urban design, planning, and urban and economic development.

Robert N. Lane is Principal of Plan & Process LLC and is Senior Fellow for Urban Design at Regional Plan Association, where he directs the Regional Design Program, devoted to reforming the metropolitan landscape through research and place-based planning and design interventions. Industrial district design and redevelopment has been a particular area of focus for research, publications, exhibitions, and lecturing. Robert N. Lane was a Loeb Fellow at the Harvard Graduate School of Design during the 2008–2009 academic year; he was also a 2013 Fellow at the Design Trust for Public Space for the Making Midtown initiative.

Nina Rappaport is an architectural historian, curator, and educator. She focuses on industrial urbanism, infrastructure, and the role of the factory worker. She is the author of *Vertical Urban Factory* (2015) which includes an exhibition and a think tank of the same name. She is co-editor of *Ezra Stoller: Photographer* (2012) and author of *Support and Resist: Structural Engineers and Design Innovation* (2007). She is Publications Director at the Yale School of Architecture and was a Fellow of the Design Trust for Public Space in 2006. She was a visiting professor at Politecnico di Torino and Sapienza University da Roma. She is a lecturer at the Michael Graves College of Public Architecture at Kean university and she has taught in many New York City area architecture programs. She writes for numerous journals and lectures internationally.

The Design of Urban Manufacturing

Edited by Robert N. Lane and Nina Rappaport

Routledge
Taylor & Francis Group

NEW YORK AND LONDON

First published 2020
by Routledge
52 Vanderbilt Avenue, New York, NY 10017

and by Routledge
2 Park Square, Milton Park, Abingdon, Oxon, OX14 4RN

Routledge is an imprint of the Taylor & Francis Group, an informa business

© 2020 Taylor & Francis

The right of Robert N. Lane and Nina Rappaport to be identified as the authors of the editorial material, and of the authors for their individual chapters, has been asserted in accordance with sections 77 and 78 of the Copyright, Designs and Patents Act 1988.

Library of Congress Cataloging-in-Publication Data
A catalog record has been requested for this book.

ISBN: 978-1-138-59371-8 (hbk)
ISBN: 978-1-138-59372-5 (pbk)
ISBN: 978-0-429-48928-0 (ebk)

Typeset in Sabon

Swales & Willis, Exeter, Devon, UK

Contents

Image Credits

Part II: The Design of Factories: The Architecture of the Places of Production

Acknowledgments

This book arose from several conversations between three colleagues who over the years, in different partnership configurations, have focused on issues related to urban manufacturing—Robert Lane, Nina Rappaport, and Colin Cathcart. The editors want to acknowledge the essential role played by Colin Cathcart in conceptualizing the structure and content of this book. It would never have happened without his essential insights.

At various stages in the development of this book, we received valuable advice from several readers and editors, key among them Alex Marshall and Ann Heid who provided valuable critique as well as Ann Holcomb who made careful edits. The insight of Christopher Hall, Jamie Chan, and Nilus Klingel is also greatly appreciated.

Numerous people contributed in different ways to the extensive documentation for the Atlas, including mapping, collecting and reviewing documents, taking site photos and conducting or sitting for interviews. A comprehensive list appears with the Atlas but noted here are the special contributions of Anna Ousler, Ellis Calvin, Minkyung Song and Ben Oldenberg.

Heavily illustrated collected volumes are complex endeavors. The book would never have been completed without the support of editorial assistant Jessica Morris who not only created a coherent package from all of the diverse materials, but offered valuable insights into the content. We would also like to thank those whose work is featured in the numerous project descriptions.

Finally, and most importantly, the editors would like to acknowledge the 12 authors of the articles in this collection who donated their invaluable time and intelligence to a complex initiative and their shared belief in the reality and potential for urban manufacturing today.

At our publisher, Routledge, we would like to thank the editors and their continued support—Krystal LaDuc Racaniello, Alexis O'Brien, Kathryn Schell, Sean Speers, and Natalie Thompson.

Contributors

Stefan Al is an associate professor in city planning at the University of Pennsylvania. He was part of the design team for the 2,000-feet tall Canton Tower, which briefly held the title of the world's tallest tower. He served as an advisor to the Hong Kong government, the Chinese government, and the United Nations High-Level Political Forum on Sustainable Development. His book on Chinese informal settlements, *Villages in the City*, was selected as one of the best books on informal urbanism by *Architectural Record* and he recently published a book on Las Vegas, *The Strip*.

Jonathan Bach is an associate professor of Global Studies at The New School in New York. He is the co-editor of *Learning from Shenzhen: China's Post-Mao Experiment from Special Zone to Model City* (2017) and author, most recently, of *What Remains: Everyday Encounters with the Socialist Past in Germany* (2017).

Frank Barkow has held teaching posts at, among others, the Architectural Association in London, Cornell University, Harvard University, and the Royal College of Art in London. Since 2016 he has been a visiting professor at the Princeton University School of Architecture. In 1993 Regine Leibinger and Frank Barkow founded Barkow Leibinger, an American/German architectural practice based in Berlin and New York. Recently completed buildings include the Smart Factory in Chicago, the Fellows Pavilion for the American Academy in Berlin, the HAWE Factory Kaufbeuren, and the Tour Total office high-rise in Berlin.

Jenifer Becker is a sustainability and economic development strategist with over 20 years of experience conducting research, developing public policy and implementing programs to support healthy and equitable communities. Becker is a long-time advocate for sustainable urban manufacturing, authoring numerous studies on the opportunities and challenges facing small manufacturers in New York City.

Beth Bingham is a visiting assistant professor at Pratt Institute. She is an urban planner and historic preservation consultant focusing on sustainability and community-based initiatives. She has worked for Partnerships for Parks, New Yorkers for Parks, and the Pratt Center for Community Development. She is a member of the Gowanus Canal Community Advisory Group, and on the board of the Historic Districts Council. She holds an MS in city and regional planning and a Certificate in Historic Preservation from Pratt Institute's Graduate Center for Planning and the Environment, and is currently working towards a PhD in environmental psychology at the CUNY Graduate Center.

Alison Conway is an associate professor in the Department of Civil Engineering at the City College of New York and the associate director for Education at the Region 2 University Transportation Research Center (UTRC). She is also a member of the research team for METROFreight, a Volvo Research and Education Foundations Center of Excellence in Urban Freight. Her recent research focus has been in the areas of sustainable urban logistics and interactions between freight, passenger and non-motorized modes in livable communities. Conway holds PhD and master's degrees in civil engineering from the University of Texas at Austin and a bachelor's of civil engineering from the University of Delaware.

Janne Corneil is a planning and urban design consultant with over 20 years' experience developing campus master plans, research parks, innovation districts, and downtown revitalization plans. Her broad range of experience working with public, institutional, community, and private clients strengthens her ability to navigate the cultural differences between universities, cities, and private stakeholders. Janne's practice focuses on working with anchor institutions and their host cities to develop planning strategies that align research, innovation, and economic development goals in a shared vision for urban revitalization and city district building. Janne speaks frequently and teaches on the topics of the changing roles of institutions in cities and the potential of innovation districts as a new model of urban economic development.

Naomi Darling is Five College assistant professor of sustainable architecture at Mt. Holyoke College and the University of Massachusetts, Amherst and principal of Naomi Darling Architecture. Naomi's teaching, practice, and research examine the intersections of climate, culture, and materiality as vital components of sustainability for the built environment.

Alexander D' Hooghe is a senior founding partner at ORG. D'Hooghe is also a professor in architecture and urbanism at MIT. He directed the Center for Advanced Urbanism at MIT, and has published internationally, including *The Liberal Monument* (2010).

Giovanna Fossa is professor of urban design and planning at the School of Civil and Environmental Engineering, Department of Architecture and Urban Studies, Politecnico di Milano. She has international experience and scholarship on issues of urban regeneration and regional planning, landscape planning, tourism, and place branding, with special focus on metropolitan regions. One of her many publications includes, *Transforming the Places of Production,* (co-author with R. Lane, R. Pirani, and D. Palazzo), 2002; and *An Atlas for Milan,* 2006.

Adam Friedman is the executive director of the Pratt Center for Community Development. He was the founding executive director of the New York Industrial Retention Network (NYIRN) in 1997, where he led efforts to strengthen the city's manufacturing sector and promote sustainable development. Earlier Friedman served as executive director of the Garment Industry Development Corporation and director of economic development for Borough Presidents David Dinkins and Ruth Messinger. He has also taught urban planning courses at Pratt Institute and Columbia University. He is Chairman of the Urban Manufacturing Alliance, a Board Member of the Brooklyn Navy Yard Development Corporation, and one of New York City's leading advocates in support of manufacturing and the employment opportunities it brings.

Sagi Golan is the senior lead urban designer for Brooklyn at the NYC Department of City Planning where he ensures a high level of design excellence in projects across the Borough of Brooklyn. Sagi's work strives to achieve the best design outcome through collaboration across disciplines and constituents for projects ranging from large scale developments, neighborhood plans and waterfront developments. He also teaches at the urban design graduate program at Columbia University, GSAPP. Sagi holds a B.Arch from Tel Aviv University and an MS in Architecture and Urban Design from Columbia University. He is the recipient of the GSAPP award for excellence, the Lucille Smyser Lowenfish Memorial Prize and the 2015 AIANY Urban Design Merit Award.

Andrew Kimball joined Industry City in August 2013 as CEO directing the transformation of the long-underutilized six-million square foot industrial facility in Sunset Park, Brooklyn. In March 2015, Industry City launched a 12-year, $1B redevelopment that will create 20,000 jobs through a unique mixed-use blend of innovation economy and modern manufacturing, retail, and academic uses. Since his arrival, Industry City has invested over $400 million in infrastructure and place-making initiatives and tripled the number of jobs to over 8,000 – adding 100 new jobs a month since 2013 – with a tenant base ranging from start-ups to Fortune 500 companies. From 2005 to 2013, Mr. Kimball served as President and CEO of the Brooklyn Navy Yard Development Corporation (BNYDC) overseeing the transformation of this 300-acre former Naval ship-building facility. Under Mr. Kimball's leadership, the Navy Yard became a national model of the creation of innovation economy jobs and sustainability. He holds a BA from Hamilton College and is a graduate of the Coro Public Affairs Fellowship program.

Adam Lubinsky is a managing principal at WXY where he has led a number of strategic planning and projects, including the Brooklyn Tech Triangle Strategic Plan and the Brooklyn Navy Yard Master Plan. Adam received his BA from Brown University and has a Master's in Architecture from Columbia University and a PhD in Planning and Urban Design from University College London.

Kobi Ruthenberg is an associate director in urbanism and manager of ORG NY. Ruthenberg specializes in complex urban design and regional planning projects which involve multiple scales of analysis and implementation.

Jefferey Shumaker has been working at the intersection of architecture and city planning for more than 20 years, in both the public and private sectors. In addition to working for many of the world's top architecture and planning firms, he served as the Chief Urban Designer for the City of New York. Jeffrey is currently the Director of Urban Planning at BIG, an international architecture and planning firm with offices in Copenhagen, Brooklyn, London and Barcelona.

John Shapiro is a professor in the Graduate Center for Planning and Development at Pratt Institute, Brooklyn, following several terms as the GCPE's chair. Previously, he was a partner in the planning consultancy of Phillips Preiss Shapiro Associates. He and his work have won over twenty awards, including the national American Planning Association's first Presidential Award.

Paul van der Grient is Studio Director of WXY, leading architectural and urban design projects. He recently managed the Brooklyn Navy Yard Master Plan, a comprehensive physical and strategic plan for the 300-acre, mission-driven industrial campus, and is currently oversee-ing the construction of West Thames Pedestrian Bridge which will connect the World Trade Center and Battery Park City.

Sarah Williams is an associate professor of technology and urban planning at Massachusetts Institute of Technology. She also is director of the Civic Data Design Lab at MIT's School of Architecture and Planning. The Civic Data Design Lab works with data, maps, and mobile technologies to develop interactive design and communication strategies that expose urban policy issues to broader audiences. She was a fellow of the Design Trust for Public Space working on the Made in Midtown Project. Previously she was co-director of the Spatial Information Design Lab at Columbia University Graduate School of Planning and Preser-vation.

Laura Wolf-Powers is an associate professor in the Department of Urban Policy and Planning at Hunter College, City University of New York, where she teaches urban economic and com-munity development. She is an academic advisor to the Urban Manufacturing Alliance and has published widely in peer-reviewed academic journals on land policy, innovation policy, and workforce issues in the manufacturing sector.

i   Introduction

Robert N. Lane and Nina Rappaport

The Challenge

Urbanism and production are inextricably linked. One could write a nearly comprehensive history of the city, from the Industrial Revolution to today, simply by tracing the changing role of industry in the city: from engine of growth to source of political and social upheaval; from concentration of economic power to symbol of urban disinvestment.

Now, in this "Century of the City," production is once again at the center of discussions about urbanism. The Brookings Institution reports that from 2015 onwards, "there has been a resurgence in American manufacturing."[1] Much of this is happening in the densest parts of the densest metros: "The location of manufacturing jobs within metropolitan areas reflects the benefits of density. Of all manufacturing jobs located in metropolitan areas with three or more counties, 88.8 percent were located in the central counties of those metropolitan areas."[2] Manufacturing is not so much returning to the city in the conventional sense as it is reinventing itself in ways that often are not recognized: "Makerspaces," "Innovation Districts," and "Vertical Urban Factories" are some of the signposts of current and future urban production.

Figure i.1 The "Berlin Block" exemplifies the way industry was completely integrated in the fabric of the city.

Figure i.2 VW Dresden factory, Henn Architekten, Dresden, Germany; a multistoried transparent factory in the city center, 2001.

Figure i.3 Technology transforms urban manufacturing, both in terms of who does the work and where it is located. Pfizer Building, Brooklyn, New York.

The potential value of manufacturing is enormous for cities and people. However, there are significant challenges for it to exist economically. Our survey of industrial policies and regulations around the world reveals the degree to which city planners and economic development agencies are struggling to come to terms with and to reframe manufacturing for a contemporary context: just what is urban manufacturing? What kinds of spaces and places of production are needed? What policies can best manage this new opportunity?

This book is offered at a moment in which deeper attention to these issues is pressing and the conditions driving the need are numerous. These issues include:

- The loss of urban manufacturing jobs has reduced economic diversity by eliminating access to living-wage jobs, contributing to income polarization. Production, along with food service and transportation, is considered one of the sectors most vulnerable to automation.[3]
- Industrial land and buildings just outside the urban core are underutilized or vacant, creating blight, which disproportionately impacts disadvantaged communities.
- Many industrial sites are in waterfront areas where people and businesses are threatened by sea-level rise.

- The nature of production has changed so rapidly that land use regulations and economy policies have not kept pace, creating uncertainty for city planners, policy makers, and industrialists. Industrial zoning, still chained to a legacy of quarantining production activities, does not enable the dynamic mixed-use patterns that support contemporary modes of urban industry, such as small and medium-sized 3D printing, laser cutting, small-batch prototyping, specialized urban food production, and media and film production.

The Design of Urban Manufacturing

In one way or another, city governments and planners have been wrestling with the decline of urban manufacturing for the last half-century and so there is substantial research and accumulated experience on this subject. The underlying presumption is that production activities have left the city for good—to suburban industrial parks, to greenfield sites in other regions, and to other countries. There are abundant redevelopment and urban design studies describing how so-called postindustrial sites can be transformed into new residential or commercial mixed-use areas, but almost *no* contemporary models for how they can be designed and managed as places of urban production. Among the few that do exist, public entities are sponsoring new designs for production districts that include comprehensive open space systems, district-wide strategies for energy, environmental, and eco-industrial best practices, and street and building design standards. However, these are very much the exception.

This is a problem because the accommodation of production in the city is as much a design challenge as it is an economic development question. We need factory and urban design solutions for working neighborhoods that enable fine-grained, mixed-use activities and maximize face-to-face interactions, while creatively solving the very real problems of goods movement and functional buildings. Mixing production with the other daily activities of the city is the ultimate mixed-use design challenge, as the following list of important design challenges suggests.

- Street designs need to accommodate goods movement while enabling other forms of interaction and mobility among producers and non-producers alike.
- Open space designs need to be flexible and able to accommodate different activities at different times of the day.
- Edges of districts need to be both well-defined and permeable.
- Building designs need to enable new modes of live-work and create transitions in scale and land use between factories and adjacent neighborhoods.
- Factories need to work efficiently for the processes within them while enhancing public streets and shared urban spaces.

If we are going to implement these new design strategies and manage them over time, these new physical interventions require a complementary set of new recommendations for policy, regulation, and economic development.

To complicate things further, production networks and the civic and regulatory infrastructures that support them are very much place-bound, as Laura Wolf-Powers asserts in her essay about the limits of federal manufacturing policy. Urban manufacturing ecologies are hyperlocal and yet globally distributed and we have derived from the research found in this book a set of diverse, typology-based, and transferrable design and policy strategies.

An Interdisciplinary Perspective

Recognizing the complexity of the urban manufacturing challenge, this book provides an inter-disciplinary approach at multiple scales. The boundaries between its three sections are inten-tionally soft.

Part I – The Design of Districts: The Neighborhood as Factory

Street and block networks, public spaces, edges, adjacencies of uses—these aspects of urban form shape the complex and flexible ecology of urban manufacturing. Recently, the term "innovation district" has been used to capture this complexity. As Janne Corneil discusses in "Manufacturing in the Innovation District" (Chapter 2), while the innovation district model in Europe is incremental and granular, in North America it is reinterpreted as the typical research office park in which production plays, at best, a minor role. Giovanna Fossa, in "Settlement as Factory: Experience and Experiment in Milan and Italy" (Chapter 3), explores similar issues in the European context, in her description of the urban places of production in Milan. Finally, since production is taking place in the city, we will need new models for streets and for moving goods even in the most compact mixed-use neighborhoods, as explored in "Goods Movement for Urban Manufacturing" (Chapter 4) by Allison Conway.

Part II – The Design of Factories: The Architecture of the Places of Production

The loft factory may well be the most iconic and familiar expression of urban manufacturing, but it is not representative of the incredibly diverse range of contemporary urban production spaces, which includes everything from expansive horizontal sheds to townhouse garages. As suggested by Stefan Al and Jonathan Bach in their exploration of informal and unplanned urban places of production in "Spaces of Informal Production in China" (Chapter 8), we need to ask not only what we mean by urban manufacturing but what an urban factory actually is today. Nina Rappaport also explores this question in Chapter 9, "Production Spaces for Industry 4.0". As described by architect Frank Barkow, in "Designing Today's Factory—Representation and Functionalism" (Chapter 6), this makes the design of new urban factories an especially chal-lenging exercise in reconciling functionality and expression. Naomi Darling, in "The Potential for the Sustainable Urban Factory" (Chapter 7), explains another layer of complexity, as archi-tects and manufacturers struggle to make their buildings sustainable as well.

Part III – The Design of Policy: Making It Happen

If the objective is an urban production district that is vibrant, adaptable, and efficient, and mixed in use, as explained by Beth Bingham and John Shapiro in "Land Use Regulation for Manufacturing" (Chapter 11), then achieving that vision will mean moving beyond conventional zoning toward policies and regulatory tools that are creative, responsive, and hybrid. Faced with extraordinary market pressures, new models are emerging that allow for

Figure i.4 Cities are finding ways to reintegrate industrial districts with other uses, Certosa, Milan.

a complex ecology of urban production both in districts and as independent building projects where the benefits of agglomeration and virtually networked relationships are not necessarily monetized in rents. These new ideas are explained in Adam Friedman's and Jenifer Becker's chapter "Mixed-Use Neighborhoods—A Challenging Strategy for Maintaining Industry" (Chapter 12). In their analysis, both mission-driven not-for-profit industrial developments and private developments that cross-subsidize manufacturing tenants have roles to play in assisting manufacturers, as do new potentials for loosening industrial zoning and locating manufacturing throughout cities. Andrew Kimball, former executive director of the Brooklyn Navy Yard and current Director of Industry City, in "Making Urban Manufacturing Pay: Developers and the Innovation Economy" (Chapter 14), describes the large-scale experiment for urban mixed manufacturing currently underway in Industry City, located along the waterfront in Brooklyn's Sunset Park. As Laura Wolf-Powers writes, urban production is place-bound, so deploying these regulations, policies, and strategies requires careful calibration to the local contexts.

At the section dividers, graphic presentations focus on specific aspects of this discussion.

- Sarah Williams, Director of Civic Design Lab, MIT, using location data collected over nine days, maps the complex and overlapping movements of designers in New York City's Garment Center.
- Sagi Golan, Senior Lead Urban Designer at the Brooklyn office of the New York City Department of City Planning, and Jeffrey Shumaker, former Director of Urban Design for the New York City Department of City Planning, speculate about the design components of an adaptable street in a mixed manufacturing district.

Figure i.5 Innovation happens where the neighborhood streets become places of production, Barcelona, Spain.

- Alexander D'Hooghe, Kobi Ruthenberg (ORG), Adam Lubinsky, and Paul van der Grient (WXY) offer both research and speculation about the allocation of space in contemporary urban factories.
- Robert N. Lane speculates on the transformation over time of "big box" structures from stores to places of production.

Part IV: Atlas: Places of Production and Design Strategies

This graphic section presents a survey of industrial districts, where cities are wrestling with their transition. The atlas is followed by a set of design guidelines for urban manufacturing districts.

This Resource

The interdisciplinary content in this volume suggests numerous avenues for future research. It will thus be useful as a teaching and learning resource for professors, practitioner-mentors, and students of policy, urban design, and architecture. More importantly, because the authors in this book are practitioners, government officials, developers, and academics, their collective perspectives and insights can help planners, architects, urban designers, economists, and government agencies understand: how innovative tools and strategies can be employed to manage the rapidly changing environment for urban manufacturing; how to design and renovate the next generation of facilities; how to express the nature of production architecturally; and how to provide the new urban manufacturers with design tools for growth.

Finally, this book recognizes the role that the academy plays in shaping the way we approach urban manufacturing. The urban factory is an exceptionally rich architecture and urban design school studio topic. This book should be used as a reader in any curriculum that deals not just with urban manufacturing, but with urbanism in general. For manufacturing to thrive, planners, designers, and policy makers need to work collaboratively to create places for production that are healthy and economically, environmentally, and socially sustainable.

Notes

1 Darrell M. West, "How Technology is Changing Manufacturing," *Brookings Techtank*, June 2, 2016, www.brookings.edu/blog/techtank/2016/06/02/how-technology-is-changing-manufacturing/.
2 Susan Helper, Timothy Krueger, and Howard Wial, *Locating American Manufacturing: Trends in the Geography of Production* (Washington, DC: Brookings Institution, 2012).
3 Mark Muro, Jacob Whiton, and Robert Maxim, *Automation Perperuates the Red-Blue Divide* (Washington, DC: Brookings Institution, March 2019).

ii   Overview of Urban Manufacturing

Robert N. Lane and Nina Rappaport

In this book, we seek to elevate the role of urban manufacturing. The case for urban manufacturing revolves around several arguments that are well-tested, but need to be qualified:

- *Equity: Manufacturing creates opportunities for disadvantaged and less-well-educated people by providing well-paid jobs with benefits and possibilities for advancement.* While there is clear evidence for this, factory automation and robotics are increasingly replacing some tasks and raising the training and education bar for others.
- *Resilience: A diverse urban economy reduces exposure to market changes that a city can neither anticipate nor control.* But urban manufacturing still has trouble competing with other economic sectors.
- *Efficiency: Manufacturing districts ensure that essential goods and services (food, fuel, construction materials, etc. do not have to be transported over long and sometimes vulnerable) routes.* The cost reduction and positive environmental impacts of goods movement are significant when supply chains are in close proximity, but job density is low in warehousing and distribution districts.
- *Sustainability: Manufacturing in cities can compress the urban footprint by reusing existing sites and buildings rather than expanding over greenfields.* The reuse of existing factories saves materials and infrastructure. Factories close to their workforce reduce the amount of fossil fuel consumed by trucks and cars potentially used by workers commuting to ex-urban industrial enclaves. However, many sites require expensive environmental remediation.

The role that urban manufacturing plays in the larger "productive ecology" of the city is the key focus in this volume.

- Knowledge-based institutions can test research applications through prototyping with local manufacturers and laboratories in cities (see Corneil, Chapter 2).
- Entrepreneurs can test the market locally through low-risk, small-batch production.
- Manufacturing activities support other creative, high-value-added sectors: for example, printing supports advertising and financial services; craft manufacturing (metalwork, carpentry, stone carving) supports architecture and industrial design; lighting and set production support the theater and film industries. These linkages support the accepted metric—that every manufacturing job supports 4.5 upstream and downstream jobs (see Figure ii.2).

- Workers coalesce in cities where resources for economic development and employment are more plentiful.

Economic geography, as the study of the relationship of land use and economics and thus land value and location for industries, had its beginnings in the late nineteenth century with theorists such as Johann H. Von Thünen and later with Alfred Weber and August Lösch. In 1933, Walter Christaller developed the idea of Central Place Theory, which spatially mapped the convenient locations for marketplace and energy resources in a series of related hexagons over a hierarchical networked territory; additionally, the geographer Chauncy Harris, in the mid-1950s, showed that industry best locates in clusters—which, when combined with Central Place Theory, reinforces the urban location for manufacturing to be essential both spatially and economically.[1] Today, although the industrial landscape is vastly different, and urban advantages, such as access to natural resources of water and steam for power, are less essential, theories of economic geography still support the fundamental premise of centrality.[2]

However, the strength and value of Central Place Theory and clustering is today undermined by the impact of digital infrastructure, thereby removing some of the necessities and benefits of spatial proximity,[3] and enabling companies to locate anywhere. With today's mass customization and just-in-time production, as well as consumer digital platforms in the digital marketplace, global trade operates in a deeper and broader, even increasingly virtual, geography. The other shift in location preference is that global trade has exponentially expanded Von Thünen's circumference of land value, spreading industry more equally around the world as now-global products are made in formerly emerging countries.

Despite the dilution of centralizing forces due to expanding digital infrastructure and globalization, there is widespread acknowledgement that production—more than other sectors of the economy—is still grounded in regional, metropolitan, and urban contexts. There is still a subset of manufacturers who continue to locate in cities for reasons that are economically advantageous, environmentally sustainable, socially just, and resilient to both financial and climate crises. Some factories are situated in cities because of pro-urban entrepreneurs engaged in small-scale "authentic" production and artisanal methods, as seen in the trend for local food

Figure ii.1 Worker in Industry City, Sunset Park, Brooklyn, 2016.

PDR Linkages to Key Sectors

INDUSTRY TYPE	Financial Sector	Residential Sector	Tourist/ Restaurant Sector	PDR Sector
Printing & Publishing				
Other Printing & Binding				
Wholesale Printing & Pub				
Photography Services				
Graphic Design, Int.Design & Signs				
Radio, T.V. Stations & Comm Svcs				
Garment Manufacturing				
Other Apparel				
Wholesale Apparel				
Transportation & Delivery Svcs				
Taxi/Limo/Shuttle				
Trucking, Freight, &Packing				
Parcel Shipping &Courier Svcs				
Utilities				
Small Scale Manufacturing & Wholesale				
Public Warehousing & Storage				
Sound Recording/Film Prod				
Wholesale Flowers				
Catering & Food Processing				
Food & Beverage Wholesale & Distribution				
Building Construction & Maintenance				
Auto Wrecking &Scrap Storage Yards				
Concrete Works				
Wholesale Construction & Distribution				
Furniture Mfg & Rpr.Wood Work				
Furniture Wholesale & Showrooms				
Appliance Repair				
Interior, Household & Appliance Wholeseller				
Large Scale Manufacturing & Wholesale				
Parking, Rental & Towing				
Theaters, Art Spaces				
Wholesale Auto Parts				
Auto Repair				
Export/Import Trading Companies				
Jewelry Wholesale Mfg				
Landscaping/Horticulture & Animal Svcs				
Chemicals/Plastics/Leather Goods mfg				
Waste Management				

Figure ii.2 Financial, residential, and tourism/restaurant-sector linkages to production, distribution, and repair (PDR).

production and the making and selling of a wide range of products locally. Other manufacturers choose their locations because of natural resources that they need to extract or process. Urban locations remain critical and resilient through the traditional passing of skill from one generation of workers to the next, as seen in the glass industry in Paris, the plastics industry in Oyonaux, France, the diamond business in Antwerp, silk manufacture in Hanoi, the sock industry in Datang, China, and the manufacture of handbags in Donggong, to name just a few. Niche products related to the design field, such as fine metal components, fashion, and furniture, remain strong in cities such as New York, Chicago, Philadelphia, London, and Toronto, where clusters of highly skilled workers meet the need for iterative processes between design and manufacturing (see Fossa, Chapter 3 and Wolf-Powers, Chapter 13). Finally, studies of the impact of automation on employment, show that the larger, more urban metropolitan areas with high education attainment such as New York, San Francisco/Oakland, Seattle, Boston, and Philadelphia—many of the same places identified through our case study research—are the least vulnerable to industrial displacement.[4]

In the United States, almost 90 percent of manufacturing jobs are located in the central counties of metropolitan areas, whereas the figure for all jobs there is about 60 percent, suggesting that the benefits of density are more important for manufacturing than for other industries.[5]

Diversity and Density

From a design perspective, two urban manufacturing characteristics are relevant in recent years.

- *Diversity: Urban manufacturers are overwhelmingly medium-sized and small.*
  Cities should offer a diverse array of production sites with flexible spaces of different sizes and configurations. Contemporary manufacturing can inhabit a broad variety of spaces in many different parts of the city.

- *Density: Proximity matters.*
  Clustering of related industries (garment, diamonds, watchmaking, metalwork), has proven to be advantageous for the manufacturers and the urban economy, despite the decentralizing impacts of digital networks. However, the periphery *is* important. Giovanna Fossa (Chapter 3) describes the synergy between the core and periphery for manufacturers in the Milan region, where product design, development, and small-batch prototyping occur in the center and large-scale production is located at the urban edge or beyond the city limits.

While there is evidence for concentration and centralization at the scale of metropolitan regions, surprisingly little quantitative evidence exists at the scale of center-city districts and buildings, in part because urban manufacturing tends to be idiosyncratic and fine-grained.[6] Often factories in a mature industry (component manufacturing, for example) benefit from economically and statistically significant agglomeration economies. Design-intensive factories experience higher benefits from urban locations where it is easier to access idea-rich specializations like product design. External economies affect factories' internal operations by facilitating information transfer between employees of different firms and by creating pools of specialized labor that many firms can draw on.

Some studies have shown that there is an increase in knowledge transfer through proximity and connectivity. For those small- and medium-sized firms that dominate US manufacturing sectors but cannot support their own formal R&D departments, proximity supports an informal knowledge exchange that fosters nonlinear innovation. Firms within the same industry located within one mile of each other see ten times the effects of information exchange, as compared to those located between two and five miles apart.[7] Instead of relying on universities, federal labs, or private consultants for innovative knowledge, firms gain commercial insight informally from other firms, from customers, and from suppliers through partnerships, reverse engineering, related contracts, or the hiring of workers with the specific knowledge the firm desires (see Wolf-Powers, Chapter 13). In a recent survey of manufacturing firms, 50 percent of respondents said that external sources were responsible for new product innovation; 27 percent that innovation was derived from customers; and 14 percent attributed innovation to companies in their supply chain.[8] Because of the high cost of real estate, large-scale factories will rarely be located in cities unless they are legacy manufacturers. However, as in the metropolitan regions of London, New York, Paris, Tokyo, and Milan, many knowledge hubs are in the center of what can be called "global cities" (see Fossa, Chapter 3).[9] Because some industries innovate through informal partnerships across supply chains, public- and private-sector leaders in cities with many unconventional industries can better strategize to link urban manufacturers, designers, and engineers within the larger manufacturing ecosystem for cross-fertilization and growth.

Finally, beyond facilitating efficient goods movement, proximity and density can also enable eco-industrial practices such as the sharing of materials and labor, and shared approaches to storm water management, energy production and distribution, and waste heat capture (see Darling, Chapter 7).

Figure ii.3 Dense areas of clustered enterprises in Seoul's garment district.

Urban Manufacturing Today

Through 2010, the number of manufacturing jobs in the United States declined by 40.7 percent from 1979 (when it peaked at 19.4 million). In 2010, the US had 11.5 million manufacturing jobs, which made up 8.5 percent of all US jobs. Since the beginning of 2010 the United States has gained manufacturing jobs. This can be attributed in part to the re-shoring of manufacturing to the US, a trend that is driven by rising labor costs abroad, rising transportation costs, poor production quality, high tariffs, political instability in other places, and the advantages accruing from the close proximity of design, production, and consumers. Unfortunately, one industry—computer and electronic products—accounts for a disproportionately large share of manufacturing growth, while traditional manufacturing has not kept pace with the rest of the economy's growth. Increases in productivity resulting from automation and robotics has resulted in fewer manufacturing jobs, especially for those less-well-educated workers who are often cited as the beneficiaries of such innovation. Other developments impacting urban manufacturing today and auguring huge changes for the future include 3D printing, materials science innovation, and enhanced internet-to-machine capabilities.

What is Urban Manufacturing?

The design and policy of urban manufacturing are made more complex by changing definitions. Certainly manufacturing has accepted categories: advanced manufacturing, value-added manufacturing, just-in-time production, lean production, mass production, mass customization, on-demand production, and prototyping, among others. However, the definition of manufacturing has expanded in ways that are not as well documented (see p. 234). Definitions of manufacturing are as diverse as the physical and policy contexts in which the activities of making take place—leading cities such as San Francisco, Somerville, and Nashville, among others—to create their own classifications for manufacturing activities to reflect local conditions, such as San Francisco City Planning's Production/Distribution/Repair (PDR) framework.[10] Other cities count film production as an industry because of its relationship to associated production such as set building and costume design.[11]

This book focuses on the production of physical products in cities. By this measure, software development, even though it is often an essential accessory activity to manufacturing, is not considered manufacturing. Similarly, warehousing, packaging, and distribution, which may also be essential to the urban manufacturing ecology, are not considered *manufacturing* even if they are generally considered *industrial* uses. Heavy industry that requires large secure precincts free of conflicts are also not part of this book's focus. While there are great challenges for manufacturers to stay in a city—higher rents and constrained space, higher labor and energy costs—these are offset by labor access, market, and expertise access.

Urban Production Places: Districts and Spaces

Today, a majority of small manufacturers are drawn to urban areas: "Unlike the days when large, vertically integrated companies dominated the nation's commodity production, today's manufacturing landscape is largely occupied by decentralized networks of small, specialized firms, many of which are hidden in plain sight in America's urban areas."[12] In the data for North America as of 2016, there were 256,363 firms in the manufacturing sector, with all but 3,626 considered small (e.g., having fewer than 500 employees). Three-quarters of American manufacturing firms have fewer than 20 employees and more than one-third of these smaller firms are in the nation's ten largest cities.[13]

The smaller size, diversity, and concentration of urban manufacturing demonstrate that, under the right conditions, manufacturing should be accommodated in a wide variety of building types and urban environments. In most cities there is, at best, only an approximate correlation between places zoned for industry and places where manufacturing actually occurs. As urban manufacturing becomes smaller, cleaner, and more diversified, it becomes more nuanced to accommodate. It is now increasingly possible for people to make things just about anywhere, as long as they are not polluting or a nuance. These "neo-cottage" industries are perfectly suited for former industrial buildings or mixed uses (see Rappaport, Chaper 9). These new realities point towards several design propositions explored here that promote a diversity of building types; create dense places with spaces for interaction and informal knowledge transfer, and make connections within and beyond district boundaries.

Districts

In keeping with the tradition of separating uses, the first generation of industrial urban renewal projects in the 1950s recreated the suburban industrial park within the city: streets were de-mapped to create inward-looking superblocks capable of accommodating large-footprint, one-story factories with ample space for off-street loading and with room for horizontal expansion. Among the first of these were the West Central Industrial District in Chicago (1952) and the Philadelphia Industrial Park (1958), created in Philadelphia's northeast. Even as late as 1982 the Port Authority of New York and New Jersey developed the Bathgate Industrial Park in the Bronx. While these projects are considered successful as site-specific industrial redevelopments that provide ease of movement for their tenants, they created precincts cut off from the surrounding neighborhoods and from the benefits of being in an urban location such as access to places to eat, shop, and relax. Today industrial district planning and design focus on redeveloping legacy manufacturing areas to protect, enhance, transform, or transition them into new modes of manufacturing. Examples of these industrial retention districts include New York's Industrial Business Zones (IBZs), Chicago's Planned Manufacturing Districts (PMDs), and San Francisco's Production, Distribution, and Repair (PDR) districts. As seen in Asian cities such as Singapore (see Rappaport, p. 192) and

Figure ii.4 Clusters of industries thrive on proximity in Antwerp's Diamond District, 2016.

Figure ii.5 Workers are visible for all to see from the sidewalks in the neighborhoods of cities such as Hanoi, Vietnam.

Figure ii.6 Older factory buildings owned by large automotive companies have been adapted for mixed-use manufacturing units in Detroit, 2015.

Shanghai with their Export Processing Zones and in Mexico with its *maquiladoras*, industrial parks are the primary economic and land use development strategies used to develop economic incentives. Mixed-use areas are becoming more possible with zoning that encourages semi-urban manufacturing mixes in districts at the urban edge similar to those in Milan and in Berlin.

In North America industrial sites that are ripe for redevelopment are primarily low-rise districts that are close enough to the urban core to benefit from integration with the city, but just beyond extreme real estate pressures (see Atlas, p. 246–7). Where public entities lead, a comprehensive industrial district plan can be designed and built, as seen in the Cornfield Arroyo Secco Plan, which will create a new mixed-manufacturing district on vacant land near Los Angeles; or the 30th Street Corridor Redevelopment Plan in Milwaukee, which will create a mix of low-rise "flex" factories and office buildings on a new street and block network that is connected to the surrounding neighborhoods.

One trend in urban industrial district planning is the "innovation district," where the configuration and mix of uses—including the manufacturing of prototypes, technology research and development, and office space—enables an anchor institution to commercialize its research (see Corneil, Chapter 2). Many such districts are affiliated with universities, as seen in Boston's Seaport Innovation District, the University of Portland Innovation District, and the Cornell Tech campus on New York's Roosevelt Island, as well as 22@Barcelona, an economic development model in Europe. However, the jury is out as to whether or not the innovation district designation actually supports urban manufacturing, or is simply a different brand of commercial gentrification (see Becker and Friedman, Chapter 12 and Kimball, Chapter 14).

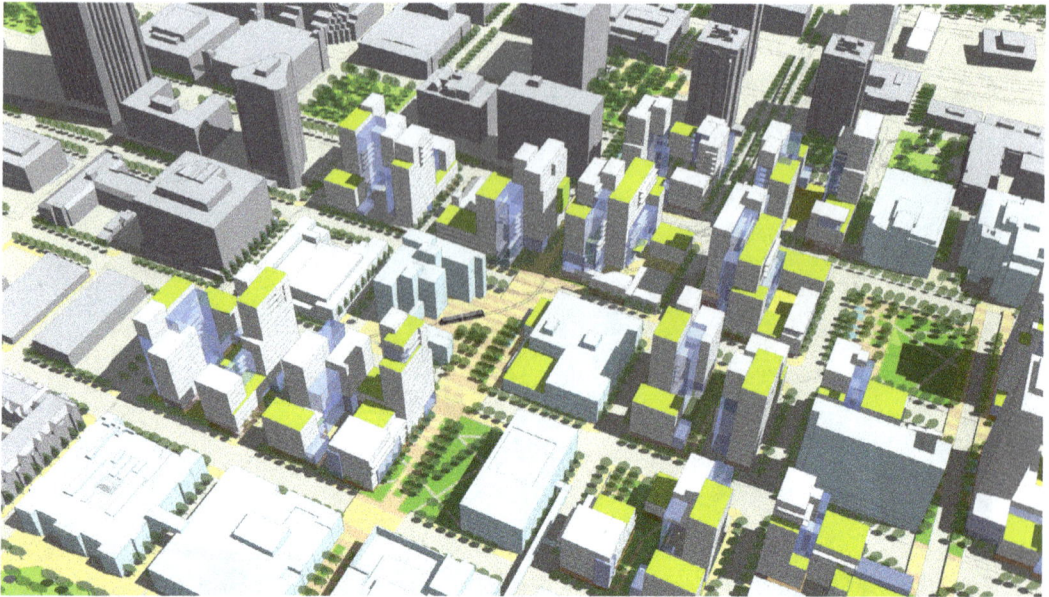

Figure ii.7 Innovation districts are meant to bring together light manufacturing, research, and marketing, Portland, Oregon.

Spaces of Production

In terms of the specific spaces for production, factories are both large and small, integrated and dispersed in industrial buildings throughout cities. They are located in buildings designed for specific companies, complexes that have been incrementally added to or expanded, or they are dispersed in small informal spaces or in former large-scale industrial buildings. Architecturally, the factory is either organized around production flow or enclosed with a wrapping in a more generic space. Both vertical urban factories and shed-like buildings accommodate production and present opportunities for architectural design in terms of organizing spatial flow to make production efficient, as well as innovative structural design to make factories that are once again accommodating to workers. Factories today are seen as high-end design, flexible, and sustainable. Factories designed by architects are efficient and also provide a sense of identity for the company, as in those of the early Modernist architects such as Peter Behrens with his innovative design of the AEG factory in 1909, Walter Gropius' Fagus Werk of 1911 in Germany, or Albert Kahn's large-scale Highland Park Ford factory of 1909 in Detroit. Today, factories such as the Trumpf Chicago factory by Barkow Leibinger (Chapter 6), or those that are attractors for visitors and the urban landscape, as in VW Dresden, provide new potentials for the return of factories to cities.

The hierarchical organization in factory management has changed over the last century from top-down management to that of closer relationships between research and development teams and the worker on the factory floor. This has influenced the design of the factory as well to be more flexible and accommodating to different tasks. Other factories are more informal, whether they be places such as garages, new makerspaces, or places in China where people can make things in informal settings (see Bach and Al, Chapter 8). The need for sustainable production has inspired some companies to make not only sustainable products but

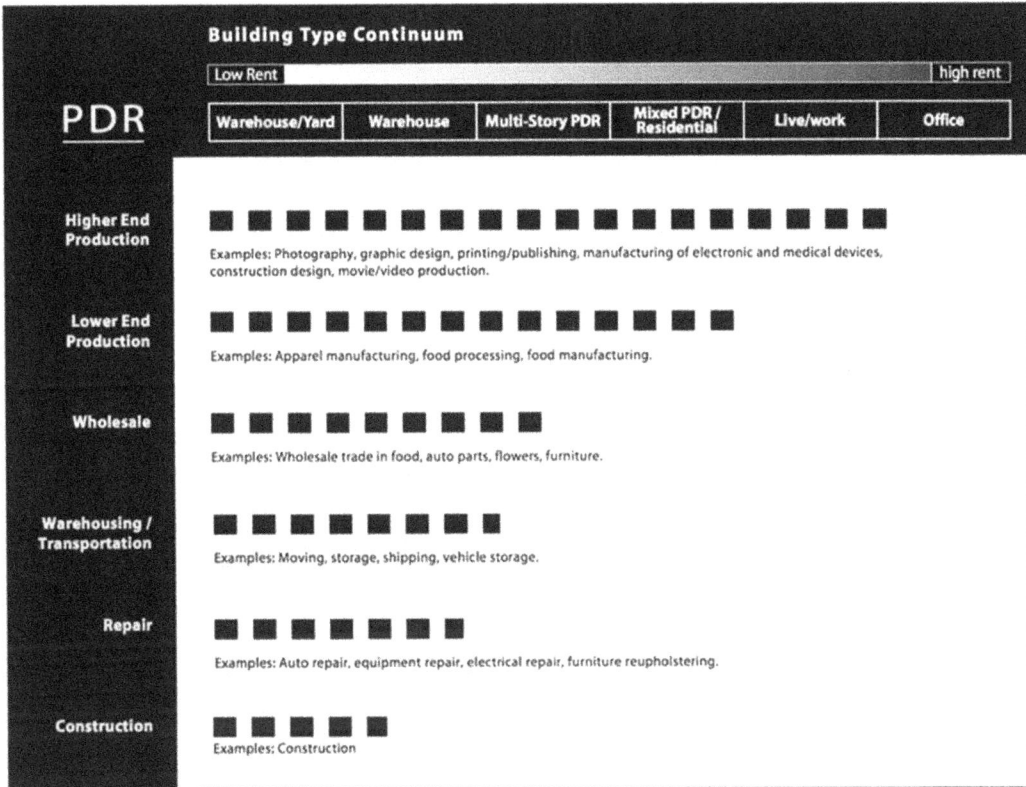

Figure ii.8 Building type in terms of production type as specified in the San Francisco Production, Distribution, and Repair categories.

also sustainable buildings (see Darling, Chapter 7). How can companies be encouraged to build, grow, and remain in cities and how can municipalities incentivize good architecture and urban design?

The Challenges

Urban design is part of the challenge of accommodating manufacturing in cities: designing street edges that balance integration and connectivity to the city while creating a clear identity and protection from commercial gentrification; designing streets that accommodate goods movement but also enable pedestrian mobility; designing spaces that adopt loading and storage areas for other uses while promoting interaction among manufacturers (see Part I).

Architectural design is another part of the challenge for manufacturing in cities: the relationship of factories to their urban context. Multistoried factories in historic loft districts enliven the streets. In low-rise districts, unrelieved and boring expanses of factory boxes prevail. The latter, however, provide a number of interesting design opportunities. The factory box can serve as the base for a multistoried building; it can be carved out and enhanced with an innovative façade; or it can be fitted with inviting and welcoming entryways that could enliven the streetscape (see Part II).

The biggest challenge, however, remains policy regulation and administration (see Rappaport, Chapter 10). Many cities are experimenting with new zoning tools for industrial mixed use, such as Pittsburgh's NDI (Neighborhood Industrial), Cincinnati's IX (Mixed Industrial), and Cleveland's R/I (Residence/Industrial) designations, all relatively recent. These cities are struggling to define manufacturing as it rapidly evolves (see Friedman and Becker, Chapter 12, and Bingham and Shapiro, Chapter 11). Is someone with a 3D printer a manufacturer? Should manufacturing uses be controlled by use lists that are soon made obsolete by a rapidly changing manufacturing sector, or should they be controlled by performance standards that are adaptable but difficult to enforce? How should cities decide what uses and in what quantities best serve the long-term vitality of the district? (see Part III).

Notes

1   Walter Christaller, *Central Place Theory in Southern Germany, Die Zentralen Orte in Süddeutschsland* (Jena: Gustave Fisher, 1933).
2   Paul Krugman, *Development, Geography, and Economic Theory* (Cambridge, MA: The MIT Press, 1997).
3   Manuel Castells and Saskia Sassen have conducted extensive research on these issues.
4   Mark Muro, Jacob Whiton, and Robert Maxim, *Automation and Artificial Intelligence: How Machines are Affecting People and Places* (Washington, DC: Brookings Institution, January 2019).
5   Susan Helper, Timothy Krueger, and Howard Wial, *Locating American Manufacturing: Trends in the Geography of Production* (Washington, DC: Brookings Institution, 2012), 10.
6   Susan Helper and Marcus Stanley, "External Economies: How Innovative Small Manufacturers Compete" (Cleveland, OH and Cambridge/MA: Case Western Reserve University and National Bureau of Economic Research, November 2010).
7   Stewart Rosenthal and William Strange, "Evidence on the Nature and Sources of Agglomeration Economies," *Handbook of Urban and Regional Economics*, ed. V Henderson and J. F. Thisse, Volume 4 (Amsterdam: North Holland (Elsevier), 2004).
8   Scott Andes, *How Firms Learn: Industry Specific Strategies for Urban Economies* (Washington, DC: Brookings Institution, 2016).
9   See also Saskia Sassen, *The Global City* (Princeton, NJ: Princeton University Press, 1991).
10 San Francisco Planning Department, *Industrial Land in San Francisco: Understanding Production, Distribution, and Repair* (San Francisco, CA: City of San Francisco, 2002).
11 See Made in New York, the promotional and technical assistance initiative of the Mayor's Office of Media & Entertainment.
12 Nisha Mistry and Joan Byron, *The Federal Role in Supporting Urban Manufacturing* (Washington, DC: Brookings Institution, April 2011), Appendix: "Case Studies From Selected U.S. Cities."
13 *Ibid.*

iii Notes from the Field: Interview with Greg Mark, Founder and CEO of Markforged

Greg Mark is the President and CEO of Markforged, a company that manufactures 3D printers for industrial applications. An MIT-educated engineer, Greg Mark founded Markforged in 2013 with the goal of reducing the time between design concept and the production of a strong, functional component. Originally started on his kitchen table in Cambridge, the company now employs 150 people in a 1950s-era, one-story, 32,000-square-foot building at the edge of an industrial zone in Watertown, Massachusetts, just west of Boston. In this interview from 2017, Greg Mark touches on many of the themes explored in this book: the advantages of an urban location, the essential features of his factory, and the role that government can play in reducing risk for a manufacturer.

What is your product and why did you start your company?

As most mechanical engineers will tell you, you can design thousands of parts for a Tesla or iPhone in a matter of minutes or hours, but then you wait four to five weeks for that part to be made. The reason mechanical engineering is so slow is because you have an almost artisanal process in which a human is crafting each individual part.

We founded the company in 2013 to make 3D printers with the goal of enabling the designer to go from idea to a strong functional part in the same day. We found a way to embed continuous carbon fiber into plastic to make it twenty-three times stronger than aluminum. Now the engineer can design the part he wants, can print it, and can use it the same day he designed it. This saves four to five weeks per iteration—in the end it saves months. Now there are thousands of these industrial 3D printers all around the world. Basically, every Fortune 100 company has hundreds of them.

What were the beginnings of the company and where did you start up?

We literally started in my kitchen. Antonio Rodriguez of Matrix Partners was the first investor. He had been the chief technical officer for consumer printing at Hewlett-Packard and he did the seed grant for MakerBot. So he knew both printing and 3D printing. When we showed him what we were doing, he was super excited to jump on board. So we did a seed round. Two things were moving in parallel: technology and fundraising. Engineering was moving, which is developing the print head, de-risking the process, and figuring out whether this thing would work. We filed for the intellectual property rights for our innovations.

Figure iii.1 Prototype parts created by Markforged 3D printers.

At the same time, we were raising money. We did a relatively small seed round of $1 million and about nine to thirteen weeks later we printed our first piece of Kevlar. The first composites were printed out of Kevlar and then a few months later we printed some pieces with carbon fiber, and then a few months after that we debuted a machine. One year after I started working on it we debuted the first prototype on the main stage at the Consumer Electronics Show (CES) in Las Vegas, Nevada in front of 6,500 mechanical engineers.

How long did it take to for this initial prototyping?

It took a year *for* prototyping and proof of concept and another year and a half to figure out how to manufacture the material at volume. Being able to make enough material for one machine was hard. Being able to make enough material for thousands of machines was unbelievably hard. And then, about sixteen months ago, we debuted the world's first "Adam Printer," a new way to print metal that is ten times less costly than traditional metal 3D printers. It's also easier to use and safer—because it encases the metal in plastic, it's nontoxic.

The piece goes through a washing station to remove some of the plastic, followed by a sintering furnace where the metal particles start to squish together. Imagine a bunch of metal marbles acting like sand in a sand castle: the water drains out but a kind of friction between the small sand particles holds it together.

What were some benchmark moments in the development of the company and the spaces you needed?

We had our first building in Somerville—an 8,000-square-foot former furniture and carpet warehouse, which felt big. Then we moved into a 16,000-square-foot-space in Alewife, which also felt big. We were there for 18 months and now we're in Watertown in a 32,000-square-foot space. We just signed a lease for an additional building—we're growing faster than we can keep up with. The nice thing about Watertown is that we can rent buildings that are within walking distance—it's like having a campus or a distributed office. At this headquarters building we have two floors. The second floor is like a software company, with desktops and laptops that can move in a day if needed. The first floor is full of industrial equipment: CNC machines, extrusion lines, vacuum ovens, tensile test machines. There are just huge quantities of materials and machinery that require a forklift to move. Our headquarters will probably stay in Watertown for a few years while we expand in this neighborhood.

What are the factors that drive your location decisions in this neighborhood and around Boston in general?

The primary factors are location and cost. We need proximity to recent graduates who want to live near or commute to our factory. In the beginning that was Somerville, and then we moved to Alewife to be within reach of both Boston and Cambridge; you can still commute from Cambridge or Boston, but people outside the city can also drive in. Alewife is like the fringe of the city today, but if you go from Alewife to the inner part of the city, your commute doubles. So we split it so that people in both the city and suburbs have easy access.

How did the move to Somerville come about?

We ran out of space. We have the combined need of manufacturing space, light manufacturing, and office space. So that puts you in a subset of locations to begin with.

Is that because of zoning or because of the kinds of buildings that are available?

If the building doesn't have elevator access or a loading dock, it won't work for us. An office park usually doesn't provide loading docks. That's something we need three times a day, every day, because we're in constant production; we have material shipping out, material shipping in, and equipment shipping in. We would have been fine in Cambridge or Boston—we would have been able to pull our employees in from the suburbs. The thing is, wherever you start, people get used to the commute, but there's increased friction the further out you move. It's

Figure iii.2 A mid-block service area away from the residential street provides adequate room for loading.

just nice to stay relatively close to where you started. Also, Watertown has been up-and-coming for decades now. In five or ten years we won't be able to afford to rent the space, but for now we can.

Is there a moment when you would contemplate having to move? Sometimes urban manufacturers complain about not being able to get leases that are long-term enough to install all of the necessary equipment. It's one thing to move a bunch of laptops; it's another to move all of the equipment required for production. Were you able to negotiate the length of the lease you wanted?

Right behind us is a small business, New England Flag and Banner. It's located in a building owned by the same company that owns our building. They got there when this place was really, really cheap. And the city has grown up around them, and it doesn't make sense for them to be here now. The reason I'm in the city is because I have software engineers who come out of MIT and want to live in Harvard Square, Inman Square, Porter Square, or Back Bay. And we also have manufacturing operations people who are physically building all of our stuff. They live outside the city where it is more affordable. They would actually rather not have to commute, even to Alewife or Watertown.

While we're in the design development phase, it's important to have engineers nearby to troubleshoot problems. But, to me, if you're making something that you've made for ten years using a very stable process, there's no reason to be in the city.

If your long-term business plan works out the way you think it will, is there a moment coming where you're going to move out of the city entirely? And, if you did that, is there some other kind of satellite presence that you would want to keep in the city? When does the calculus of being in the city versus a suburban office park change?

I believe that we would move manufacturing out of the city when we have to triple our space requirement. It's actually more efficient to have all of the people on the manufacturing line there. Rent in the city is like two to three times what it is outside. So if we can move manufacturing to a low-cost region it's better for the people who work there. Farther out in the suburbs you can buy more. You can literally buy warehouse space and throw heaters in there. The floor's already a nice slab. So our first floor is for contract manufacturing and the second floor is an office building. If we moved manufacturing out of the city we'd still need engineering here for at least a good profit margin.

Would you keep a certain amount of the prototyping in the city?

There's a problem with that. The more you fracture your workforce, the less efficient it is, and then all those kids you hired as grads five years ago get married and have kids and want to move to the suburbs too. So it fits with the natural dynamic of how the company evolves.

We've been doing research across the country about "innovation districts." They seem to be very much like what you're describing in Watertown—they're not in the core where real estate is just too competitive, but they're often in legacy industrial areas at the edge of the core, where they're striking a balance between proximity to research institutions, talent, young people, less-expensive real estate, and access to highways. We're interested in the role this kind of neighborhood and district plays for the manufacturer. What's interesting is the campus model you described, where you can expand by having an agglomeration of several little sites that are close to each other. Does anybody who works for you actually live here? How do your workers get to you?

Not only do people live here, most of the people in the market for houses are looking to buy here. The two main factors are a) it's a great commute and b) it's an up-and-coming neighborhood. Watertown is a great place to invest your dollars. We moved 150 people in when we first moved here and we're going to move another 150 people in over the next few years. In fact, we have six employees looking for houses right now. The real estate market is going to get hotter, and Markforged is going to drive some of that growth. Six to ten houses per year is not a trivial fraction of the inventory on the market.

So what are some of the important features of the neighborhood for you as a manufacturer?

The first thing is parking: no parking, no good. We have plenty of parking spaces. And the city of Watertown has been great—when we first came here, we had a bunch of city officials visit the site to see what we were doing. We've also had some of the high schools come by to show the students what 3D printing is. So that helps inspire them to go into engineering. We think it's a productive thing to do.

Were you offered any incentives when you were making this move; did the city actually offer anything other than being enthusiastic?

I didn't ask for that. The city has replaced some trees outside of our building. I don't know if they were planning on doing that anyway or not, but you can tell when you are being tolerated or actually wanted. Watertown is super happy to have us here, and we're super happy to be here. That is not always the case.

Can you tell me specifically some of the ways in which that plays out?

I believe that if we ever needed help—say we needed more power to the building—the city would be more than happy to work with us. Entrepreneurship is about getting rid of risk, right? And when I think about other places we might move to and the different kinds of risks, I feel like we have a civic partner. I feel like everything is about how the city can help, as opposed to looking for reasons to get us out of here.

Figure iii.3 Façade improvements and streetscaping make the Markforged factory a good neighbor.

What other kind of businesses are in the neighborhood and what are some of the community's other assets? Are there any conflicts? Do you have truck access? Sometimes people say that one of the advantages of urban manufacturing districts is that there actually are some amenities—first and foremost, you can get something to eat. Parks and street life just don't exist in the suburban industrial park.

When we were in Somerville there was great food everywhere. You could take clients and employees out for dinner or for drinks. The atmosphere was great. When we were in Alewife, there were only chain restaurants. Here in Watertown, just 100 feet from our door, there's a little family-run restaurant called Striptease. They've got great food. Our workforce comprises probably 20 to 30 percent of their customer base. Every other week we order lunch for our entire staff from them. The Striptease chefs and wait staff all have that "we work in a funky restaurant" attitude. It gives the restaurant a great vibe, with a lot more character and charm than a chain restaurant.

On the business side, AthenaHealth bought a huge campus from Harvard for $169 million—they're another great neighbor. We've already talked to them about a few different projects we could do together. One of the spaces we're moving into in what we call our distributed campus is actually in one of their buildings. Again, it's the same as with the city of Watertown; they've been very supportive, very encouraging.

What other businesses are in this industrial area?

There is a used-equipment business that's right behind us that we buy from and sell to. We've bought furnaces from them and other equipment that we've urgently needed. If we're upgrading they will take the old equipment—maybe you get just sixty cents on the dollar but it's better than trying to sell on Ebay. The transaction is immediate and you rock and roll.

Is there anybody who is literally connected to your supply chain?

Our contract manufacturers are all local, but most are located outside of the city and can't afford to live in the city. So there's no immediate synergy in that sense.

What are some of the materials that you have to have delivered to you? Do you have good highway access?

Plastics, carbon fibers, metals. Actually we don't have great highway access, but that hasn't really affected the shipping prices. We don't seem to get charged for that last mile.

I see you're surrounded by a residential neighborhood. You are right at the edge of an industrial district.

Yes, it's a bit weird. But when a customer like Siemens or Porsche comes to visit us it feels more like Europe, where cities have grown up with factories and houses side-by-side or across from each other. In the case of Porsche, the company has a beautiful plant surrounded by farms and a little city. In the US, which is much, much younger, things tend to be way outside the city in industrial parks, and then things change over time: you drop a manufacturing building on the outskirts, the city expands to meet it, then all of a sudden the value's disappeared.

Necco was manufacturing candy in Cambridge, and then they sold it to a developer. You know, quite honestly, they probably should have held onto it for about four more years, but selling allowed them to buy a new building and move outside the city. In retrospect this doesn't seem like such a great deal considering that the site is now class-A biotech space.

Do you have conflicts with your neighbors? Or are your processes quiet, clean, and odor-free?

We don't do anything that is toxic, our CNC machines are quiet, and we're not running jack-hammers or anything like that. We're not an obnoxious neighbor. In fact, if anything, we have probably increased property values. This building was super creepy before we gutted and renovated it—now we have people looking for houses in the neighborhood. Our workers can be right across the street from work, which is a great asset. It just snowed two feet here… wouldn't it be nice to just leave your car in the garage or driveway? In fact, why would you even own a car? Now when you walk by and look in the front windows you see nice people doing interesting things.

That's one of the things we've heard from other people about urban manufacturing—one way to get people to value it is to make it more visible. You can see that there's stuff going on. And when you bring some students in from some of the local schools, you are helping make manufacturing

Figure iii.4 "Nice people doing interesting things."

a more visible and valuable thing. What works in your building and what would you change about it? If you could have the urban factory of your dreams, how would it be different?

We always need more space and of course more parking spaces. If I had unlimited money and we had to stay in this location, I would knock down the building behind us, add three floors to this building, add more engineering space, and then put a parking lot somewhere.

Can you imagine a situation where any of the production happens on upper floors?

Moving to a large warehouse makes sense because of the concrete slab. You don't want to have to build a freight elevator that goes up to the second floor. In fact, our loading dock is large, has a freight elevator, and goes from the parking lot to the first floor. But it doesn't go up to the second floor, which can't support the weight of CNC machines or loaded pallet racks. The pounds per square inch on those floors have to be sustained or they might pop through the wood floor; manufacturing wants to be done on a concrete floor. Some of these old mill buildings are different. They have more solid floors—you can put industrial equipment on them. We worked in another building where we had CNC manufacturing on the second floor. It's doable. But if we had five floors, we would never put a CNC on the fifth floor. Maybe in Japan, where real estate is at a premium, but in America we've just got too much space.

If you wanted to promote urban manufacturing, what do you think are some of the key policies to support it?

Urban manufacturing to me feels like a transition toward revitalizing the neighborhood. But it's a process that goes through a series of steps. The city wants to attract manufacturing talent. Step one: the city invests in a site or building that needs renovation but adds value, then a manufacturer like us moves in. We bring employees who buy houses and spend money. Step two: the neighborhood gets increasingly expensive. Step three: as the manufacturer grows, the neighborhood grows around it. In addition the type of tenant changes from industrial manufacturing to software, biotech, or pharma, all of which have higher dollar-per-square-foot capacity. It's a natural progression.

Look at Watertown. If I had a crystal ball … in five, ten years, I may not be able to afford the space, right? So we're part of that lifecycle.

Are there things that can be monetized that are currently not being monetized such as efficiency, job training opportunities, access to talent, or access to labor?

I know why a manufacturer wants to be in a city. I don't know why the city wants to have manufacturing, except for two main things: you want diversity of economy and the stability of manufacturing, which tends to stay around for a long time.

So, as the world changes, if you're building stuff, you want to sign a ten-year, not a two-year, lease. Software companies come and go. Manufacturing has a lower margin, but it has a longer lifecycle.

Part I

The Design of Districts

The Neighborhood as Factory

1   Urban Design for the Manufacturing District

Robert N. Lane

Landscapes of Urban Production: Loft Districts, Industrial Parks, and Working Neighborhoods

Scenes of urban manufacturing:

> *From the window of the train as it passes through the edge of the city, a commuter sees imposing loft factories, most of which are gradually being overtaken by nature and graffiti artists. But it looks like some are still being used—not by the original manufacturer, whose majestic rooftop sign is gradually fading away—but by five, six, or seven businesses, each with their own smaller signs in the windows.*
>
> *From the elevated highway a driver looks across a wide expanse of flat featureless roofs on windowless one-story buildings. The approaching exit—never to be taken by this driver—says "truck route."*
>
> *Across the counter of a small shop downtown a customer catches a glimpse of the jeweler working on a lathe in a back room, or catches a whiff of varnish on newly sanded wood furniture.*

These places of production in the city are as diverse as the cities themselves. In most people's minds the only urban manufacturing districts are "loft districts" like SoHo in New York City, symbols of the "postindustrial" city, where striking multistory factories, abandoned by their original owners and subsequently pioneered by artists, are now occupied by well-heeled residents, office workers, and shoppers.

Despite the fact that loft districts are the places that come to mind when people think of urban manufacturing, most industrial real estate in American cities, and almost all of the still-active industrial areas, are more like the low-rise districts our driver saw from the elevated highway—the expanse of single-story "boxes" with open storage and loading areas.

The streets of these "industrial parks," in contrast to the bustling sidewalks of the loft district, are gritty and eerily quiet, the sidewalk pavement broken up under the weight of the trucks that are parked half on top of them or stacked with pallets of materials obstructing the paths of pedestrians. Cigarette butts around a windowless steel door suggest that there is something happening behind these mute facades, and there is—inside are anywhere from five workers to sixty, making everything from plumbing fittings to electronic components.

At the edge of the industrial park the blocks of one-story windowless factories give way to streets, where workshops and factories of every scale are mixed up with small apartment buildings and townhouses in which people live above workshops or cheek-by-jowl with small

Figure 1.1 A working loft district, Garment Center, New York City.

Google Earth

Figure 1.2 An active loft district street.

Figure 1.3 A low-rise industrial district, Spring Creek Industrial Park, New York City.

Figure 1.4 Typical street in a low-rise industrial district, Los Angeles.

factories. Here is the "manufacturing neighborhood," where the factory is the neighborhood itself—products don't move so much from floor to floor as from building to building: a metalworker delivers a piece of ornamental hardware to the jewelry maker down the block; two cabinetmakers meet at a nearby coffee shop, and one of them whose business is a bit slow at the moment agrees that some of his workers can help out in the other guy's shop until he gets through the big order he has just landed.

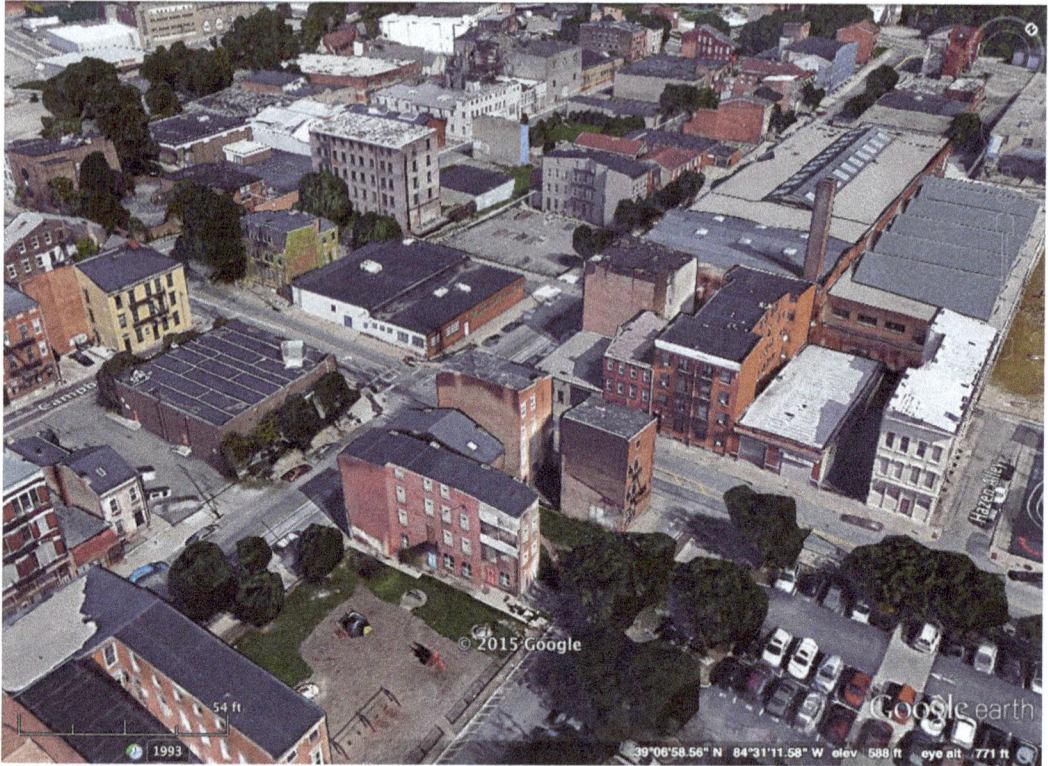

Figure 1.5 A working neighborhood, Over-the-Rhine, Cincinnati, Ohio.

Google Earth

Figure 1.6 Manufacturing neighborhood street, Dogpatch, San Francisco.

Manufacturing neighborhoods evolved in the same unselfconscious and unplanned way as the rest of the city. While in some cases these complex patterns have been memorialized in various zoning regimes,[1] in general, these would not be considered designed industrial districts if by

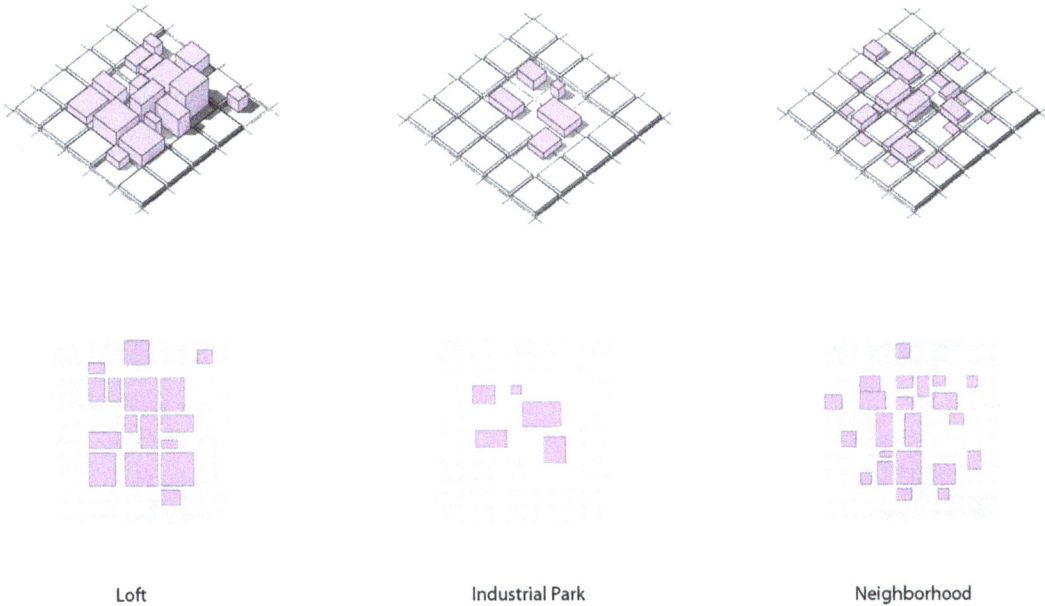

| Loft | Industrial Park | Neighborhood |

Figure 1.7 A typology of industrial districts: lofts, industrial parks, and neighborhoods.

that we mean a comprehensive design strategy for new streets, buildings, and public spaces across a large enough area to be considered a district.

There are some examples of designed urban industrial districts built by single manufacturers who required multiple buildings and who had larger land holdings, often next to rail yards or port facilities—places like Porta Genoa in Milan, Industry City in Brooklyn (see Kimball, p. 235), and the Pershing Road Industrial District in Chicago—where the factories and the adjacent workers' neighborhoods were designed in concert.[2]

Most of the planned urban manufacturing districts in North America were not loft districts. Despite our association of the one-story "pancake factory" with suburban industrial parks, new low-rise manufacturing districts were pioneered not in the suburbs in the 1950s but in downtowns in the 1930s at places like the Crawford Industrial District in Chicago (1931).[3]

From the Machine in the Garden to the Machine Next Door: The "Urban-Suburban" Industrial Park

The troubled history of urban renewal is familiar: in so-called "blighted" places, streets were de-mapped to create superblocks capable of accommodating high-rise towers in precincts that

Figure 1.8 Houses and factories side-by-side, Newmarket, Boston.

Figure 1.9 Pershing Road, Chicago, one of the first planned industrial districts in the US.

were disconnected from the physical and social fabric of the surrounding neighborhoods. Less familiar is the fact that a parallel process was under way in the world of industrial redevelopment: of the 676 federally assisted urban renewal projects planned or underway in 1962, 119 were industrial, representing 23 percent of the acreage of all urban renewal projects. A photograph of one of these projects appeared on the 1955 cover of *Commerce Magazine*, with a caption that boasted, "Slums like these make way for modern industrial plants."[4]

To create larger sites for industrial urban renewal, the solution was the same as for other urban renewal projects: de-map streets to create superblocks capable of accommodating large-footprint, one-story factories with ample space for off-street loading and with room for horizontal expansion. By closing some streets but allowing others to remain open, the superblock represented a compromise between the perceived need to create a secure limited-access precinct for manufacturing and the need to connect to a dense urban context. One of the first of these was the West Central Industrial District in Chicago, planned and developed in the 1920s. In New York City, experiments with industrial urban renewal date to 1959, when the city began to study the feasibility of an industrial park on sixteen blocks of what became the Flatlands Industrial Park in Brooklyn. These early projects established what would become, and in many places remain, the model for the planned urban manufacturing district: replicating the suburban industrial park within the city—the "Urban-Suburban Industrial Park." The prime example in New York is the Bathgate Industrial Park, developed by the Port Authority in 1982. From a purely industrial-redevelopment perspective, Bathgate may be considered a success, but it is nevertheless an inward-looking precinct with long expanses of blank wall repelling the surrounding neighborhood.

Connect or Protect: Industrial District Design Today

Whether urban manufacturing needs to be connected and integrated with the city or isolated and protected is the fundamental issue for industry in the city, as it has been since the origins of modern town planning. In terms of urban design, the edge of the district is the frontier where this tension plays out: a porous edge makes it easier for manufacturers to connect to skilled labor, designers, researchers, academics, retailers, and other complementary businesses and the

Figure 1.10 "Slums make way for Industry." Cover of *Commerce* magazine, 1955.

Figure 1.11 Bathgate Industrial Park, New York City, 1982; industrial redevelopment brings the suburban model to the city.

markets they serve. On the other hand, a hard edge satisfies the perceived need to isolate manufacturing from adjacent activities because of noise, dust, and traffic, and especially to establish a defense against displacement by "higher and better uses." Ironically this leads advocates to push for protected single-purpose precincts with restrictive regulations even though this is not the best environment for urban manufacturers, especially those who want to innovate.

Trying to balance these two intentions—integration or protection—shapes both policy and urban design, in particular around the degree to which uses should be mixed, the degree to which edges of the district are hard or soft, and the degree of street network connectivity between industrial and nonindustrial areas. One solution to the challenge of industrial mixed use is the "industrial campus," where a mission-driven entity has control over real estate and can deliberately "curate the ecology" of the district. Examples include the Brooklyn Navy Yard and the Greenpoint Manufacturing and Design Center in New York, the Philadelphia Navy Yard, the Menomonee Valley Industrial District in Milwaukee, and the Breda district in Milan. However, in most cities where planners struggle to strike the delicate balance between connection and protection they must rely on a range of more conventional land use regulatory strategies (see Rappaport, Chapter 10 and Becker and Friedman, Chapter 12).

Because large manufacturers are no longer building their own precincts in the city and because city planners have their hands full just trying to manage the transition to new forms of urban production, there are almost no examples of new industrial districts being planned and designed from scratch in the US and Europe. Rather, industrial district planning and design today focuses more on legacy manufacturing areas where cities, in the face of a rapidly changing production economy, wrestle with strategies to—by degrees—either protect, enhance, transform, or transition away from manufacturing. This is the case in Europe as well as in North America. Industrial district design in these places tends to focus on a relatively small subset of concerns: enabling some level of waterfront access, managing the often jarring transitions in scale between industrial and nonindustrial buildings, and making the edge of the district apparent.

In the few places where new urban industrial districts are being created by public entities, the design, architecture, and land use administration challenges described above can be managed because the public entities, not the real estate markets, drive the redevelopment process: a comprehensive open space system can be created; district-wide strategies for energy, natural systems, and eco-industrial practices can be implemented; street and building standards can be more detailed. Examples include the City of Los Angeles's initiative for Cornfield Orroyo Seco, which will create a new street network with blocks capable of accommodating both factories and office buildings.[5]

Similarly, the city of Milwaukee is redeveloping the 30th Street Corridor as a mix of office buildings and new low-rise "flex" industrial buildings, creating a series of campus-like environments that are both inward-looking and create successful urban edges with the surrounding neighborhoods. The Menomonee Valley Industrial Center, also in Milwaukee, is organized around a new greenway that provides access for workers as well as the public brownfield remediation and green infrastructure services.[6] These projects are noteworthy for their break with the previous generation of industrial redevelopment projects such as the Bathgate Industrial Park, which created closed precincts exclusively for industry. Instead, connections are made to the surrounding context and uses are mixed.

In the last few decades several new models have emerged for industrial district design: "Eco-industrial Parks" and "Innovation Districts." Eco-industrial parks are places where the by-products from some processes (materials, waste heat, and water) become inputs for others

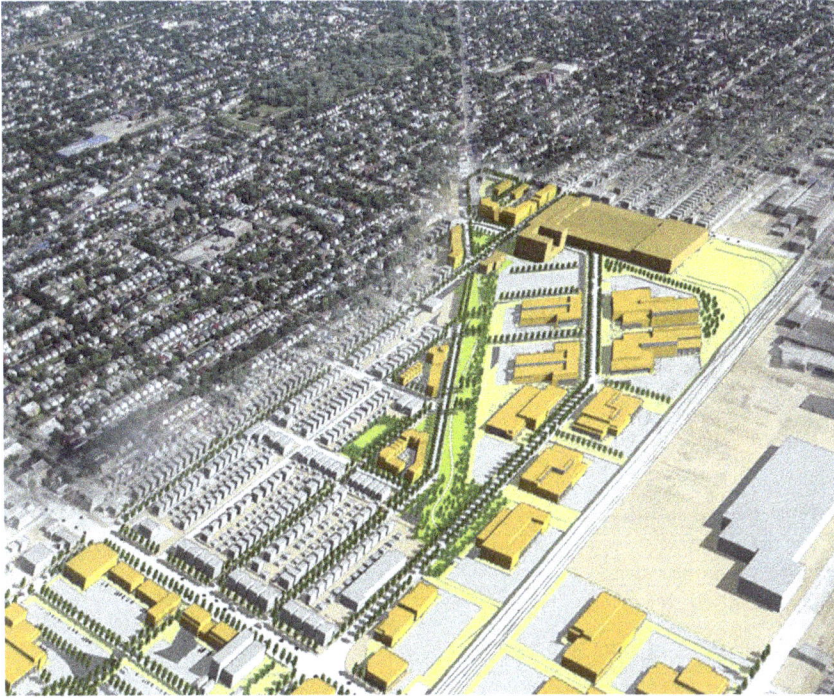

Figure 1.12 Urban design is part of this industrial district redevelopment initiative in Milwaukee, Wisconsin.

as a way to reduce waste and increase efficiency. While the proximity and connectivity of an urban manufacturing district are not the only prerequisites for eco-industrial practices (or even the most important), some eco-industrial practices do in fact depend on proximity—including shared approaches to storm-water management, shared energy production, materials and products distribution, and waste heat capture.

Innovation districts are places where the configuration and mix of uses, including the manufacturing of prototypes, enable an anchor institution to ground-test their innovations, and perhaps even commercialize its research. Several innovation districts are planned or underway in the US, including the Boston Seaport Innovation District, the Cleveland Health-Tech Corridor, the University of Portland Innovation District Master Plan, and Cornell Tech on New York's Roosevelt Island; 22@Barcelona is the flagship international example (see Corneil, Chapter 2).

This concept seems to embrace the kind of dynamic mix of activities that can support creative urban production in its many forms. However, as suggested by Adam Friedman and John Shapiro, absent a long-term commitment to manufacturing or control of real estate by a mission-driven organization, the innovation district "brand" may simply be the harbinger of industrial displacement through market-driven mixed-use redevelopment. The Barcelona and Milan case studies described by Corneil and Fossa (Chapters 2 and 3) suggest that government has a large role to play. However, Andrew Kimball, in his essay (Chapter 14), makes the case for a private-market model for industrial mixed use.

Figure 1.13 This covered storm water collection trench in an industrial district allows for truck crossings, loading, and parking.

Figure 1.14 A mixed-use street in the Aramingo district of Philadelphia, Pennsylvania.

Industrial District Design: Edges, Streets, and Spaces

Industrial districts are thought of as the disconnected, leftover spaces of the city fouled with noise, dirt, and truck traffic, better suited to movies about the shadowy underside of Gotham than to the parks, street trees, and other amenities often deployed by the urban designer. Certainly, every city has those kinds of menacing and forbidding places—dominated by warehouses, concrete batching operations, fuel storage tanks, electrical substations, sewage treatment plants, and the last surviving "heavy manufacturers" of things like paint or canned foods. The urban design of the manufacturing districts hosting these kinds of uses has received little attention.

Some cities are beginning to address the urban design of manufacturing districts—design guidelines accompany new innovative zoning strategies. However, our research suggests that even the "Manufacturing-Aware Cities"[7] approach industrial district urban design from the timeworn defensive city-planning posture that manufacturing is a nuisance to be tolerated rather than an asset to be celebrated. Thus most of the urban design energy is focused on the mitigation of both real and perceived negative externalities at the edge—noise, dirt, odors, trucks—not on promoting a supportive environment within the district. Even where new manufacturing districts are planned, the approach to space-making relies on the same formal language one finds in an office district, not on the particular ecology of production.[8]

For those districts where there is significant employment in light industrial activities, urban design has an essential role to play in organizing the activities of the district and in reconciling competing demands on real estate, room on the streets, and the uses of public spaces. In these places the urban design of the manufacturing district has an impact on the quality of life for the people who work there by enabling access to transit and to amenities, such as places to eat or gather. Industrial district design can make manufacturing visible by creating views into buildings, displaying products, and celebrating the "making" of things and in that way educate a public that may not understand or appreciate the importance of urban manufacturing. A well-designed manufacturing district can also attract investments that support the manufacturing ecology, such as building upgrades, new information infrastructure, and new interactive places to meet and share intelligence.

What, then, are the urban design considerations for industrial districts in the city? How is the core issue of integration/agglomeration versus protection/isolation manifested in the urban form of manufacturing districts?

- *Edges.* The edge of the district is where the essential dilemma of urban manufacturing meets the ground: integration and agglomeration with the urban economy, or segregation and protection from encroachment. How discrete and identifiable is the edge—is it closed or open, a wall or a filter?
- *Streets.* Industrial district streets are where workers, residents, and goods all compete for space, not only to get in and out of the district but to move within the district to share resources and information. Do the streets constrict or enable the dense interactions of the urban manufacturing district?
- *Spaces.* Most urban manufacturing districts are littered with outdoor staging and storage areas that no longer function as they were intended to. How can these leftover spaces be repurposed for a diverse range of activities and tied together to create a new kind of industrial-district public realm that supports innovation, interaction, and communication?

Edges

Scenes of urban manufacturing:

> *Modest townhouses with stoops give way to a one-story brick building with a strip of steel windows just below the edge of a flat roof. A large roll-down door is open, affording a glimpse of three people making a furniture frame. Almost imperceptibly the street keeps changing—fewer houses, more factories—until the destination is reached: a large bread factory that is shipping its products on tractor trailers from loading docks, but which also has a storefront selling baguettes and croissants. This is the messy reality of the "soft edge" that is common around urban manufacturing districts where mixed-use blocks with both factories and houses display a chaotic range of building types and scales. Finding the edge is confounded even further by the land use pattern, which reveals many "non-conforming" manufacturing uses outside of the district.*
>
> *As evening approaches, the choice of sidewalks is clear: on one side the light from ground-floor apartments spills out onto the pavement; on the other side a long expanse of almost windowless brick wall casts an intimidating and unrelieved shadow. Occasionally one of the neighborhood cross-streets creates an opening in this relentless wall of buildings, affording a view down streets lined with more featureless brick walls. A large truck sits across half of the street, the rest of its length buried in the one- or two-story factory where it is picking up its cargo. Here is the Maginot Line between living and working*

HARD (medium pruple)
  Industrial
  Residential
  Plugged-in building
  Lobby/Office/Retail (Industrial Building)
  Lobby/Office/Retail (Residential Building)

SOFT

MIXED

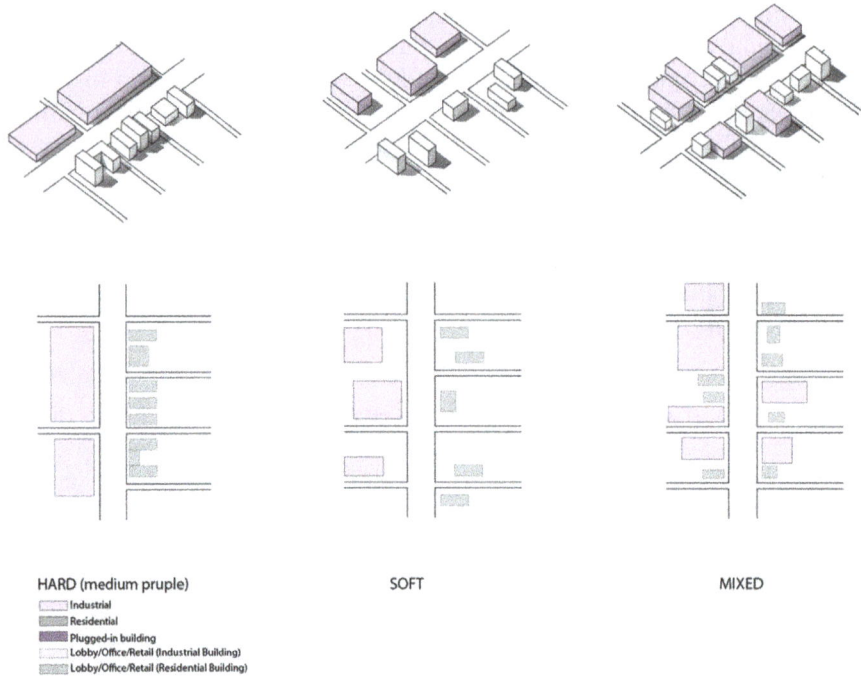

Figure 1.15 A typology of industrial district edges: hard, soft, and mixed.

Figure 1.16 A soft edge between industrial and residential uses in Berkeley, California.

Figure 1.17 A hard-edge street in Newmarket, Boston.

coveted both by city planners who want to keep noise, dust, and odors away from the neighborhood and by advocates for industrial preservation who want the limits of real estate pressure to be clearly defined.

The residents of the dense Breda neighborhood in Milan remember when almost everyone worked for the Breda aircraft and machinery manufacturing company. As with other urban campuses, the edge of the Breda district is at once definitive and porous: the large sign over the gate is hardly needed to create a sense of entry into a precinct where the buildings are arranged in ways that recall the logic of the original production processes (see Fossa, Chapter 3). Many of the neighborhood streets pass directly into the campus but there is also some measure of discontinuity with the surrounding street network: dead-end streets are created by a rail line, highway, or canal, or shifts in the size and orientation of the blocks—legacies of an earlier incarnation of the district when oversized lots were needed for larger factory buildings. Many urban industrial districts follow this kind of "industrial park" model bounded by a hybrid edge that is at once both hard and soft.

As the case studies in the Atlas reveal (Part IV), it is rarely the situation that industrial uses, regulatory boundaries and building massing all align in such a way that the edges of the industrial district are unambiguous. It is true that urban industrial districts may have one or more hard edges defined by some large-scale infrastructure such as an elevated highway or rail line. There is often some level of discontinuity in the street pattern as grids give way to the larger blocks found in the "campuses" such as the Brooklyn Navy Yard or the Breda district in Milan. However, it is more typical for the edges to be messy—a mix of land uses and building types and configurations—and for some number of streets to extend seamlessly into the district. This soft edge, which is typical of traditional manufacturing neighborhoods like Chicago's Clybourn Corridor or San Francisco's Mission District, often reflects the creative ecology of an active urban production neighborhood and the extension of the surrounding street grid into the industrial district promotes interaction and agglomeration. However, those same streets and roads can become avenues of commercial gentrification. Interestingly, in Portland's Central Eastside—perhaps the single most resilient urban manufacturing district in the US—all of the surrounding residential streets extend into the district. In Barcelona, the famous Cerdà grid continues uninterrupted into the 22@ Innovation District.

Design at the Edge: Strategies and Best Practices

Because so much of city planning is preoccupied with the separation of land uses, district boundaries of all kinds are fundamental. So it is no surprise that the boundaries of industrial districts are addressed by most cities. However, as is the case with industrial street standards (described below), the standards and guidelines for industrial district edges offer a set of familiar techniques, such as deep landscape buffers, that are targeted toward mitigating externalities rather than creating a well-designed interface between the district and its context. An exception is the proposed form-based code for Cincinnati, Ohio, where edge designs consider the entire street context and are calibrated to different kinds of production.[9] Where altogether new districts are created through redevelopment plans, active urban edges can be designed in ways that are not easily accomplished through standard zoning tools (see Bingham and Shapiro Chapter 11).

One way to avoid the jarring changes in scale that can occur across the two sides of a street is to map district boundaries through the middle of the block or at the back of what are often deeper parcels along the ends of blocks facing an avenue (see design guidelines, p. 270). In this way the properties facing the nonindustrial street can match the uses and scales of the buildings

Figure 1.18 Mid-block alleys enable transition from industrial and residential neighborhoods, Strathcona, Vancouver.

on the opposite side of the street. The transition to the industrial buildings and uses occurs on the side streets just behind the larger properties facing the avenue. Of course, this is easier to do where the street and block system includes a mid-block alley, creating both a transitional zone for massing and a service zone for manufacturers who can then have active street frontages. This is the case in the Strathcona district in Vancouver.

As effective as these strategies can be, they rely on finding a fairly clear line between land uses. However, what should be done where the edge is truly "soft"—where uses are mixed, as they are in traditional working neighborhoods? One ambitious strategy is to enable mixed industrial/residential infill buildings, which by filling gaps can give definition to the edge and be designed to manage the transition in use and scale. Architect Nicole Pandolfo has developed a series of prototypes for horizontal mixed use in which neighborhood-oriented residential buildings and factories of different scales back up against each other or interlock.

This builds on a strategy of carving into or clipping onto the factory shed to moderate the scale of the box, an approach that was pioneered in the so-called "artisans' settlements" in Modena, Italy, and has been the basis of several design explorations, including one for new municipal workshops in Toronto and a new urban industrial district in Morrisania in the Bronx by Robert N. Lane (see Figure 1.20). In the Strathcona industrial district of Vancouver, a new building puts housing over light manufacturing and creates a mid-block transition between a mixed-use corridor and the rest of the industrial district behind.[10]

In addition to architectural solutions such as new mixed-use and hybrid buildings, new openings, or additions for existing buildings, there are lighter solutions to both softening and articulating the edge, including changes in streetscape and street landscape treatment. The City of Philadelphia's Mural Arts program engaged artists, youth, residents, and other community partners to design and create a series of murals in old industrial neighborhoods that depict the city's expansive history in brewing, textiles, tool-making, railroads, and other key industries. The "inside-out" murals painted on windowless expanses of brick walls reveal the processes that took place within them. This is an interesting variation on the "urban industrial chic" graffiti that often signals the frontier of commercial gentrification and industrial displacement. Here the artwork is of and for the community, celebrating and communicating the value of urban manufacturing.

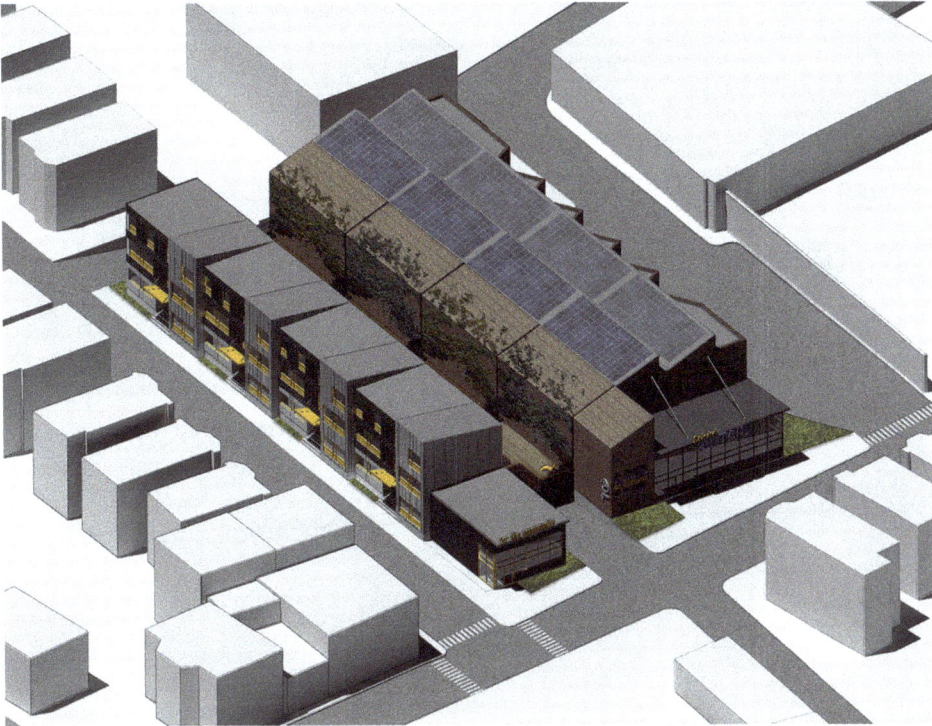

MANUFACTTURING: ▓   **RESIDENTIAL:** ▓
LOAD/UNLOAD: ▓   **EXISTING:** ▓
ADMINISTRATION: ▓

HEAVY INDUSTRIAL
GROUND FLOOR
BUILT / UNBUILT RATIO: 0.82
MANUFACTURING SF: 2,300 SF   45.0 %
LOAD / UNLOAD SF: 1,150 SF   22.5 %
ADMINISTRATION SF: 575 SF   10.0 %
RESIDENTIAL SF: 1,150 SF   22.5 %
TOTAL SF: 5,175 SF

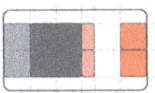

HIGH DENSITY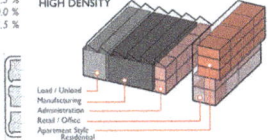

LOW DENSITY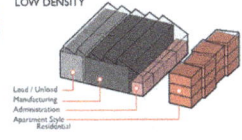

LIGHT INDUSTRIAL
GROUND FLOOR
BUILT / UNBUILT RATIO: 1.00
MANUFACTURING SF: 3,450 SF   55.0 %
LOAD / UNLOAD SF: 1,150 SF   18.0 %
ADMINISTRATION SF: 575 SF   9.0 %
RESIDENTIAL SF: 1,150 SF   18.0 %
TOTAL SF: 6,325 SF

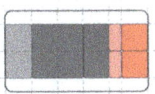

HIGH DENSITY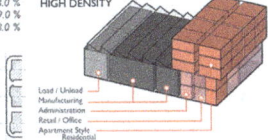

LOW DENSITY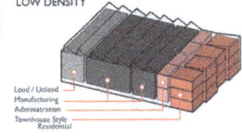

CLEAN INDUSTRIAL
GROUND FLOOR
BUILT / UNBUILT RATIO: 1.00
MANUFACTURING SF: 4,600 SF   72.5 %
LOAD / UNLOAD SF: 1,150 SF   18.0 %
ADMINISTRATION SF: 575 SF   8.5 %
RESIDENTIAL SF: --- SF   0.0 %
TOTAL SF: 6,325 SF

HIGH DENSITY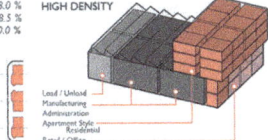

LOW DENSITY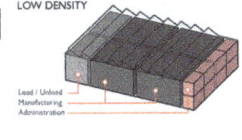

Figure 1.19 In the design study, new industrial mixed-use buildings create the transition between industrial and residential areas.

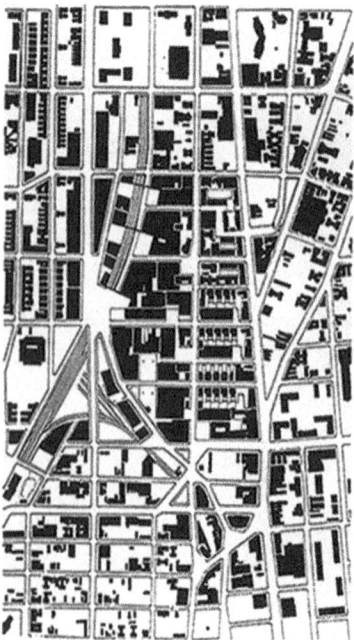

Figure 1.20 This proposal for a manufacturing neighborhood seamlessly integrates industrial and residential buildings at a variety of scales. Robert Lane.

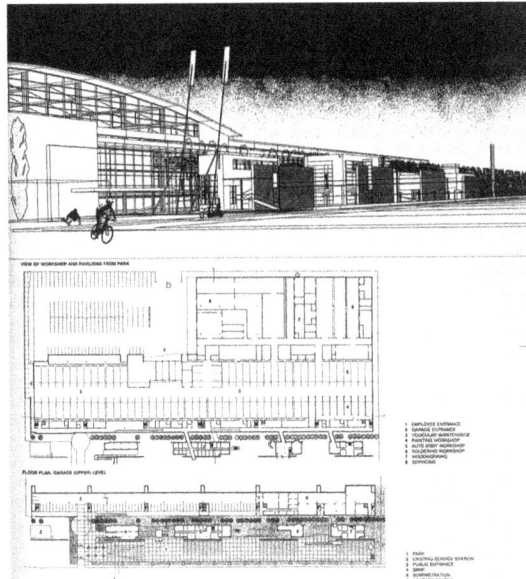

Figure 1.21 This proposal for municipal workshops in Toronto softens the factory shed with "clip-on" program elements.

Streets

In the loft district near the center of the city, trucks line the curbs on one side of the street. Deliverymen wait for an opening in the steady streams of businessmen rushing for the subway and shoppers heading for stores where products made on the factory floors above are sold. Across the street a delivery cart is exploiting the clear path of what is supposed to be a bike lane.

In the industrial park beyond the center of the city, tractor trailers block the street with impunity as they maneuver into loading docks, riding over curbs and sidewalks as they do. The one-story, almost windowless buildings along the sides of the street create a corridor that is relentless in its uniformity, but for the occasional open spaces where trucks are parked or materials stored. However, in a few places the owners have opened their buildings out onto the street, branding their presence with a new awning and planters.

In the manufacturing neighborhood, workers and residents, panel trucks, and cars at once make way and get in the way of each other. Here it seems that the street has itself become a kind of open factory where the pavement is the lobby, corridor, conference room, and cafeteria.

The competition for space on the street is fundamental to the urban condition. Nowhere is this more apparent than in industrial districts where workers, residents, drivers, and pedestrians compete for street space with goods movement, not only to get products in and out of the district but to move materials within it. Streets also play a critical role in how industry is perceived in the city: is the street a forbidding experience or a window into essential production activities?

In the older loft districts the streets are defined not by windowless one-story buildings but by human-scaled facades that reveal activity within. Many of the buildings in the older loft districts have been adaptively re-used, sometimes anchoring low-rise districts, as is the case with the GMDC in Brooklyn, the Global Dye Works in Philadelphia's Aramingo district, and the Showplace Square building in San Francisco's Dogpatch neighborhood (see Part IV, Atlas). There are some examples of contemporary vertical factories that relate well to the street, such as Ryhove in Ghent, Belgium by TRANS Architecture, or Lafayette 148 in Shantou, China by Mehrdad Hadighi and Tsz Yan Ng Architects (see Part II).

However, in general, industrial district streets are lined with the single-story, almost window-less "production boxes" that remain the staple urban factory type, creating an intimidating pedestrian experience and transmitting the mistaken impression that the buildings are abandoned or underutilized.

Industrial district street design also has to accommodate goods movement. The typical "complete streets" prescription, which attempts to accommodate all modes and integrate green infrastructure, needs to be recalibrated for industrial users. As bicycle transit has expanded, so have accidents between trucks and bicycles. Manufacturers often object to street trees or other forms of greening that interfere with their on-street and on-sidewalk operations.

Best Practices

Some cities do address the design of industrial streets. Both in West Berkeley, California, and the Midtown Mixed-Use district in Cleveland, new industrial developments—like new commercial and mixed-use developments—must meet a set of form-based design guidelines that address typical urban design issues such as street wall continuity and transparency. The new form-based code in Cincinnati includes a series of three-dimensional digital models showing street-oriented massing, setbacks, parking/loading locations, and street wall transparency[11] (see Part IV, Atlas).

Where new industrial redevelopment districts are being planned or are underway, such as the Menomonee Valley Industrial Center[12] and the 30th Street Corridor[13] in Milwaukee and the Tukwila Manufacturing/Industrial Center[14] in Seattle, it is possible to design new multimodal streets. In the Cornfield Arroyo Seco district in Los Angeles, where the city is advancing a district-wide plan for a new manufacturing and mixed-use district, a new street classification system creates street types calibrated to different land use conditions. This includes a Local Industrial Modified Street type that allows for an automobile travel lane in each direction as well as a bike lane, but still is designed to facilitate truck access to industrial properties. Typical features include limited on-street parking, sidewalks, and street trees.[15]

While these guidelines work for new mixed-use areas, they do not address the particular programmatic and design requirements of manufacturers in existing, more consolidated industrial districts. In Portland's Central Eastside, as in other low-rise districts, the street experience is challenged by breaks in the street wall for loading and storage areas and by long expanses of unrelieved and windowless wall. Yet, many of the streets are still successful because of robust street plantings, facade improvements, and the occasional strategic punched opening to the inside. There are also intersection improvements, such as clear crosswalks, ramps, and corner bulb-outs, which are designed to be mounted by trucks. Changes in practices related to urban goods movement are helping to resolve some of these conflicts, including the use of smaller vehicles, freight consolidation, and reallocation of space on the street[16] (see Conway, Chapter 4).

Figure 1.22 Industrial district streets can be designed to be flexible and adaptable.

Figure 1.23 New lightweight mixed-use buildings on top of monumental loft factories, Robert N. Lane.

Embrace the Messiness

In Europe, where many more generations of urban manufacturing are layered on top of one another, a kind of messiness is apparent in the streetscape; vehicles of every size, from light trucks to scooters and bicycles, share space on the street. A mix of old, new, and repurposed structures creates a chaotic street wall. This lively but diverse environment is not easily managed or planned for. However, in New York City the Urban Design Division of the Department

Figure 1.24 In Europe, streets are often appropriated for production.

of City Planning is pioneering a new model that attempts to capture this diversity for existing mixed industrial streets. In this exploration a kind of "kit of parts" may be deployed for different frontage conditions along the street. These parts are designed so that they can still be aligned with one another to create a continuous streetscape (see Graphic Essay 1, p. 93).

To address this complex challenge, industrial street design needs to move beyond the curb lines and rethink the street as not merely a right-of-way but as a public space that can accommodate multiple agendas simultaneously or at different times. For example, by acknowledging that goods movement is itself part of the identity and branding of the district—the rolling sample racks that are an indelible part of New York's Garment District, for instance—the visibility of goods movement becomes an industrial retention strategy by communicating the vitality of urban production. In that spirit, as part of the Making Midtown initiative (sponsored by the Design Trust for Public Space and the Council of Fashion Designers of America), the now almost ubiquitous New York City bike lanes were made wider and re-branded to accommodate—and celebrate—the movement of goods on garment racks or small motorized delivery vehicles like those described by Alison Conway (see Conway, Chapter 4).

In one design study from Making Midtown the industrial street becomes a fashion show runway. As suggested below, there may be conditions in which the industrial district street is taken over for production activities in the same way, becoming a kind of "working street." The strategy of designating streets within a district as either loading/working streets or entrance/service streets is part of design studies for both Fort Point in Boston and Central Eastside in Portland.[17] This is not too far from reality. In the Breda industrial district described by

Giovanna Fossa (Chapter 3), a formerly private street in the interior of the campus has become the mixed-use armature for the district, mediating between the manufacturing uses on the north side and the institutional and cultural uses on the south side.

Spaces

> *On the loading dock where identical oversized crates had once been stacked, smaller containers of different sizes and colors are scattered about. Between these, folding chairs create a kind of "meet-up" space for workers, fueled by coffee just purchased from the food truck down the street.*
>
> *In the course of the day the food truck attracts workers, designers, and cargo brokers to an oddly shaped space created by the curve of a now unused rail spur barely visible though the asphalt. Grass pokes through cracks in the broken pavement and a few papers have blown up against the bottom of a chain-link fence. The edges of the space have been appropriated for storage, although it's not clear by whom.*

Storage yards for materials and equipment, aprons at loading docks, front-yard setbacks, and yards between generations of building additions and demolitions: this is the messy inventory of open spaces in the urban manufacturing district. The construction of simple rectangular factory boxes on irregularly shaped blocks creates the reduced coverage and idiosyncratic open space patterns found in even the more centrally located industrial districts. In their desire to impose an aesthetic order, urban designers may feel compelled to either occupy or design these leftover spaces. In fact, these spaces serve an essential role in driving up the "interactions per block" metric. In Milan, as Fossa describes (Chapter 3),

> marginal, residual spaces have always been useful for small manufacturing activities. Cellars or stores underneath residential buildings, where better uses are restricted, sometimes host maker laboratories; it could be thought of as the Italian and more urban version of the garage in the United States, as an instant informal space for hosting start-ups.

Thus, the role of the urban designer in this condition is not so much to redesign or fill these spaces as it is to enable appropriation for the widest range of entrepreneurial activities. As Corneil explains (Chapter 2), many of the chamfered corners of the blocks in Barcelona's 22@ district have become informal work yards, which "do not follow the conventions of sidewalks, tree plantings, or lighting patterns, creating a quality of 'unfinished' which, many would argue, is essential to inspiring creativity and hands-on activities."

In some high-density production districts, such as loft districts in or near the core of the city and the more densely built-out low-rise districts, there are few opportunities to create either formal or informal open spaces. However, even in these conditions there are opportunities to repurpose leftover spaces. Loading docks and passages to freight elevators can become production spaces, places for workers to eat, gather, and interact, or if the right management tools are in place, can become platforms for pop-up retail, restaurant, art, and performance activities. As part of the previously mentioned Making Midtown initiative for the Garment District, these leftover spaces were reimagined to provide relief from the compression of the canyon-like streets in much the same way. Even the narrow slots between the district's monumental factories were linked together, both at ground level and above, to provide additional mid-block passageways for goods movement, worker mobility, and display of production activity.[18]

Figure 1.25 In Berkeley, California, leftover spaces are redesigned as part of the public realm.

Courtyards and "De Facto Superblocks"

In Europe, where internal courtyards are a common feature of the urban fabric, such spaces play a key role in the life of the district as places for mixing activities at different times of the day and creating opportunities for strategic building modifications and additions. In Milan many of these inward-looking spaces are being reconnected to their surrounding neighborhoods and reimagined not only for production uses but for trade fairs and cultural activities. In Barcelona the interiors of the blocks and the alleyways are full of workshops and productive activities.

The courtyard form is less common in North America, but there are other opportunities to create interactivity by utilizing the aforementioned leftover spaces around buildings and creating new openings into the factory sheds that frame them. Another strategy is to repurpose selected streets as outdoor working spaces. In the same way that pedestrian-only zones are created in the commercial centers of cities, noncommercial traffic would be eliminated on those streets in manufacturing districts, creating a kind of "industrial superblock" linked to the surrounding neighborhood but enabling the unfettered movement, interaction, and activity typical of an industrial park. This dedicated "factory-street," together with the other irregular spaces that abut it, can create a kind of internal mid-block courtyard where manufacturers can share resources, consolidate goods movement and delivery, and host informal amenities such as food trucks.

Creating the Public Realm

In the few places where new industrial districts are being created, such as the 30th Street Corridor in Milwaukee, a comprehensive and deliberate public realm can be designed. These design studies create green streets, shared "campus" spaces, and internal courtyard spaces for logistics. The question is whether this more rationalized design will support greater creativity and productivity.

Figure 1.26 In American cities, groups of blocks may create interior courtyard spaces, Los Angeles, California.

In the many existing largely low-rise districts, the imposition of a rational and comprehensive order might not only kill the informal creative ecology of the district but might unintentionally abet commercial gentrification. Nevertheless, in the search for balance between integration and protection, there is a role for creating a new kind of public realm that supports creative interaction and favors production-related activities while still creating access for the public and visibility for manufacturing in the city. Such a strategy would knit together the leftover spaces into an idiosyncratic network of interconnected courtyards and passageways. Landscaping and lighting treatments would create a unique identity for this open space system.

An exemplary model is the Bayer campus in Berkeley, California. Here the leftover spaces between buildings were knit together to create a new public realm. Because many of these spaces were bounded by the blank walls of the factories, the industrial sheds were carved into, clipped onto, and otherwise transformed to animate the reimagined public spaces. This same strategy was adopted in the city of Stamford's Master Plan for the Waterside district and is also the basis for a 1998 design study for a new mixed industrial district in the Bronx.

Landscape design plays a central role in the repositioning of industrial lands, from Emscher Park in the Ruhr Valley (Germany) to Fresh Kills on Staten Island (New York). However, in urban conditions as well, landscape treatment helps create the new industrial district public realm. At the Bayer campus, landscape design embraces overhead utility racks and other elements of the production infrastructure. There are sometimes opportunities for larger-scale landscape interventions.[19] In the Ansaldo district in Milan, abandoned rail yards are being transformed into a public greenway. Milwaukee's Menomonee Valley Industrial Center converted fallow industrial acreage into a new greenway network, tying the district together and providing an amenity for residents and workers alike.

The creation of new public corridors through formerly closed districts or along industrial waterfronts is a powerful expression of the reintegration of industry and the city. In Portland's Central Eastside, Clay Street links the Ladd's Addition neighborhood to the Eastbank Esplanade waterfront greenway. Mountable curb ramps accommodate trucks, bicycles, and pedestrians. At the Bayer facility, the Dwight Way corridor through the campus links Berkeley to the Aquatic Park path. Along Portland's industrial Columbia South Shore, the proposed Slough Trail follows a streambed as it winds its way between, and connects, two industrial sub-districts.[20] Corridors along the waterfront, which are a universal objective in dense urban areas, may not

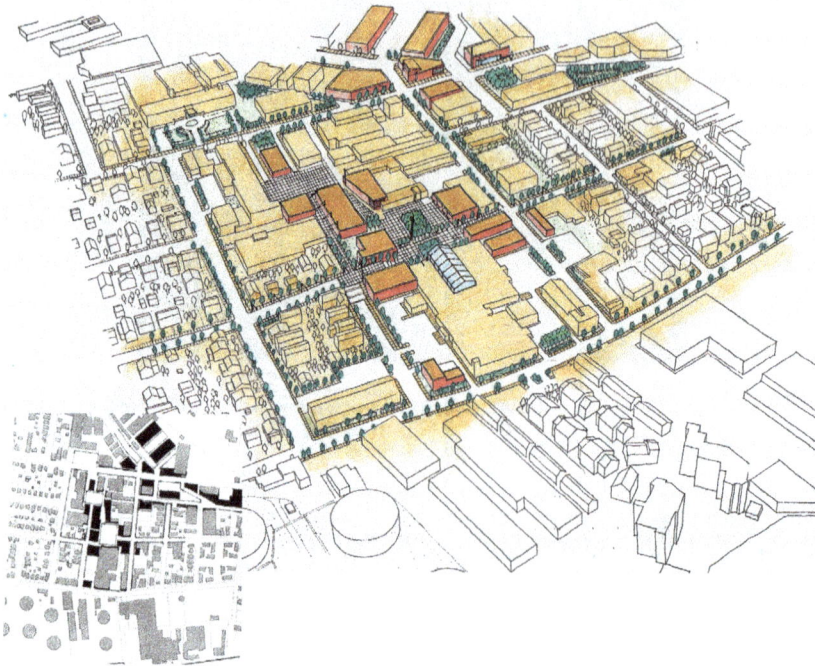

Figure 1.27 Strategic insertions create a public realm in this design study for the City of Stamford
Master Plan, 2003, Robert N. Lane.

be suitable where larger-scale shipping is anticipated. However, even where continuous access
along the waterfront is not desirable, properly designed corridors can lead to smaller parks and
plazas at the water. The Industrial Strategy for the city of St. Paul includes design studies that
reconcile industrial uses with waterfront access[21]—and in Paris, surprisingly, small freight loading areas along the Seine cohabitate with the classic French canal-front promenade.

As with mixed-use streets, an attractive and accessible public realm raises the challenge of
commercial gentrification and industrial displacement. Once again, the role of a mission-driven
entity in programming these spaces and managing this tension is essential.

What is Industry-Supportive Urban Design?

Taken together, this research points to a variety of best practices that in part would be broadly
applicable, but which also are calibrated to the special conditions of the urban manufacturing
district.

Manage the edge.

Create an edge that is well-defined and creates identity but is also porous enough to make
connections with the city. The urban design of the edge of the district helps resolve the fundamental conflict a bulwark against encroachment by other uses.

Create a diversity of block sizes and configurations.
This enables the flexibility needed for a rapidly changing sector—expansion, contraction, re-use, renovation, adaptation to new production methods. Both the subdivision into smaller blocks and the assembly of larger "superblocks" should be anticipated. (See Design Guidelines in Part IV: Atlas.)

Maintain and link flexible and irregular spaces.
With minimal interventions around technology and amenity, leftover spaces like loading docks, which are generally ignored or reconfigured by the urban designer, can support the production ecology by enabling flexible and shared uses at different times of the day or be linked together to create an armature for the district.

Create a connected street network.
Compactness and connectivity make it more efficient for workers and goods to move around the district and enable strategic points of connection to the surrounding neighborhoods as well as "eco-industrial" practices.

Activate selected streets and open spaces.
While many industrial district streets may be lined with largely featureless walls and storage lots, along key connecting corridors and open areas, spaces should be animated by windows into production spaces, entrances, front offices, and loading docks, all of which promote the kinds of incidental interactions that create the flexible ecology of a vibrant urban manufacturing district.

Make manufacturing visible.
Enable public access to selected streets and spaces where manufacturing processes can be seen. This is essential for fostering public understanding and appreciation of urban manufacturing.

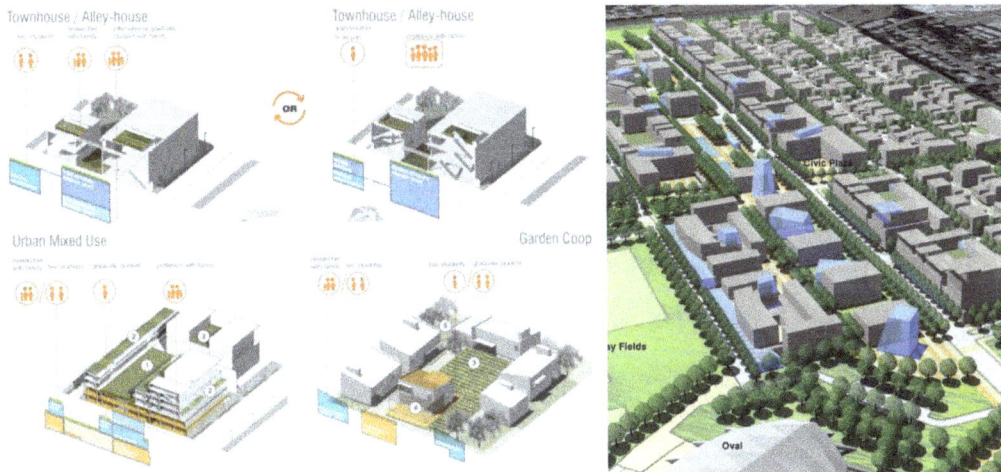

Figure 1.28 Industrial district housing types enable new living and working configurations in the Portland Innovation District master plan.

Create amenities with production workers in mind.
Create amenities that may be accessed by the general public but are targeted to the needs of production workers—places to interact, have lunch, take breaks.

Design streets that enable pedestrian amenity but prioritize and celebrate goods movement.
With the exception of selected connecting corridors, design elements such as street trees, lighting standards, bike lanes, and reduced crossing distances should not interfere with production-related operations. In fact, truck parking and loading operations should be thought of as elements that raise the visibility of manufacturing (see Conway, Chapter 4 and Department of City Planning, Graphic 1a).

Notes

1 City of Berkeley, "Chapter 23E.80 MU-LI Mixed Use-Light Industrial District Provisions," *Berkeley Municipal Code* (Berkeley, CA: City of Berkeley, 2015).
2 Robert E. Boley, *Industrial Districts: Principles in Practice* (Washington, DC: Urban Land Institute, 1962).
3 Robert E. Boley, *Industrial Districts Restudied: An Analysis of Characteristics*, Urban Land Institute Technical Bulletin Vol. 41 (Washington, DC: Urban Land Institute, 1961).
4 *Ibid.*
5 Department of City Planning, *Cornfield Arroyo Seco Specific Plan* (Los Angeles, CA: City of Los Angeles, 2012).
6 Department of City Development, *30th Street Corridor Economic Development Master Plan* (Milwaukee, WI: City of Milwaukee, 2011).
7 C.S. Dempwolf, N.Z. Hoelzel, B.R. Kraft, and N.G. Leigh, *Sustainable Urban Industrial Development* (Chicago, IL: American Planning Association, 2014).
8 City of Cincinnati, "1703 Use Districts," *Land Development Code* (Cincinnati, OH, 2014), 3–1–3–134.
9 *Ibid.*
10 General Manager of Planning and Development Services, "RTS No. 9736, CD-1 Rezoning," *Policy Report Development and Building* (Vancouver, BC: City of Vancouver, September 11, 2012).
11 See City of Cincinnati, "1703 Use Districts," *Land Development Code.*
12 Ron Henken and Joe Peterangelo, *Redevelopment in Milwaukee's Menomonee Valley: What Worked and Why?* (Milwaukee, WI: Public Policy Forum, 2014).
13 *30th Street Corridor Economic Development Master Plan* (2011).
14 Puget Sound Regional Council Growth Management Policy Board, *Tukwila Manufacturing/Industrial Center* (Tukwila, WA: Puget Sound Regional Council Growth Management Policy Board, 2012).
15 See *Cornfield Arroyo Seco Specific Plan* (2012).
16 Bureau of Planning, *Central Eastside Industrial Zoning Study* (Portland, OR: City of Portland, 2003).
17 Hacin + Associates Inc, *Seaport Square: Setting the Standard for Innovation on the Waterfront*, Seaport Square Master Plan (Boston, MA: Hacin + Associates, Inc., 2010).
18 Andrew Bernheimer, Colin Cathcart, Kei Hayashi, and Robert N. Lane, *Making Midtown: A New Vision for a 21st Century Garment District in New York City* (New York, NY: Design Trust for Public Space, 2012).
19 Todd W. Bressi, "Effective Industrial Growth in a Progressive City," *Places* (New York, NY: Design History Foundation, 1995).
20 Bureau of Planning and Sustainability, *Columbia South Shore Plan District* (Portland, OR: City of Portland, 2015).
21 Laura Wolf-Powers and Interface Studio, *An Industrial Study for The City of Saint Paul* (Boston, MA: Initiative for a Competitive Inner City, May 2012).

2 Manufacturing in the Innovation District

Janne Corneil

The "innovation district" has emerged as a promising strategy for cities searching for new economic prospects in the postindustrial context. The innovation-district model, where universities and business partners commercialize discoveries and products developed by faculty, researchers, and entrepreneurs in a tight-knit and diverse urban context, holds promise for localities that have struggled to attract new industries and maintain living-wage jobs. In the past decade cities with well-endowed research universities like Cambridge, Massachusetts and Seattle are cornering new markets with innovative technologies while tech-savvy cities like Chattanooga and Kansas City are charting their own success by investing in networks of web-based entrepreneurs and start-ups. Cities like Barcelona and Detroit, through partnerships between municipalities, community organizations, and anchor institutions, are consciously building on local assets and skills to devise new economies that link community and innovation. All of these cities are investing in their innovation-district strategies and rebuilding their urban neighborhoods to accommodate the innovation economy.

An economic development strategy that links locally grown invention, ideas, and talent to global opportunities and markets requires a human-scaled, urban, and mixed-use setting to nurture the "innovation ecosystem" of people, programs, and places. Innovation-district strategy is necessarily focused on intellectual capital, human interaction, and collaboration—and, as a result, urban designers and planners focus on creating buildings and public places that foster social interaction and diverse activities at all times of day and night. Nurturing ideation is at the root of the innovation-district strategy. In our excitement to embrace these cerebral functions we have overlooked the daily act of making things. Manufacturing in the innovation process is one of the essential activities of this new economic model that has more recently attracted the attention of policy makers and economists. We as urban planners and designers need to understand the evolution of manufacturing activities in order to help shape the future of our cities in a more intentional manner.

This chapter will discuss the nature of manufacturing in the innovation economy and will elaborate on the district-building outcomes of urban design and planning policy, or lack thereof, in two very different examples from the US and Europe. It will illustrate how cities and universities are integrating manufacturing uses into their districts and, if not, what opportunities there may be to rekindle urban production as an essential component of urban innovation. In addition it will consider the role that urban design plays in enabling the complex network of relationships and activities that support manufacturing in an innovation district.

Manufacturing Matters in the Innovation Economy

The place of manufacturing in the innovation process is an ongoing topic of diverging viewpoints. Nurturing the early stages of product innovation in proximity to the research is accepted as best practice, but many argue that once a product reaches a certain stage of development the manufacturing process is more dependent on labor and tends to migrate to places where the cost of business is lower. Richard Locke and Rachel Wellhausen's research as part of MIT's Production in the Innovation Economy (PIE) Commission on manufacturing and innovation asserts that "innovation takes place not merely in the early phases of product development and design but throughout the value chain, including on the shop floor, as products are modified for new applications as well as through repeated interactions with customers."[1] Advanced manufacturing is an essential part of the process of innovating—the feedback loop from research to design to production provides inputs essential to sustaining innovation and the development of new ideas and products. Maintaining manufacturing activities close to innovation hubs is essential (see Markforged interview, p. 19).

Understanding the Changing Nature of Manufacturing

The kind of manufacturing that shaped our cities in the nineteenth and early twentieth centuries was inclusive of invention, design, prototyping, and production, including mass production. Workers, product engineers, management, and their families lived in a dense, pedestrian and mixed-use urban environment. Over the last fifty years, we lost that tight-knit productive community to zoning, suburbanization, and global pressures. The innovation-district model tries to recapture that kind of environment by co-locating small-scale manufacturers capable of rapid prototyping and small-batch production with institutions and designers in a neighborhood rich with amenities. As Chris Anderson, founder of *Wired* magazine, describes in his 2012 book *Makers*, "The idea of a 'factory' is, in a word, changing. Just as the Web democratized innovation in bits, a new class of 'rapid prototyping' technologies, from 3-D printers to laser cutters, is democratizing innovation in atoms."[2] The economic boom in the "Internet of Things" is accelerating the need to accommodate spaces and design approaches that support advanced manufacturing and fabrication activities in innovation districts.

A Tale of Two Innovation Districts

Kendall Square, the "most innovative square mile on the planet,"[3] is a 210-acre area adjacent to the Massachusetts Institute of Technology (MIT) in Cambridge, Massachusetts. MIT has an enrollment of 11,300 students and undertook approximately $697 million of sponsored research in 2015. During the academic year, roughly 3,750 researchers, including visiting faculty and scientists, work with MIT faculty and students on projects funded by the government, private and independent foundations, and industry. Cambridge is home to over 300 life sciences- and technology-related firms, including Sanofi/Genzyme, Pfizer, Baxter, Biogen, Microsoft, Google, and Facebook. According to the Kendall Square Market Profile prepared by the city of Cambridge, 20,634 employees live within a half-mile radius of the Square.[4] Although the number of manufacturing jobs in the area is very low, the activities that researchers and new enterprises engage in include different kinds of fabrication and prototyping as

USES & AFFILIATION

- Residential
- Mixed-use
- Other commercial
- Innovation companies
- Co-working / Accelerators
- Academic co-founded companies
- Academic affiliated institutes
- Academic department & institutes
- Government / Civic
- Industrial

MANUFACTURING ACTIVITY

- Laboratories
- Prototyping
- Production
- Energy

Figure 2.1 Kendall Square is home to a mix of academic, research, some residential, and industry partners that are engaged in new kinds of advanced manufacturing activities.

part of their research and early-stage product development. The latest master plan for Kendall identifies an additional capacity of 4 million square feet of mixed-use development including commercial, residential, research, retail, and other amenities.[5]

The 22@ innovation district in Barcelona encompasses over 490 acres of a nineteenth-century urban industrial district adjacent to downtown Barcelona, of which roughly 70 percent has been transformed or is slated for redevelopment. A very ambitious plan, with capacity for over 43 million square feet of new or redeveloped space, is planned for 22@ including 8.6 million square feet of housing and other urban amenities. There are ten educational institutions with over 25,000 students located in the district as well. Between 2000 and 2015, approximately 4,500 new businesses were established, 47.3 percent of which began as start-ups in the district. Approximately 93,000 people work and 90,000 live in the district as of 2015. 22@, with its holistic approach to urban regeneration, has become a global model of sustainable urban economic development and many cities around the world have been trying to replicate its success (see Part IV).[6]

Figure 2.2 Advanced manufacturing activities are happening, hidden away in the hallways of MIT and deep in the superblock complexes of the biotech companies and research institutes in Kendall Square.

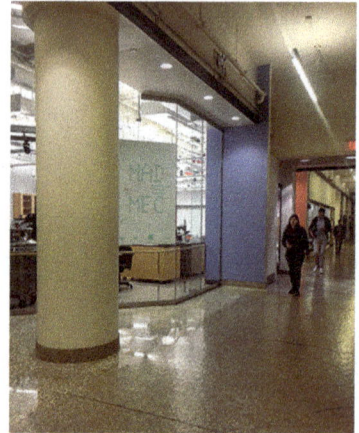

Figure 2.3 The Poblenou neighborhood of Barcelona's 22@ innovation district accommodates a medley of new and old uses including industry, education, research, and civic uses where more traditional manufacturing coexists with advanced manufacturing activities.

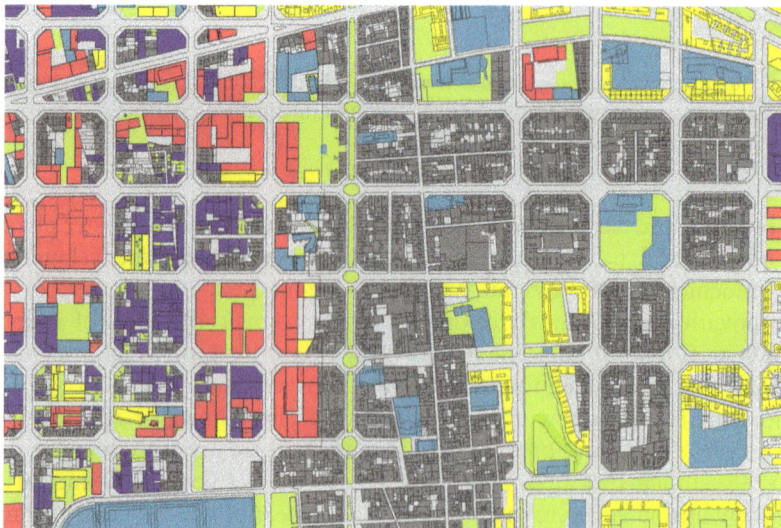

Figure 2.4 Barcelona's @22 innovation district accommodates a medley of new and old uses including industry (purple), civic and education (blue), commercial (red), residential (yellow), and existing workshops and historic (grey) where more traditional manufacturing coexists with advanced manufacturing activities

Figure 2.5 22@ Barcelona is a lively, mixed-use district where new academic buildings are woven together with historic industrial buildings.

Figure 2.6 An alley street in 22@ Barcelona supports a mix of small workshops and housing; new street design accommodates both loading bays and apartment entrances.

These two examples have very similar high-level goals of promoting economic development by attracting global talent and nurturing a ground-up innovation economy. Both places have been studied extensively by urban planners and recognized for their economic success. Despite having similar goals the planning history and urban morphology of these two districts is starkly different; it is in these contrasts that we can start to understand how historic context and planning policy create opportunities or obstacles to supporting a range of contemporary manufacturing uses in the innovation economy.

The "Hands-On" Mission of Anchor Institutions

We associate the research and commercialization of new knowledge that happens at and around universities with theoretical and highly controlled activities, when in fact a significant proportion of research pursuits involve the messy processes of designing, building, and testing physical things. After decades of moving toward computer modeling and simulation, many universities are rebuilding their "experiential" curriculum to support "learning-by-doing" academic strategies.

William Barton Rogers, MIT's founding president, believed that education should be "both broad and useful, enabling students to discover and apply knowledge for the benefit of society ... and ... should be within easy reach of works, mills, forges, machine shops and mines."[7] Not only was it essential for the education to be experiential and hands-on; the connectivity with urban manufacturing was a founding principle of Rogers' plan for MIT from the outset. In 2012 there were almost 200 principal investigators (PIs) undertaking research in the broad category "manufacturing, design, and product development."[8] Faculty pursuing the commercialization of materials, advanced manufacturing processes, and research-based companies with significant manufacturing components are collocating in Kendall Square to benefit from close proximity to cutting-edge research.

Since 2000, 22@ Barcelona has attracted ten universities with over twenty-five centers focused on research or training in five industry clusters: IT, medtech, design, media, and energy. These facilities are located on infill sites throughout the district. Through a deliberate integration of higher education, research, entrepreneurship, start-up business, and established businesses collocated in complementary clusters of industry, the 22@ effort has reaped significant economic development and urban regeneration results. The academic facilities in 22@ are primarily geared toward practical and professional fields, providing satellite programs for Catalan higher-education institutions that focus on training, internship, and entrepreneurship.

The presence of an anchor institution in an innovation district is essential to that district's ability to innovate and grow new companies. However, it is the particular focus of the academic mission of the anchor on "hands on learning" and engagement with industry, specifically, that determines the degree to which an innovation economy will embrace manufacturing and fabrication as an essential component of the innovation ecosystem. Both MIT and the 22@ academic institutions and research centers embrace manufacturing activities; the extent to which they have connected the old workers and businesses with the new and the local community with global expertise has a lot to do with the redevelopment process and the specifics of planning policy.

Contrasting District Redevelopment Models

Kendall Square and 22@ Barcelona offer two starkly different redevelopment approaches: one born of an era of urban renewal (Kendall Square in the 1960s), the other a product of a more cautious era of incremental transformation (the Poblenou neighborhood of Barcelona in the 2000s). The need to build the social infrastructure into the urban context is recognized in both districts, although the history and policy in both cities has resulted in quite different contemporary urban conditions.

Kendall Square began with the hasty clearing of 29 acres in 1964 in preparation for the possibility of NASA's electronics research facility moving to Cambridge. Although East Cambridge's industrial areas were in decline, urban renewal resulted in the displacement of many large and small companies employing more than 2,750 people. When the NASA deal fell through the Cambridge Redevelopment Authority was left with a large and blighted area of assembled property with little developer interest. During the early '70s the city underwent a number of planning efforts using various appointed task forces and citizen advisory committees to create a land use vision for the area. Despite the general consensus by effected parties to create a mixed-use diverse urban district, political forces in support of focusing exclusively on job creation prevailed.[9] Cambridge Center, developed by Boston Properties, was the first of several internally focused office and research buildings built on large superblocks as planned urban development (PUDs). The office/campus character of Kendall Square, with its superblocks and wide multi-lane streets continues to dominate. Nineteenth-century manufacturing—after decades of decline—was all but eliminated in Kendall Square, clearing the way for modern research-based industry. Some nineteenth-century small factories still exist at the edges of Kendall in Campbridgeport and north of Binney Street, but for the most part the large factories were eliminated. Since the 1970s a new form of urban manufacturing has emerged as part of the innovation uses surrounding MIT. Advanced manufacturing activities occur throughout Kendall but, other than a few loading bays and storage yards, there is little recognizable trace of them. Over the last four to five years an effort to increase the diversity of uses in the Kendall Square area has been ongoing. The city of Cambridge has increased the amount of housing and improved the pedestrian quality of streets and public spaces. New retail along important pedestrian corridors is giving Kendall a more vibrant urban quality.

In contrast to Kendall Square, the regeneration strategy adopted by the City of Barcelona in 2000 for its Poblenou neighborhood embraced a surgical approach to urban infill while retaining the enduring nature of Ildefons Cerdà's Eixample urban grid. Cerdà's city block has proven to be a highly flexible urban structure, accommodating just about any land use from housing and universities to markets, churches, and public plazas. Many of the blocks in Poblenou have a mixture of housing and factories. The industrial uses range from small semi-detached workshops to large factories that take up entire blocks. Before 2000 the "22A" zoning only allowed for industrial uses so it was impossible to legally apply to build or renovate any use other than industrial. The name "22@" comes from a complete makeover of the 22A zoning. In 22@ today there are a variety of development incentives and procedures that allow for a broad range of development types and program mixes. The most significant zoning change was the density up-zoning that gave private developers increased capacity in exchange for land concessions that would ensure that additional "innovation" amenities (subsidized space for uses associated with learning, research, and entrepreneurship), new social housing, and public open space would be built.

Equally as important to the character of this urban district is the Poblenou "Industrial Heritage Protection Plan" that calls for the preservation of 114 historic industrial buildings in the district. Not only does new development need to respect the historic fabric of the neighborhood, it also has to work around a plethora of existing businesses, neighborhood institutions, and existing residents. To streamline the complex development scenario, the city created a toolkit of development incentives and procedures and simplified the permitting and design review process to make it relatively easy to pursue projects of any scale, thus promoting a very diverse and incremental transformation of the district.[10]

The 22@ strategy is unique in that it considers urban regeneration, economic development, and social improvement together. There was from the outset a conscious goal of linking the global firms and employees that would be attracted to the district with the local businesses and communities that had called Poblenou home for decades.[11] This does two things that are important. It ensures that the historic fabric of the city—the factories, work yards, and industrial structures of a time gone by—are refurbished and integrated into the new urban context. It is complicated, messy, and expensive but makes for a richer, more enduring urban environment that is attractive to the young and the talented. It also embraces the people that live and work in a neighborhood who would otherwise be displaced as the city develops physically, economically, and socially. The redevelopment strategy that embraced the historic fabric of the industrial district and engaged in a regeneration strategy that was strategic, catalytic, and incremental allowed for a gentle and inclusive transition to an innovation economy.

Kendall Square   Barcelona Poblenou

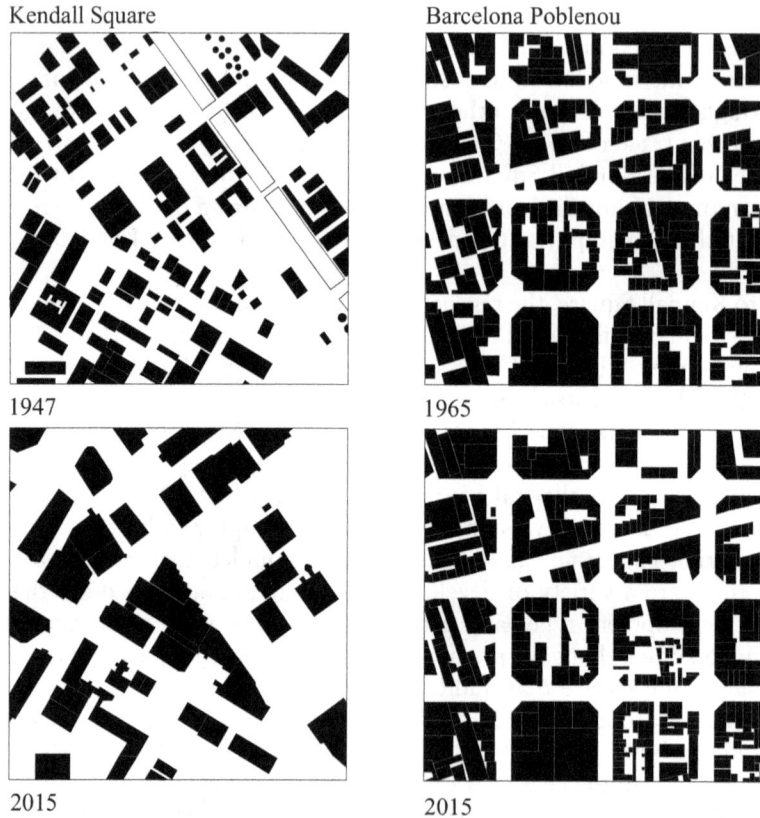

1947   1965

2015   2015

Figure 2.7 A comparison of historic and current urban form in Kendall Square and @22 Barcelona
        highlights the dramatic differences in outcomes between the redevelopment approaches.

Considerations of Urban Form

The redevelopment of Kendall Square, dominated by campus-like corporate offices and research facilities until recent years, has attracted global companies and nurtured the growth of an incredible innovation economy. The urban structure of big, flexible blocks has created opportunities for the city of Cambridge to accommodate very large corporate footprints in a dense, fine-grained, and walkable urban context. Conversely, large block development sites do not lend themselves to incremental small-scale change. As a result, Kendall over the years has not integrated existing small-scale enterprises, nor organically nurtured a fabric of new smallholders. In the past decade, however, through the deliberate efforts of outfits like the Cambridge Innovation Center, a burgeoning start-up scene has emerged. The city of Cambridge and MIT have more recently worked together to transform Kendall Square from its suburban and car-dominated scale of blocks and streets into a more pedestrian-scaled environment with a greater mix of residential and small-scale uses like co-working, start-up accelerators, restaurants, and retail. The streets and public spaces are evolving in classic form, with more narrow drive lanes, wider sidewalks with nice paving, more street trees, human-scaled lighting, benches, and bike lanes. Some very comfortable pedestrian streets like 3rd Street have been refurbished in the last couple of years. The occasional loading bay or service drive is apparent but the presence of manufacturing is nearly absent in the urban fabric of Kendall Square.

The 22@ innovation district in Barcelona is a different kind of place altogether. The combination of an infill redevelopment strategy and the nuanced manifestations of the Cerdà block in the Poblenou neighborhood has created a number of opportunities for a distinctive urban form that not only accommodates the flexible arrangements needed for urban manufacturing but also reflects the "working" character of its productive population. The mixed-use blocks with frequent alleyways support the "front door–back door" idea, where space is given to activities that happen in the public realm of both: along the main streets, four- to six-story housing above stores and restaurants; in the alleys and on the side streets, workshops and studios. Many blocks in the district that look at first glance to be primarily residential are on closer inspection embracing a "nesting" of workspaces and productive activities centered most frequently around the alleyway. The streets accommodate the external requirements of both activities. Similarly, the unique chamfered corners of the Cerdà block, known as *illes* in Catalan, were designed to provide sunlight and ventilation in the tight-knit street grid but in Poblenou have also created a very distinct "working district" condition at the corners of the blocks. Many of the older factories that face these corners have large rolling doors on their diagonal sides, turning the chamfered intersection into a "work yard" where trucks, workers, and the general public navigate the space. In addition many of these spaces do not follow the conventions of sidewalks, tree plantings, or lighting patterns, creating a quality of "unfinished," which many would argue is essential to inspiring creativity and hands-on activities.

Google Earth

Figure 2.8 The urban design elements like streets, alleys, and squares define the distinctly different character and patterns of use in the two districts.

Towards a New Model of Urban Manufacturing in Innovation Cities

The Kendall Square and 22@ Barcelona innovation districts are two of the most recognized examples of urban economic engines in the world. It turns out that manufacturing plays an important role in sustaining innovation—transforming new knowledge to economic prospects, generating new businesses, and nurturing entrepreneurs. In summary, the major factors that support the continued presence of manufacturing uses in an innovation district context are as follows:

Academic anchors with "hands-on" missions.

The physical presence of a university or college, either as a whole campus or as a satellite center, is critical to nurturing and sustaining productive activities in an innovation district. Institutions with a particular focus on experiential learning, local engagement, and, in general, the interaction between academia, research, and commercial enterprise will play a significant role in creating the educational and social infrastructure necessary to incorporate manufacturing opportunities into an economic agenda. Cities seeking to develop an innovation district where manufacturing is desired should engage with their local universities and colleges to identify programs and initiatives with "hands-on" approaches to learning and research. Aligning education, research, and industry in ways that are focused on "making" and developing collocation strategies will nurture manufacturing as an important component of urban innovation.

Holistic urban redevelopment approach.

Embracing development policies that integrate economic, social, and environmental ambitions with a redevelopment agenda rather than approaching these separately will ensure a more holistic approach to urban regeneration. If we can influence development so that it embraces the culture of the local community while accommodating the ever-changing nature of work patterns in an ongoing manner, we are more likely to achieve a balanced and equitable regeneration strategy. Policy that creates opportunities for capturing the increased value of private property for public benefit, combined with strong proactive leadership and an empowered district management entity that is both effective politically and well connected with the local social and economic ecosystem, will go a long way toward achieving equitable progress.

Relaxed zoning.

Land-use zoning that prevents other uses from encroaching on industrial land (sometimes labeled employment land) or protects residential neighborhoods from the noise, traffic, and pollution associated with industrial uses has addressed legitimate urban challenges. Nevertheless, the control of negative externalities through active "on-the-ground" management of development rather than through restrictive zoning regulation has proven a much more flexible approach to encouraging innovation activities, including manufacturing. Determining the negative impact of a particular land use, not by restrictive land-use zoning but rather through careful review and advocacy of program goals, is a more effective method of nurturing sustained economic growth in an innovation district.

Affordable land

Without some way of providing affordable rents it will be very difficult to nurture small-scale and manufacturing enterprises in the mix of an innovation district. It is critical to create opportunities for start-up activities with little or no capital and to lower the barriers to entry for low-profit businesses. There is a range of collaborative workspace—co-work, fab labs, makerspaces, accelerators, etc.—that has emerged to create some of these opportunities even without subsidy, but creating policy and development tools that result in affordable land or rent will build more socially and economically diverse districts, ones that can accommodate manufacturing uses. Redevelopment policy that exacts land in exchange for increased density from private landowners and developers and uses that land for the public good is effective, as are regulations that encourage cross-subsidy of high- and low-rent space within the district.

A flexible urban structure.

No matter how progressive planning policy is in support of a diverse range of innovation activities including manufacturing, if the physical setting creates functional challenges or is inhospitable and unattractive, an innovation district will not be successful. The urban structure—size of blocks and width of streets—that nurtures diversity of use and scale of development will provide a range of spatial opportunities that encourage the organic growth of human activity including "making" activities. If people are too spread out they will not interact and collaborate. If public spaces are uncomfortable or uninspiring, or if there is nothing interesting to do, people will not linger and engage. Devising an urban design framework that fits into and supports a holistic redevelopment strategy that embraces environmental, social, and economic goals will improve outcomes. Place matters.

The sheer magnitude of the innovation economy in Kendall Square far surpasses that of 22@ Barcelona. The "Innovation Cities Program" rankings[12] have Boston consistently in the top five, while Barcelona's ranking over the last five years has improved from 56th to 13th globally. The flexible superblocks at the doorstep to one of the world's most innovative universities have allowed Kendall Square to become an engine of global innovation. New advanced manufacturing activities are abundant and contribute to Kendall's success, although their presence is not obvious in the urban context of this primarily redeveloped innovation district. 22@ Barcelona does not attract global companies with the same magnitude as Kendall Square but its economic strategy reaches beyond the elite class of highly educated innovators to extend opportunities to the local manufacturing companies and existing skilled workers. In 22@, the integration of physical regeneration, historic preservation, economic development, and social improvement as pillars of an incremental district redevelopment strategy has a strong presence in the fabric of the city and in the life of the neighborhood.

The success of this new urban economic development paradigm, the innovation district, depends on a multitude of factors beyond urban design, but it is apparent that the policies, redevelopment process, and approach to scale and land use play a significant role in creating opportunities for manufacturing activities in the innovation economy. The urban design of an innovation district—its scale, public realm, and distribution of uses—supports the integration of manufacturing into the daily life of an innovation district. The policies that embrace the integration of urban regeneration, economic development, and social advancement determine how the existing is included in the new economy. Together they will have an impact on a city's ability to bring manufacturing, the urban fabric, and history, the productive traditions and skills embedded in the working community, along with us into the twenty-first-century innovation economy.

Notes

1 Richard M. Locke and Rachel L. Wellhausen, eds. *Production in the Innovation Economy* (Cambridge, MA: The MIT Press, 2014), 5.
2 Chris Anderson, *Makers: The New Industrial Revolution* (New York, NY: Crown Publishing Group, Penguin Random House, 2012), 19.
3 Michael Blanding, "The Past and Future of Kendall Square," *MIT Technology Review*, August 18, 2015, www.technologyreview.com/s/540206/the-past-and-future-of-kendall-square/.
4 City of Cambridge Community Development Department, *Just the Facts: A Demographic and Commercial Information Resource about Cambridge, Massachusetts* (Cambridge, MA: City of Cambridge, Spring 2017), www.cambridgema.gov/~/media/Files/CDD/EconDev/WhyDoBusiness/justthefacts2017.pdf?la=en.
5 Cambridge Community Development Department, *K2C2 Kendall Square Final Report* (Cambridge, MA: City of Cambridge, 2013), www.cambridgema.gov/cdd.
6 Ajuntement de Barcelona, "22@Barcelona, The Innovation District," www.22barcelona.com/documentacio/22barcelona_eng_nov08.pdf.
7 Committee on Educational Survey, *Report of the Committee on Educational Survey to the Faculty of the Massachusetts Institute of Technology* (Cambridge, MA: MIT, December 1949).
8 Richard M. Locke and Rachel L. Wellhausen, eds. *Production in the Innovation Economy* (Cambridge, MA: The MIT Press, 2014), 236.
9 Cambridge Redevelopment Authority, *Background of the Kendall Square Urban Renewal Area* (Cambridge, MA: City of Cambridge, 2011), www.cambridgema.gov/~/media/Files/CDD/CRA/backgrounddocuments/cra_kendallsq_background.pdf?la=en.
10 Ajuntement de Barcelona, *22@ Barcelona Plan: A Programme of Urban, Economic and Social Transformation* (Barcelona, Spain: 22@Barcelona Urban Planning Management, June 2012), www.22barcelona.com/documentacio/Dossier22@/Dossier22@English_p.pdf.
11 Nick Leon, "Attract and Connect: The 22@Barcelona Innovation District and the Internationalization of Barcelona Business," *Innovation: Management, Policy and Practice*: 10 (eContent Management, 2008), 235–246.
12 2thinknow Global Innovation Agency, from the "Innovation Cities Program Index 2016–2017." Based on 2thinknow analyst interpretation of 162 standard indicators from 2thinknow City Benchmarking Data set, www.innovation-cities.com.

3 Settlement as Factory

Experience and Experiment in Milan and Italy

Giovanna Fossa

The Italian Context

Art and craft production has always been part of the Italian experience and has to be seen in a historic framework of diverse and small-scale agriculture.[1] At the beginning of the nineteenth century, limited-size enterprises appeared, integrated in the local territory. In the early 1900s, large producers emerged and played a big role in Italian manufacturing until the energy crises and digital revolution of the 1970s, when they began to decline. Then, in the 1980s, Italian production rediscovered its roots in the districts featured by enterprise networks. Their flexibility and resiliency have allowed them to endure globalization in the 1990s and the recent economic crisis (2008). Compared with similar industrial European regions (Baden-Wurttemberg, Bavaria, Catalonia, Rhone-Alps), the Milano region has a higher density of manufacturing enterprises with fewer employees; its structure is characterized by a diffusion of small and medium-sized enterprises.[2]

Italian districts are historically based on family networks and the combination of home and factory—"how to make" is a value to be transmitted from parent to child and co-workers (Cavalli 2014). The production is bottom-up, an expression of the freedom and creativity of many independent entrepreneurs. Continuous innovation is rooted and shared in the local community.[3] Most of the districts are specialized, focusing on a specific type of product; local manufacturing systems provide different components of the final product. District production is supported by adaptive logistic chains, specialized facilities, identity cultural networks, and trained skilled labour.

Most of all, products of the Italian districts are based on artisan competence that is rooted in the territory and it is this that distinguishes the Italian experience.[4]

The Milan Case: The Symbiotic Relationship of Core and Region

The Milan core plays the role of a center of excellence for its regional districts (Bonomi 2012), a production system functionally and physically integrated within a radius of about 35 km.[5] "Mother" factories are fed by regional networks of smaller factories. Manufacturing districts in the Milano region are highly integrated mixed-use settlements based on complementary and synergistic local networks, similar to ecological networks. Their on-going clustering interconnects universities and research centers located both in the regional districts and in the metropolitan core; innovation and internationalization of clusters is supported by regional government and enterprise associations.[6] Technological evolution is incremental, upgrading

Figure 3.1 In Gallarate, manufacturing and residential buildings have grown around the Enrico Sironi
historic factory, still making specialized cotton and linen.

but not substituting the fundamental support of the artisan competence; the knowledge goes
along with the know-how to make it, even by hand.

Plans and policies promoted by industry associations foster multicenter development and regional
accessibility in ways that enable the flexible evolution of production sites and supply chains. Important brands with the core of their production in the Milan regional districts generally prefer to
keep their creative departments and showrooms attached to the factory, using spaces and facilities of the city center for special exhibits and meeting events.[7] Famous brands that now have
the mass of their production out of the Milano region or abroad often keep in the Milan core
the highest value-added manufacturing phases and their headquarters, quality/research centers,
factory museums and showrooms.[8] International designers don't just send their designs to factories but are asked to come to the factory site in order to develop their concepts in partnership
with the factory R&D center, which can produce prototypes and calibrate production techniques. This physical integration between design and production, together with the proximity
to a world-class service center such as Milan, guarantees the excellent quality of the products.

The Regional Landscape

Production districts in the metropolitan region feature a variety of factory building types (Fossa,
Lane et al. 2001): traditional models such as workshops inside, or as additions to, single-family

Figure 3.2 The sustainable wooden skin reflects the furniture manufacturer in the recent showroom/museum building by Citterio in the Riva1920 factory complex, Brianza.

houses; historic loft factories, many with their evocative brick chimneys; artisans' workshops and showrooms at the ground floor of apartment buildings; one-story factories with shed or flat roofs, more common in peripheral expansion zones.[9] At the end of the 1970s the availability of large, underutilized factories enabled quick adaptive re-use by multiple artisans. The more contemporary model is to build complexes with many single-enterprise factory "boxes," often with a separate service center, or multi-enterprise buildings including also housing-related complementary uses. Contemporary interventions prefer an architectural language that communicates interest in issues related to environmental sustainability.

Open spaces like inner courtyards and outside gardens are included in the production site. Buildings in new industrial developments generally align with surrounding streets. Factory complexes are transformed by adding new buildings, either for production uses, offices or new programs associated with the innovation economy such as showrooms, outlets, museums, and meeting and event spaces.

These buildings are added in the same factory site if it is large enough or otherwise in close proximity in the same municipality or immediate surroundings. Since 2000, in the reuse of former industrial complexes, a soft production mix emerged that includes independent uses ancillary to the manufacturing activities as well as general services. Contemporary manufacturing incubators are located inside landmark abandoned factories, which become the symbols of the district innovation: they usually host a creative mix that balances high-tech manufacturing start-up and innovative services with facilities supporting all enterprises of the district, with collective indoor spaces open to the general public.[10]

Urban Manufacturing Districts in Milan City

Milan city manufacturing activities are found in the following typical configurations.

- Makers, most of them developing prototypes for things like innovative hardware components (Maffei 2015): their spaces are fab labs, high-tech incubators, co-working environments with associated support services, and temporary workshops. The City, the Chamber of

Commerce, and industry associations support these innovative urban manufacturing activities mainly by making space available on a competitive basis. Few of them own their space.

- High-end historic manufacturers who continue to stay in the city for the proximity to their clients and major institutional partners, for the brand value of their historic factory buildings, or for the locational advantages of their sites, which were once at the city edge and are now in quite central neighborhoods where they benefit from urban density.[11]
- Traditional handicraft workshops, high-quality and custom-oriented, which stay in the Milan center because of the proximity to their clients and customers. These workshop spaces are either privately owned or rented.

Figure 3.3 Old meets new: a recent addition to the Savaré chemical factory by Zanuso Pascoe, in the Certosa district.

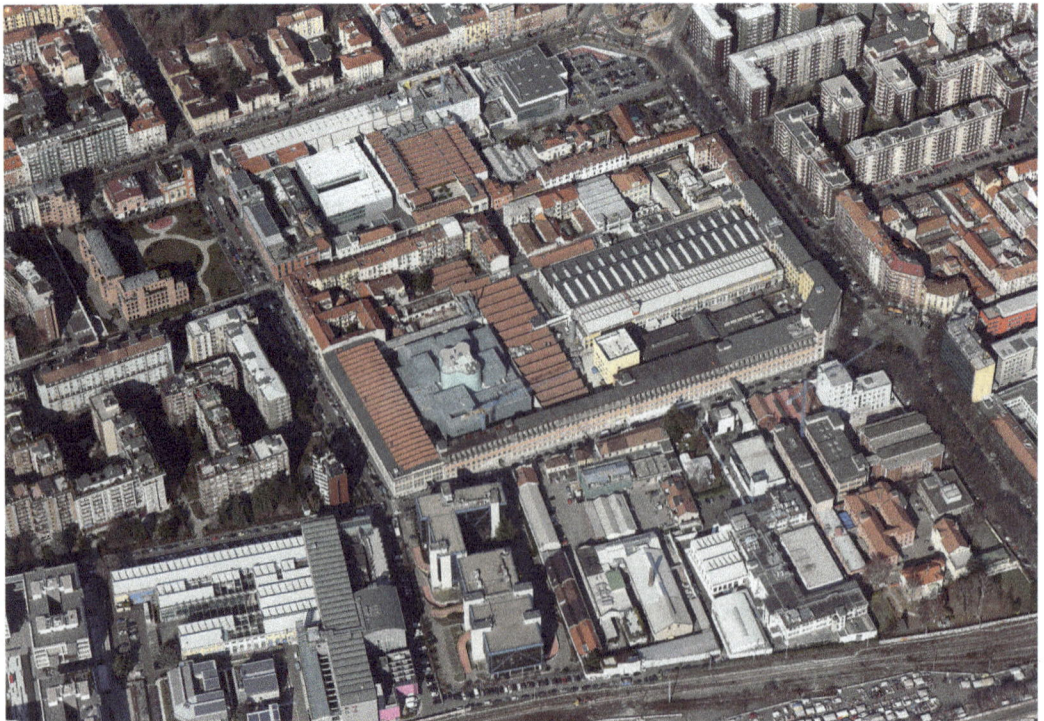

Figure 3.4 The Ansaldo complex in the Navigli district: it contains co-working, start-up incubators, creative labs, dedicated temporary housing, city offices, a museum.

All of these typologies are integrated in urban manufacturing districts where productivity is based not just on the density of high-value human interactions and the extraordinary variety of uses and users, but on inspiring events and cultural/educational world-class facilities that provide the ecosystem for creativity and innovation. Shared knowledge, cross-fertilization, and the circular economy are reinventing the family-based model of the regional manufacturing districts for the maker communities of the urban creative districts.

Most of Milan urban manufacturers are located inside historic industrial neighborhoods, close to railways and their yards.[12] In these places the regular urban texture of the late 1889 Beruto Plan of Milan, with streets characterized by continuous built fronts and often lined with trees, is still evident. The urban skyline is signified by shed roofs and lofts, and the street fronts are defined by Liberty "palazzinas" originally dedicated to residential and office uses related to the factory. Some blocks are still occupied entirely by single historic factories with their original buildings adapted to the evolution of their production and marketing needs.[13] Famous former industrial buildings occupying an entire block are bought by the city and reused, mixing production activities with programs for the general public celebrating industrial archeology.[14] In some significant cases, former industrial blocks are privately redeveloped with a creative mix of light manufacturing, showrooms, services, and even live/work studios.[15]

Even though the recent Milan city plan allows for more use flexibility, the change of use from industrial to other more conventional mixed uses is inhibited by the cost of cleaning the sites to residential standards and volume incentives accorded to production and production-supporting activities.

Usually former industrial buildings with high-quality architecture are preserved and adaptively reused. This choice in part is driven by practical considerations—keeping the existing high-ceiling spaces provides more volume than new construction. However, it also reflects a desire to capture this historic identity for new creative production activities. Indeed, in some cases, new construction features elements from the surrounding industrial landscape—bridges between buildings, freight elevators, daylight roofs, high ceilings.

The trend is to recreate the inspiring mix of the industrial district within the buildings themselves and even within the interdisciplinary co-working spaces hosted in those buildings. The continuous layering and synergies between various uses of the urban creative districts generate a hybrid architecture of adaptive reuse that has a specific creative character based on functional flexibility and resiliency. This includes opening facilities to the public with outlet stores, museums, or ways for visitors to move through the production sites. This also means integrating

Figure 3.5 New factories by Tortato in a former forging site, in the Certosa district.

start-up incubators and service centers oriented to support small factories engaged in high-tech innovation and promoting access to international networks and emerging markets, clustering, and local cooperation for global competitiveness.

At the neighborhood scale, redevelopment initiatives do not change the design of the blocks but try to make them permeable, opening connections between collective outdoor spaces in the interiors of the blocks and the surrounding neighborhood context.

Urban design strategies go beyond the factory walls; the contemporary urban factory is made permeable and visible to its immediate context, even when only the exterior wall is preserved and the interior is completely redeveloped. Collective shared spaces of the factory, both indoor and outdoor, are connected to each other and to the surrounding streets and public spaces, engaging them in the creative/productive process (Cibic 2010). The innovative re-use by the city of monumental industrial complexes promotes creative urban neighborhoods (Oevermann and Mieg 2015). The on-going redevelopment of historic industrial infrastructures such as underutilized railway yards or the renewal of canals have the potential to reconnect streets once cut off by these barriers and to regenerate the urban texture (Fossa, Lane et al. 2002).

Cultural institutions play a significant role in supporting urban manufacturing districts; actually, the decision to locate the Human Technopole (biotech research center) in the former expo area kicked off its on-going development as a Milan innovation district including also private start-ups. A similar smart-incubator role is played by the Politecnico for the Bovisa gas tank neighborhood.

The Urban Design of Production

Streets

Important streets often become the centers of the industrial districts. In the Breda complex, the private road that enters through the historic gate to the factory site signifies the border between creative re-uses on the south side (Milan) and primarily manufacturing uses on the north side (Sesto S. Giovanni), subsidized by industrial policies of the City of Sesto. This wide historic industrial road, planted with trees, is becoming the vibrant heart of the district; extending between two subway stations, this road welcomes many pedestrian users—students, workers, employees, and residents in on-site social housing—and at the same time gives vehicle access to independent manufacturers who are reusing existing industrial buildings. Conflicts with cars and trucks are avoided by limiting through-traffic for vehicles and traffic-calming. This street is a public space axis, lined with historic industrial buildings and connecting common courtyards. The recent reuse of some buildings also on the north side for university classrooms for Bicocca University, which is located about one kilometer south, portends that creative activities will expand step by step into the north side of the road, driven by the real-estate market.

Edges

The Certosa boulevard is part of the Napoleonic axis that shaped the Milano urban form in the late 1800s, leading northwest from the central Foro Bonaparte toward the Simplon pass and Paris. The boulevard is now the most direct connection between the city center and the main highway access to Milan. This historic road is the armature for the mixed-use productive

Figure 3.6 The huge Breda complex is now divided between, on one side, machine and glass bottle factories, and on the other side workshop lofts, social housing, and university departments.

Figure 3.7 The historic boulevard Viale Sarca now enables public access to the Breda factory complex.

Figure 3.8 An inner road allows access to industrial courtyards in the Breda district. A contemporary art museum is at the opposite end.

neighborhood along it, anchoring transverse roads that branch off from there to the edge created by railways and highway bridges. The accessibility of this area, located right at the highway gateway to the Malpensa airport, keeps this area attractive for high-value-added production as well as more traditional production in existing historic factories—this despite the presence of non-industrial uses. Recently a former forging site was redeveloped with studios, workshops, and factory lofts for medical machinery, introducing a contemporary landscape approach to the redesign of an urban edge bounded by infrastructures.

Figure 3.9 Courtyards on the south side of the Breda complex house soft production and creative activities.

Figure 3.10 At Breda, solar-panel-clad buildings house a cable manufacturer's head-quarters as well as creative industries.

Figure 3.11 At the urban edge, the historic fabric of Certosa meets rail lines and highways.

Public Spaces: Courtyards and Informal Spaces

An essential feature of the urban "factory settlement" is the productive role played by the courtyards. In residential/mixed-use blocks, inner courtyards interact with manufacturing activities by creating openings to ground-floor workshops and allowing room for additions.

Figure 3.12 Certosa mixed use: aerospace and chemical companies mix with traditional manufacturers, car services, social housing, and a hotel.

Sometimes the workspaces are behind a residence, maintaining an active front to the courtyard without access gates breaking up the street wall. Inner courtyards are especially strategic where historic factory blocks are adaptively reused by many independent enterprises. In these cases, courtyards offer not only space for logistics or complementary outdoor production but they also support interaction and synergies between various creative local activities. These spaces offer the possibility to host special events, acting as outdoor showrooms connecting indoor manufacturing spaces and the surrounding streets.

This trend of integrating public space with the contemporary creative factory system is particularly evident at manufacturing fairs when streets and courtyards become a continuous space (Milano Design week). It gives clients, tourists, and citizens the chance to experience the manufacturing identity of the Milan districts. In the Navigli district, sections of sidewalk and bike paths are redesigned and curated by adjacent manufacture-brand buildings, as part of their marketing strategy.

Hundreds of small art and crafts shops are in the historic city fabric inside the seventeenth-century Spanish wall ring as well as within postwar buildings with good road access. Marginal, residual spaces always have been useful for small manufacturing activities. Cellars or stores underneath residential buildings, where better uses are restricted, sometimes host maker laboratories; it could be thought of as the Italian and more urban version of the garage in the United States, as an instant and informal space for hosting start-ups (see Janne Corneil, Chapter 2).[16]

Figure 3.13 One of the hidden courtyards in the 5 Vie district hosting small workshops and creative activities.

Figure 3.14 Ansaldo inner courtyard hosting a creative hub, in the Navigli district.

Recent Trends of Urban Manufacturing in Italy and Latest Experiments

The integration of design and manufacturing continues to evolve.[17] Industry 4.0 fosters the integration of art and design while minimizing the time to market of the products. In a reversal of the Warhol critique, the contemporary urban factory is getting close to producing unique art pieces and custom-made products. Art is considered an inspiring partner in the urban creative mix; artists are hosted together with artisans and makers in contemporary incubators. A mix of uses integrating traditional artisans and international artists is part of an innovative approach to urban regeneration. Major Italian manufacturing brands are opening contemporary art museums.

Famous brands, as part of their marketing strategy, are investing in the architecture of their flagship factories designed by world-class architects whose signs on the project add the value of their architecture brands to the manufacturing brand. These contemporary factories communicate an environmental approach and a social sensitivity including amenities to promote worker well-being, sometimes related to their product identity.[18] For start-up and temporary factories, enterprises managing co-working and incubator spaces for rent are emerging at the national level, offering locations in all major Italian cities as "space makers" (see Rappaport, Chapter 6).

Urban planning and policy trends promote creative urban districts allowing changes of use, fostering an innovative mix including homes dedicated to creative users working in the same place and giving various incentives for manufacturing activities such as expedited approvals, higher allowable building ratios, and access to land and spaces.

Production based on artisan pride (Micelli 2011) is giving rise to new fertile interfaces. The leading Italian districts are exploring the cultural and touristic value of manufacturing activities, not just the products but the processes themselves and their artisan character. The Brianza Design District just opened a web platform for a tourism experience; similar experiments are "Made in Piemonte" and "Ferrari and Pavarotti Land" in the Modena district.

This suggests a contemporary version of the "Grand Tour"—one based on Italian landscapes of production (Leone 2012); factories do not need to be hidden or isolated in zones surrounded by green belts. Manufacturing districts should not be considered part of an amorphous metropolitan periphery, but rather part of an integrated landscape, with the potential to keep and attract innovative manufacturing activities through story-telling, architecture, and place-making. In this way, production offers an authentic territorial experience that it is otherwise difficult to find in the crowded conventional Italian tourism market. The factory is becoming a cool tourism destination and not only for food production. A consequence of the model of the production district that is rooted in a specific territory, there is a strong connection between production brands and the landscape of production not only at the national level—Made in Italy—but more and more at the regional and urban district level. Thus place-branding strategies need to be integrated with the landscape design of the contemporary places of production.

The physical proximity between design and manufacturing as well as between high-tech and the "know-how to make by hand" is a pre-condition for the quality of the products. The main location criterion for contemporary creative, high-value-added industries is to be in a place where this integration between knowledge and know-how is possible, which generally means a dense, mixed-use, vibrant place. This is true even when the production phases are fragmented at the global scale: at the least, prototyping and the scaling-up phases of manufacturing demand urban spaces with these qualities: an integrated, dynamic, and connected—urban—ecosystem. Using ecology as a metaphor, mixed use is to the manufacturing neighborhood what biodiversity is to the environment (see Milan case study in Part IV).

Notes

1 See, for example, the origin of the textile production in the Milano region, based on mulberry and silkworm cultivation at the family scale.
2 Source: Assolombarda/Politecnico di Milano, *Per un territorio attrattivo* (2015) and Assolombarda Research Department Booklet *Italy, Lombardy and Milan*, N°5 (2018). According to the Italian National Institute of Statistics (Istat, 2015), about 97 percent of Lombardy manufacturers have fewer than 50 employees and 3 percent have fewer than 250.
3 An icon of home and factory is the fashion brand Missoni, which is a family enterprise. The Missonis have lived and manufactured in the same place (Sumirago VA) since the beginning (end of the 1950s), and still do so today. In 1997, Italian family enterprises created their own association, AIDAF.
4 The territory feeding manufacturing districts is not just a geographic entity but also a cultural landscape.
5 The most famous manufacturing districts of the Milano region are Brianza (wood/design) and Simplon (mechanical/textile/fashion), key to Milan's competitiveness.
6 The strategic plan of the Lombardia Industrial Association (Confindustria, *Lombardia 2030/Strategic Plan, Vision and Guidelines for Manufacturing in Lombardia* (2015)), in order to foster the continuous innovation of the SMEs, interprets the cluster concept with a focus on culture and services, extending the interpretative scale for reading manufacturing networks from traditional districts to the whole region.
7 For example, the Molteni compound in Giussano (designer furniture) includes, beside the production sheds, a multistory building dedicated to research, design, prototyping, and the factory museum; also, surrounded by the garden, there are the visitor center, the showroom, the archive building, and the owners' family house. Similar combinations of factory and R&D/museum on the same site are typical of other major brands in the Brianza design district, such as Riva in Cantù.
8 Examples are fashion groups like Prada and Armani, or Mapei (chemical) and Branca (spirits).
9 Brick chimneys are no longer in use but under preservation constraints for their historic value.
10 An example of the new generation of incubators is "Como Next," Lomazzo (CO) in the Brianza district, hosted in the historic building of the former Somaini cotton factory.
11 Examples of these typologies could be, respectively, the Pomellato jewelry factory; the Opera House Labs, which manufacture large-scale products for the La Scala Theater; the Branca historic factory (spirits), Savaré and Mapei scale-up manufacturers and headquarters (chemical).

12 Significant urban manufacturing districts in Milan are: the creative district along the Navigli canals (design and fashion), Lambrate (design and food), Breda (glass and mechanical factories bounded by creative activities), Certosa (aerospace, chemical, car services), Lancetti (beverages, chemical, and craft), Porta Romana (pharmaceutical and smart start-up). All these districts are attached to different railway yards. Other districts are: Mecenate (event/media) and the handicraft district in the medieval core of Milan, called "5 Vie" (art and design).

13 For example, the factory of Branca (spirits), Lancetti district.

14 For example, the case of the former Ansaldo locomotive factory, Navigli district.

15 For example, the regeneration of the former Richard Ginory pottery factory, Navigli district.

16 An example of "neo-cottage industry" is the Noah Guitars Lab, which inhabits a seventeenth-century cellar in the Lambrate district.

17 The contemporary evolution of the integration between design and manufacturing was pointed out by the 2016 XXI Milano Triennale exhibit entitled "Design after Design," with a program dedicated to "New Craft."

18 Examples of workers' well-being facilities could be the gym spaces inside the Technogym Village in Cesena or the team-building-by-cooking initiatives in the Barilla pasta factory, Parma.

References

Bonomi, A., *Milano: Le tre città che stanno in una* (Milan: Bruno Mondadori, 2012).

Cavalli, A., *Il valore del mestiere* (Venice: Marsilio, 2014).

Cibic, A., *Rethinking Happiness* (Milan: Corraini, 2010).

Fossa, G., Lane, R., Palazzo, D., and Pirani, R., *Transforming the Places of Production* (Milan: Olivares, 2002).

Fossa, G., Fossati, A., and Lane, R., *Beyond the Box* (Milan: Clup, 2001).

Leone, N.G. (ed.), *Itatour* (Milan: F. Angeli, 2012).

Maffei, S. et al., *Makers' Inquiry* (Milan: Politecnico di Milano, Libraccio, 2015).

Micelli, S., *Futuro artigiano: l'innovazione nelle mani degli italiani* (Venice: Marsilio, 2011).

Oevermann, H. and Mieg, A.H. (eds), *Industrial Heritage sites in Transformation* (New York: Routledge, 2015).

4 Goods Movement for Urban Manufacturing

Alison Conway

As cities become increasingly densely developed and urban transportation systems become more multimodal the urban freight movements to support urban manufacturing and other freight-dependent industries will only become more complex. Movement of locally or regionally sourced inputs, product samples, or end products destined for local or regional markets will rely almost exclusively on road transport. While high-volume loads will move by truck, small shipments may be completed by commercial vans, automobiles, or even motor- or human-powered cycles. These movements will occur on streets shared with multimodal users conducting a variety of personal and commercial activities.

A new body of international research and practice known as "city logistics" has emerged to address the increasing complexity of goods movement in cities. A frequently cited definition of city logistics is provided by Eiichi Taniguchi, Russell Thompson, Tadashi Yamada, and Ron Van Duin.

> City logistics is the process for totally optimizing the logistics and transport activities by private companies in urban areas while considering the traffic environment, the traffic congestion, and energy consumption within the framework of a market economy.[1]

City logistics solutions frequently involve a variety of stakeholders and rely not only on changes in private-industry behavior but also on local policy initiatives or infrastructure investments to support efficient freight operations.

Emerging Challenges for Urban Goods Movement

In cities, widespread traffic congestion causes frequent trip delays, unreliable arrival times, and missed connections. The American Transportation Research Institute estimated that in 2013 the US trucking industry bore $9.2 billion (or an average $864 per truck) in excess operating costs due to traffic congestion.[2] In recent years, as many cities have sought to increase passenger movements by public transportation and non-motorized modes and to encourage dense, mixed-used development, a variety of challenges to urban goods movement have emerged or been exacerbated.

Reduced Lane Capacities and Lost Curb Access

In densely developed urban areas commercial vehicles must compete with a variety of passenger modes for limited road and parking space. With rapid implementation of Complete Streets

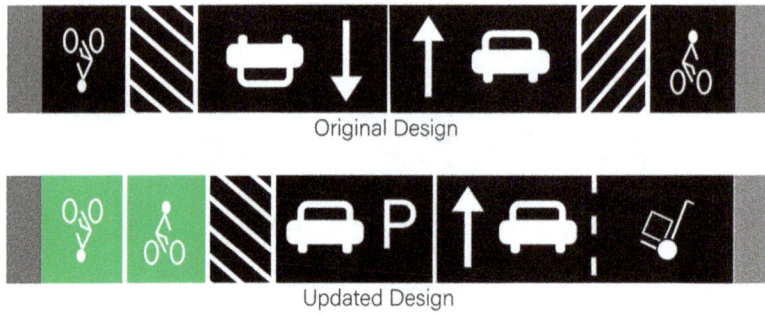

Figure 4.1 Street space reallocated for bicycles and freight.

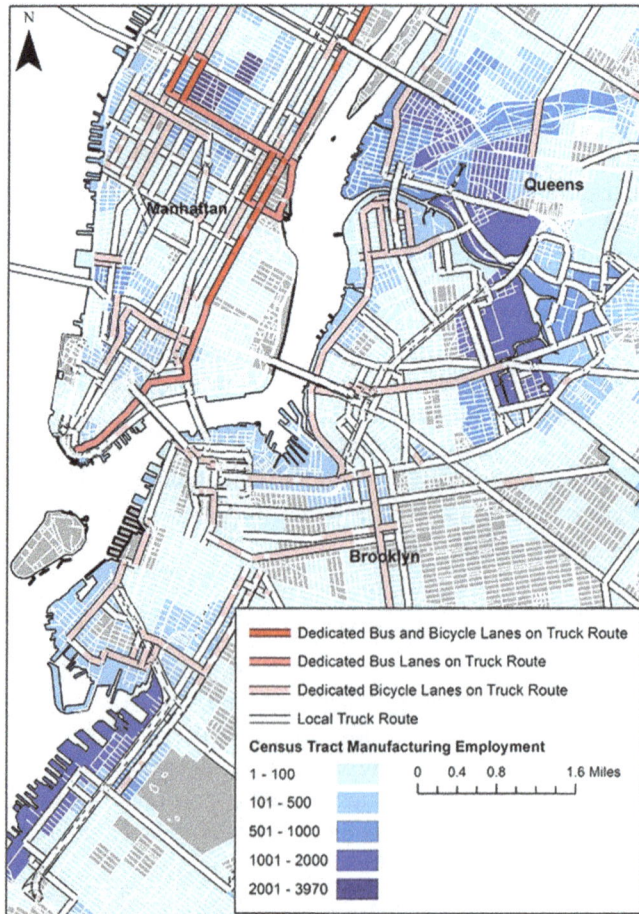

Figure 4.2 Street space allocation changes on New York City local truck routes, 2005–2015 (NYCDOT Local Truck and Bicycle Network Maps, US Census Bureau LEHD Data).

policies since 2003, many cities throughout the US have quickly reallocated space previously designated for motor vehicle travel to new pedestrian-friendly street designs, bicycle lanes and paths, and dedicated public transit infrastructure.[3]

While ultimately these cities aim to achieve congestion improvements by encouraging passenger mode switches to these now-prioritized green modes, the immediate impact for commercial vehicle movements is often lost lane capacity. For example, in New York City, bicycle lanes and bus lanes have proliferated since 2005 on segments of the city's local truck route network in Manhattan, Brooklyn, and Queens; these routes are critical to the movement of goods to and from the city's manufacturing centers (see Figure 4.2).

Roadway Geometry

In addition to reducing lane capacities street design changes can present new navigation and parking challenges for commercial vehicles, particularly when freight operational requirements are overlooked or explicitly deprioritized. Trucks with lengths and wheel bases considerably larger than passenger vehicles require wide lanes and large turning radii that are inherently incompatible with pedestrian-friendly street designs that favor short crossing distances at intersections. Some bicycle lane designs require intersection mixing zones that can consume curb lengths equivalent to up to six passenger parking spaces per block.[4] Curbside transit or bicycle lanes may completely prohibit direct curb access for curbside loading/unloading. Even at buildings with loading docks, conversion of curbside parking to another lane type may leave inadequate space for a parked truck. Facing high costs for delay and few alternatives for parking, commercial vehicles will frequently park illegally, risking high fines while partially or fully obstructing one or more travel lanes.

Rezoning

Changing urban land uses have also generated new challenges for both intra- and interregional goods movements. In many cities, large-scale rezoning efforts have introduced residential and commercial development in formerly industry-dominated areas. New zoning classifications have also permitted industrial and residential developments on adjacent or shared tax lots or even in different levels of a shared building. Changing land uses—whether through new zoning or through permitted variances—can affect transportation and logistics operations for existing manufacturers and constrain future development.

As urban centers become increasingly dense with residential and commercial activities, warehousing activities—which often have high space requirements, relatively low job densities, and generate lower tax revenue per square foot than other uses—are pushed to the periphery.[5] A number of studies have documented global patterns of "logistics sprawl," the spread of warehousing away from urban centers to suburban and exurban locations where land is more affordable.[6] For urban manufacturers remaining in the urban core this trend may lead to trade-offs between paying high costs for centrally located storage facilities or high costs for travel to and from distant warehouses.

Exacerbating losses in roadway capacities, in recent years many cities have introduced plans for both residential and recreational developments along underutilized waterfronts and in abandoned rail right-of-way.[7] While these developments may contribute positively to quality of life in the surrounding area, they can also limit access to rail networks and waterways and may remove existing freight infrastructure such as docks (see design guideline p. 269).

Externalities

A final impact from mixing residential, commercial, and industrial land uses is that externalities from manufacturing operations—including transportation of manufactured goods—are no longer isolated from these other land uses. Large freight vehicles impose higher congestion costs on the surrounding transportation network than passenger vehicles. Trucks, especially those running on diesel fuel, are major generators of particulate matter, carbon monoxide (CO), nitrogen oxides (NO_2), and hydrocarbons.[8] These pollutants can cause short- and long-term health problems for nearby residents, and contribute to urban visibility problems.[9] Additionally, trucks moving, loading, and unloading can generate loud noises that are bothersome to nearby residents, especially when these activities occur during nighttime hours. As the number of bicyclists and pedestrians traveling on shared corridors with commercial vehicles increase, so too will the interactions between these modes. Studies have documented the severity of accidents between large vehicles and bicycles or pedestrians.[10] As truck drivers sit higher in their vehicles than passenger car drivers, bicycles and pedestrians may fall into blind spots, leading to collisions—especially during right-turn movements. While researchers have noted that both truck drivers and nonmotorized users would prefer to operate on separate facilities, provision of these is difficult when space is constrained.[11]

Best Practices for Urban Goods Movement

A variety of city logistics approaches can be employed to improve efficiencies for and reduce externalities from manufacturing goods movements; many of these require changes in shipper behavior or cooperation between multiple stakeholders. Four frequently discussed solutions include mode shifts to alternative vehicles, mode shifts to non-highway modes, off-hour deliveries, and joint distribution strategies. Other strategies rely on public-sector interventions to enable efficient goods movements and incentivize responsible operations.

Alternative Vehicles

Manufacturers moving relatively small volumes of goods locally can use a variety of alternative motorized and human-powered vehicles. Electric trucks and vans are much quieter and

Figure 4.3 Cargo cycle in Amsterdam.

produce much less local air pollution than their diesel-powered counterparts. Human-powered bicycles and tricycles can also be employed for small local movements; these vehicles produce no local pollutants, and often have more flexible options for parking and moving through congested traffic than motorized vehicles.[12] While electric and human-powered vehicles are difficult to implement for long-distance trips due to human and battery limitations, they work well for deliveries to dense markets within a limited radius. As an added benefit these vehicles can be branded with advertising, providing a relatively slow-moving billboard on an eye-catching vehicle and demonstrating a company's commitment to sustainable logistics operations.

However, some constraints to use of these vehicles do exist. Electric trucks and vans are generally more expensive to purchase than diesel-powered vehicles. While small vans and bikes consume less space than large trucks and vans they also offer lower economies of scale; more vehicles, drivers, or trips may be required to move the same volume of goods, increasing transportation costs. To address the resulting cost differential, public agencies can employ a variety of public policy solutions including rebate programs for the purchase of green trucks, time-based bans or pricing on truck operations, or formal recognition schemes for "green" operators.

Non-Highway Modes

Multimodal solutions utilizing rail or water modes for last-mile delivery are uncommon due to the high cost of transloading and to limited capacities on local infrastructure. A number of cities have tested concepts for using public transportation vehicles to move freight; however, many of these have been unsuccessful due to constraints such as limited excess vehicle and route capacities during peak hours and challenges in providing adequate access for freight loading.[13] However, operators in a few cities have developed successful location-specific multimodal solutions, often at a high cost borne by shippers willing to pay a premium for these alternatives. In Dresden, Germany, a CarGoTram operating on infrastructure shared with passenger trams carries goods between Volkswagen's "Transparent Factory" and its distribution center.[14] In Paris, "part-time transit ports" on the Seine River enable movement of goods into the central city by barge during certain hours; last-mile deliveries are then conducted from these ports via truck.[15] Also in Paris, Vert Chez Vous operates a delivery barge that makes five stops along the Seine from which natural gas-powered vans and electric cargo cycles make final deliveries of goods.[16]

Multimodal solutions are more cost-competitive and therefore more common for interregional movements to and from an urban area. In recent years a number of cities have sought to maintain manufacturing and logistics activities through implementation of master-planned industrial campuses in both brownfield and greenfield locations accessible by highway, rail, water, and/or air. For example, the Philadelphia Navy Yard, the home of the Tasty Baking Company's new manufacturing plant, is accessible to the I-95 highway corridor and includes both an intermodal rail terminal and marine port facilities.[17]

Off-Hour Deliveries

Off-hour delivery schemes seek to shift freight delivery activities to off-peak time periods when there are fewer multimodal demands for urban street and parking space. A pilot study conducted in New York City evaluated the benefits of shifting goods deliveries to evening,

Figure 4.4 Part-time transit ports, Seine River, Paris.

overnight, and early-morning hours for a number of operators carrying goods to restaurants and small and large retailers in Manhattan from regional distribution and manufacturing facilities.[18] The study found significant cost savings, including reduced fuel consumption, fewer delays from congestion, and fewer parking fines for carriers, as well as reductions in congestion, emissions, and peak-hour exposure to heavy vehicles in the city. However, the study also identified a number of constraints that limit off-hour operations, including high costs to retailers to have staff available for deliveries made outside of typical business hours and noise impacts on local residents.

Joint Distribution

The most common joint-distribution strategy for urban goods movement is implementation of an urban consolidation center (UCC). Julian Allen, Garth Thorne, and Michael Browne define a UCC as "a logistics facility that is situated relatively close to the area that it serves (be that a city center, an entire town, or a specific site) from which consolidated deliveries are carried out within that area."[19] UCCs may be implemented by wholly private entities or through a

Figure 4.5 Sustainable urban delivery, Portland, Oregon.

Figure 4.6 Loading docks can also be active
public spaces.

public–private partnership. In general, goods are delivered to a UCC by truck from multiple shippers; at the UCC they are sorted and reloaded onto smaller, usually "green" vehicles for last-mile urban delivery. Some UCCs also offer additional value-added services such as storage, packaging, and reverse logistics of waste streams. UCCs can provide benefits both to shippers and to the urban area in which they operate. Generally UCC implementation will reduce the number of heavy vehicle miles traveled in an urban area (and associated costs and externalities) and will enable better utilization of delivery vehicle space, as fewer empty or partially empty trips are made when deliveries from multiple shippers are coordinated. Many UCCs utilize the alternative "green" vehicles described above. While UCCs have primarily been implemented to manage retail and construction goods movements, urban manufacturers conducting less-than-truckload deliveries to local businesses or end consumers can also benefit from their operations. For example, in Portland, B-Line Sustainable Urban Delivery conducts last-mile deliveries for the Portland Roasting Company and a variety of other customers via cargo cycle from their centrally located urban warehouse.

While UCCs can produce benefits both for cities and for shippers, they are also challenging to operate. They often (but not always) require cooperation and financial support from multiple stakeholders and frequently are not financially self-sustaining, due to expensive space and labor for transloading in centrally located areas.[20] The public sector (or landlords) can support UCCs by mandating their use or by providing access to space at a reduced cost.[21]

Manufacturers requiring on-demand movements may also take advantage of an emerging form of joint distribution: the use of new shared-mobility services. Manufacturers have historically relied on messenger services for small-scale local movements. For example, fashion samples frequently move via messenger between New York City's midtown Garment District where production occurs, and downtown where corporate offices are located. Now technology-driven services such as UberRush and Zipments have simplified the process of requesting these on-demand movements. Emerging applications have also enabled on-demand requests for larger-scale shipments; Cargomatic matches shippers making larger-scale movements to carriers with available space on a truck. Like UCCs these services can improve truckload utilization factors and limit extra miles and empty trips.[22]

Public-Sector Decision-Making

The public sector can also improve conditions for urban goods movement by implementing effective planning, design, and traffic management policies. To ensure that goods movement needs are recognized and addressed, urban planners and engineers should first involve a broad range of freight stakeholders—including shippers and manufacturers, carriers, receivers, and 3PLs and 4PLs (third party logistics providers and companies that manage 3PLs)—in the earliest stages of planning. A number of best practices have emerged in recent years for involving freight stakeholders in the planning process. In Philadelphia the regional metropolitan planning organization, the Delaware Valley Regional Planning Commission (DVRPC), holds quarterly meetings of its Goods Movement Task Force, which includes multimodal freight stakeholders from the public and private sectors.[23] The Central London Freight Quality Partnership was established between the Central London Partnership—a nonprofit aimed at improving business conditions—and Transport for London in 2006.[24] In Paris, when major freight industry concerns emerged following massive reorganization of the city's streets to prioritize transit and non-motorized modes, a formal consultation process was developed; a series of outreach efforts ultimately culminated in the 2006 signing of a comprehensive Freight Charter committing forty-seven signatory stakeholders to accommodate efficient freight operations while also reducing freight-related externalities.[25] A new charter was signed in 2013.[26]

Once goods movement needs are identified agencies should implement infrastructure designs and street and curb regulations that enable efficient operations while minimizing freight impacts on the surrounding neighborhood. In many American cities impacts have traditionally been minimized by mandating separation between residential and industrial land uses; for example, in Chicago's Planned Manufacturing districts residential development is prohibited.[27] However in many cities physical separation is not maintained, or cities are actively seeking to mix residential and industrial land uses, which makes traditional solutions such as sound walls and grade-separated crossings infeasible.

In mixed-use areas where goods movements should be prioritized, dedicated infrastructure capacity can be provided. While many cities provide priority travel lanes for buses and bicycles, goods vehicles are rarely given access to priority lanes in the urban core; one exception is in Newcastle, England, where lorries (trucks) are permitted to operate in bus lanes, previously called "no-car" lanes.[28] A few cities have published guidelines for accommodating large vehicles at intersections. The City of Portland's official guidelines, "Designing for Truck Movements and Other Large Vehicles," provide geometric design recommendations for various classes of roadways that carry different types of freight movements.[29] The City of San Francisco's Better Streets Plan identifies lane width and intersection design requirements specifically for freight routes and for industrial streets.[30]

Other cities recognizing freight loading and unloading needs through practical experience have developed innovative solutions to provide curb access on multimodal streets. In Paris, when rapid implementation of dedicated bus lanes prevented trucks from loading and unloading at the curbside, new types of delivery bays—the "Lincoln" and "Half-Lincoln"—were implemented.[31] In New York City, many bus lanes are now "floating" lanes that maintain direct curb access for local deliveries.[32]

To ensure access to space for loading and unloading activities in an urban area, both parking regulations and land use policies can also be implemented. For land uses such as urban manufacturing where frequent truck trips are expected, zoning requirements should recognize

Figure 4.7 Context-sensitive design for isolating freight activity from other street activities.

Figure 4.8 "Lincoln" delivery bay, Paris.

Figure 4.9 Floating bus lane, New York City.

Figure 4.10 Typical loading area.

minimum parking space required for the freight trips generated by the site and should mandate inclusion of off-street loading docks where possible. Broader land use policies may also be implemented at a city or regional level to ensure available space for logistics activities; for example, the local government in the City of Paris supports "urban logistics spaces (ULS)"— small areas in the central business district reserved for transloading and cross-docking activities that are provided to operators at a reduced rent.

Where space is limited and multimodal demands high, innovative parking policies can also be employed to promote flexible use of space. Time-variable parking regulations can prioritize commercial vehicle loading only during certain periods of the day. Examples include delivery windows implemented in New York City and signalized "flex" lanes operating in Barcelona, Spain.[33] Pricing can also be used to encourage efficient turnover of existing space; recent examples include Washington, DC's Commercial Curbside Loading Zone program and New York's implementation of commercial metered parking.[34]

Concluding Remarks

Urban manufacturers depend on efficient freight movement to support their operations; however, urban goods movements also generate a number of undesirable externalities in urban areas. City logistics solutions can be employed to support goods movement efficiency while minimizing externalities.

To overcome access challenges and reduce negative impacts on surrounding areas, urban manufacturers can:

- employ "green" vehicles for local goods movements;
- locate in areas with good multimodal access for rail and waterborne shipments and implement multimodal delivery networks;
- work with goods receivers to implement off-hour delivery strategies;
- collaborate with other shippers and public agencies to implement consolidated goods movements; and
- take advantage of new shared-economy goods delivery alternatives.

To ensure adequate access for goods vehicles and promote responsible operations by local urban manufacturers, public agencies can:

- implement stakeholder outreach strategies to engage manufacturers in planning; implement street designs, land use regulations, and road and curb management strategies that recognize and prioritize goods movements and encourage efficient use of space; and
- evaluate public policy options including vehicle restrictions, direct financial subsidies, and recognition schemes to incentivize use of freight modes that minimize externalities.

Notes

1 Eiichi Taniguchi, Russell Thompson, Tadashi Yamada, and Ron Van Duin, *City Logistics: Network Modelling and Intelligent Transport Systems* (London: Pergamon, 2001).
2 American Transportation Research Institute (ATRI), *Cost of Congestion to the Trucking Industry* (Arlington, VA: ATRI, 2001).
3 "History of Complete Streets in the United States," *New Jersey Bicycle and Pedestrian Resource* (Alan M. Voorhees Transportation Center, Rutgers University, n.d.), http://njbikeped.org/services/history-of-complete-streets-in-the-united-states/ (accessed February 27, 2018).
4 *New York City Street Design Manual* (New York: NYC Department of Transportation, 2015), 58.
5 Laeitia Dablanc, "Logistics Sprawl and Urban Freight Planning Issues in a Major Gateway City," in *Sustainable Urban Logistics: Concepts, Methods and Information Systems*, eds Jesus Gonzalez-Feliu, Frédéric Semet, and Jean-Louis Routhier (New York: Springer, 2014), 49–69.
6 Julie Cidell, "Concentration and Decentralisation: the New Geography of Freight Distribution in US Metropolitan Areas," *Journal of Transport Geography* 18 (2010), 363–371. Nancey Green Leigh and Nathan Hoelzel, "Smart Growth's Blind Side: Sustainable Cities Need Productive Urban Industrial Land," *Journal of the American Planning Association* 78, no. 1 (2012), 87–103. Laetitia Dablanc, Scott Ogilvie, and Anne Goodchild, "Logistics Sprawl: Differential Warehousing Development Patterns in Los Angeles, California, and Seattle, Washington," *Transportation Research Record: Journal of the Transportation Research Board* 2410 (2012), 105–112. Jean-Paul Rodrigue, "Transportation and the Urban Form," in *The Geography of Transport Systems 4th Edition*, ed. Jean-Paul Rodrigue (New York: Routledge, 2017), https://transportgeography.org/?page_id=4609 (accessed April 15, 2018).
7 RBA Group, *Brooklyn Waterfront Greenway Implementation Plan* (New York: New York City Department of Transportation, 2012), www.nycdotfeedbackportals.nyc/sites/default/files/Brooklyn%20 Waterfront%20Greenway%20Implementation%20Plan_for%20WEB_0.pdf (accessed April 15, 2018). Delaware River Waterfront Corporation, *Master Plan for the Central Delaware* (Philadelphia, PA: Delaware River Waterfront Corporation), www.delawareriverwaterfront.com/planning/master-plan-for-the-central-delaware/full-plan (accessed April 15, 2018). Friends of the High Line, "About the High Line," www.thehighline.org/about (accessed April 15, 2018). Seattle Department of Transportation, "Burke-Gilman History," www.seattle.gov/transportation/projects-and-programs/programs/bike-program/burke-gilman-trail-missing-link-project/burke-gilman-trail-history (accessed April 15, 2018).
8 Alan C. Lloyd and Thomas A. Cackette, "Diesel Engines: Environmental Impact and Control," *Journal of the Air and Waste Management Association* 51, no. 6 (2001), 809–847.
9 Arden Pope and Douglas W. Dockery, "Health Effects of Fine Particulate Air Pollution: Lines that Connect," *Journal of the Air & Waste Management Association* 56, no. 6 (2012), 709–742. Joachim Heinrich, Per E. Schwarze, Nikolaos Stilianakis, Isabelle Momas, Sylvia Medina, Annike I. Totlandsdal, Leendert von Bree, Birgit Kuna-Dibbert, and Michal Krzyzanowski, "Studies on Health Effects of Transport-Related Air Pollution," in *Health Effects of Transport-Related Air Pollution*, eds Michal Krzyzanowski, Birgit Kuna-Dibbert, and Jürgen Schneider (Copenhagen: World Health Organization, 2005), 125–165.
10 Leze Nicaj, Jenna Mandel-Ricci, Soloman Assefa, K. Grasso, Patrick McCarthy, Anna Caffarelli, Wendy McKelvey, Catharine Stayton, and Lorna Thorpe, *Bicyclist Fatalities and Serious Injuries in New York City: 1996–2005* (New York, NY: City of New York Departments of Health and Mental

Hygiene, Parks and Recreation, and Transportation, and the New York City Police Department, 2006). Darren N. Moore, William H. Schneider, Peter T. Savolainen, and Mohamadreza Farzaneh, "Mixed Logit Analysis of Bicyclist Injury Severity Resulting from Motor Vehicle Crashes at Intersection and Non-Intersection Locations," *Accident Analysis and Prevention* 43, no. 3 (2011), 621–630.

11 Alon Bassok, Chris Johnson, Matthew Kitchen, Rebeccah Maskin, Kris Overby, Daniel Carlson, Anne Goodchild, Edward McCormack, and Erica Wygonik, *NCFRP Report 24: Smart Growth and Urban Goods Movement* (Washington, DC: Transportation Research Board of the National Academies, 2013).

12 Alison Conway, Jialei Cheng, Camille Kamga, and Dan Wan, "Cargo Cycles for Local Delivery in New York City: Performance and Impacts," *Research in Transportation Business & Management* 24 (2017), 90–100.

13 Keith Cochrane, *Freight on Transit Handbook* (Toronto: Metrolinx, 2012), www.metrolinx.com/en/regionalplanning/goodsmovement/FOT_Handbook-Best_Practices_Summary.pdf (accessed April 15, 2018).

14 European Commission, "Cleaner Cargo Distribution in Dresden (Germany)," *Eltis Platform Website*, 2015, www.eltis.org/discover/case-studies/cleaner-cargo-distribution-dresden-germany (accessed February 27, 2018).

15 Laetitia Dablanc, *Commercial Goods Transport, Paris, France* (Nairobi, Kenya: Prepared for United Nations Global Report on Human Settlements, 2013), http://unhabitat.org/wp-content/uploads/2013/06/GRHS.2013.Case_.Study_.Paris_.France.pdf (accessed February 27, 2018).

16 BestFact Consortium, "BestFact Best Practice Case Quick Info: Green Logistics and Co-Modality: Vert Chez Vous," 2014, www.bestfact.net/wp-content/uploads/2014/02/Bestfact_Quick_Info_Green-Logistics_VertChezVous.pdf (accessed February 27, 2018).

17 Philadelphia Authority for Industrial Development, Philadelphia Industrial Development Corporation, Liberty Property Trust, Synterra partners, Robert A.M. Stern Architects, Michael Van Valkenburgh Associates, and Pennoni Associates (2013), *The Navy Yard Master Plan 2013 Update*, www.navyyard.org/master-plan-2013/ (accessed February 27, 2018).

18 Jose Holguín-Veras, "Necessary Conditions for Off-hour Deliveries and the Effectiveness of Urban Freight Road Pricing and Alternative Financial Policies in Competitive Markets," *Transportation Research Part A: Policy and Practice* 42, no. 2 (2008), 392–413. Jose Holguín-Veras, Xiaokun Wang, Michael Browne, Stacey Hodge, and Jeffrey Wojtowicz, "The New York City Off-Hour Delivery Project: Lessons for City Logistics," *Procedia—Social and Behavioral Sciences* 125 (2014), 36–48.

19 Julian Allen, Garth Thorne, and Michael Browne, *BESTUFS Good Practice Guide on Urban Freight Transport* (Rijswijk, the Netherlands: BESTUFS Consortium, 2007), 59–78.

20 Marta Panero, Hyeon-Shic Shin, and Daniel Lopez, *Urban Distribution Centers: A Means to Reducing Freight Vehicle Miles Traveled* (Albany, NY: New York State Energy Research Development Authority and New York State Department of Transportation, 2011), www.dot.ny.gov/divisions/engineering/technical-services/trans-r-and-d-repository/C-08-23_0.pdf (accessed April 15, 2018).

21 Laetitia Dablanc, *Transferability of Urban Logistics Concepts and Practices from a Worldwide Perspective—Deliverable 3.1—Urban Logistics Practices—Paris Case Study. Prepared for the European Commission* (Lisbon: TURBLOG Consortium, 2011), www.transport-research.info/Upload/Documents/201307/20130703_154506_25800_D3.1_casestudyParisFrance.pdf (accessed February 27, 2018).

22 Uber, (2015), "UberRush Website," www.uberrushnyc.com/ (accessed February 27, 2018). Zipments, (2018), "Same Day Delivery Service," https://zipments.com/ (accessed April 15, 2018). Cargomatic, (2017), "Instantly Connecting Shippers with Local Carriers," www.cargomatic.com/ (accessed April 15, 2018).

23 Delaware Valley Regional Planning Commission, "Delaware Valley Goods Movement Task Force," 2018, www.dvrpc.org/Freight/DVGMTF/ (accessed April 15, 2018).

24 Maria Lindholm and Michael Browne, "Local Authority Cooperation with Urban Freight Stakeholders: A Comparison of Partnership Approaches," *European Journal of Transport and Infrastructure Research* 13, no. 1, (2013), 20–38.

25 Laetitia Dablanc, Diana Diziain, and Hervé Levifve, "Urban Freight Consultations in the Paris Region," *European Transport Research Review* 3 (2011), 47–57.

26 City of Paris, "*Charte en faveur d'une logistique urbaine durable*," conclusion date September 18, 2013, https://api-site.paris.fr/images/80326 (accessed April 14, 2018).

27 Sophie Hartshorn and Christopher Lamm, *Freight and Land Use Handbook* (Washington, DC: US Federal Highway Administration, 2012), 3–14, https://ops.fhwa.dot.gov/publications/fhwa-hop12006/fhwahop12006.pdf (accessed April 15, 2018).

28 Fraser McLeod and Tom Cherrett, *Modelling the Impact of Shared Freight-Public Transport Lanes in Urban Centres* (Southampton: University of Southampton, 2015), www.researchgate.net/profile/Tom_Cherrett/publication/265991892_MODELLING_THE_IMPACTS_OF_SHARED_FREIGHT-PUBLIC_TRANSPORT_LANES_IN_URBAN_CENTRES/links/54b9069e0cf269d-8cbf72a41.pdf (accessed April 15, 2018).

29 Sorin Garber, Chuck Green, Patrick Sweeney, and Christopher Hemmer, *Designing for Truck Movements and Other Large Vehicles in Portland* (Portland, OR: City of Portland Office of Transportation, 2008), www.portlandoregon.gov/transportation/article/357099 (accessed April 15, 2018).

30 City of San Francisco, *Better Streets Plan* (San Francisco, CA: City of San Franciso, 2011), 126–128.

31 Christophe Ripert and Michael Browne, "La Démarche Exemplaire de Paris Pour le Transport de Marchandises en Ville," *Les Cahiers Scientifiques du Transport 55* (2009), 49.

32 New York City Department of Transportation, "Third Avenue Bus Lane Improvements," presentation, Manhattan Community Board 6 Transportation Committee Meeting, New York, May 5, 2014, www.nyc.gov/html/dot/downloads/pdf/2014-05-third-ave-bus-mn-cb6.pdf (accessed April 15, 2018).

33 New York City Department of Transportation, *Urban Freight Initiatives* (New York, NY: New York City Department of Transportation), http://home.nyc.gov/html/dot/downloads/pdf/2015-07-20-ur-ban-freight-initiatives.pdf (accessed April 15, 2018). City of San Francisco, *Better Market Street: Existing Conditions and Best Practices: Part II—Best Practices* (San Francisco, CA: City of San Francisco, 2011), 103–104, www.bettermarketstreetsf.org/docs/BMS_P2-4_BestPractices_12072011.pdf (accessed April 15, 2018).

34 US Department of Transportation, Federal Highway Administration, *Commercial Loading Zone Program Fact Sheet* (Washington, DC: US Department of Transportation, Federal Highway Administration, 2017), https://ops.fhwa.dot.gov/publications/fhwahop17022/fhwahop17022.pdf (accessed April 15, 2018). Bruce Schaller, Thomas Maguire, David Stein, Willa Ng, and Manzell Blakeley, "Parking Pricing and Curbside Management in New York City," in *Compendium of Papers, 90th Annual Meeting of the Transportation Research Board*, Washington, DC, January 23–27, 2011 (Washington, DC: Transportation Research Board of the National Academies, 2010).

GRAPHIC ESSAY 1

Mixed-Use Streets: A Conceptual Design Framework

NYC Department of City Planning

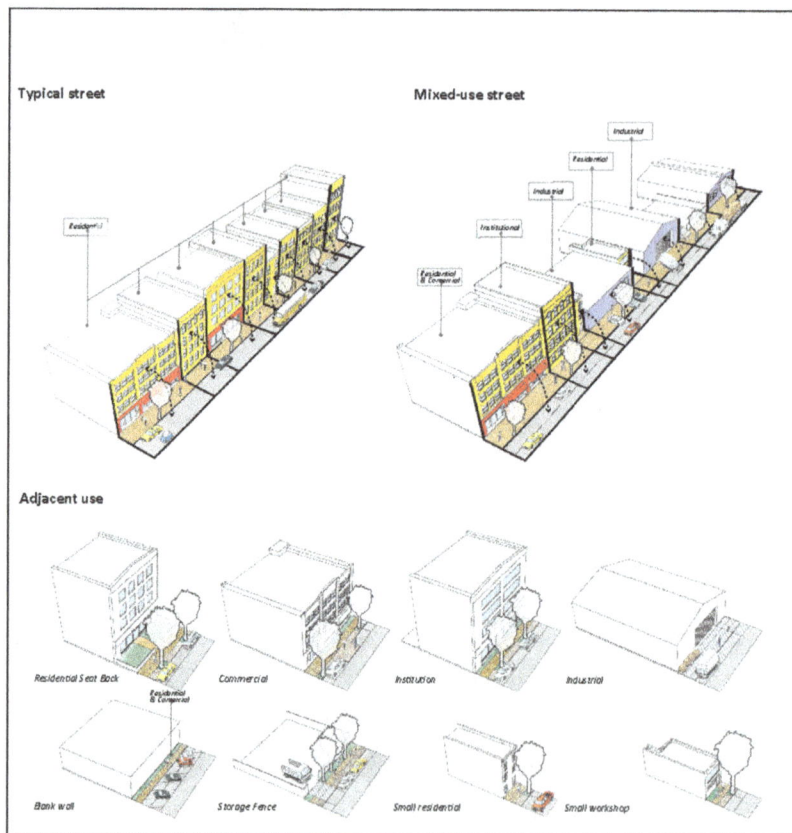

Proposed frontage kit of parts

In October 2014, the Department of City Planning (DCP) released the draft recommendations for a transportation study for Western Queens. Part of the study's scope was to develop a conceptual framework for existing "mixed-use" streets. These streets represent a unique challenge since they cater to urban environments that are in flux, with a diversity of land uses that include manufacturing, light industrial, commercial, community facilities, and residences. This poses an inherent conflict between the needs and use of the public realm. At the same time these streets offer a unique opportunity for a more fine-grained approach to design that recognizes and enhances their unique character.

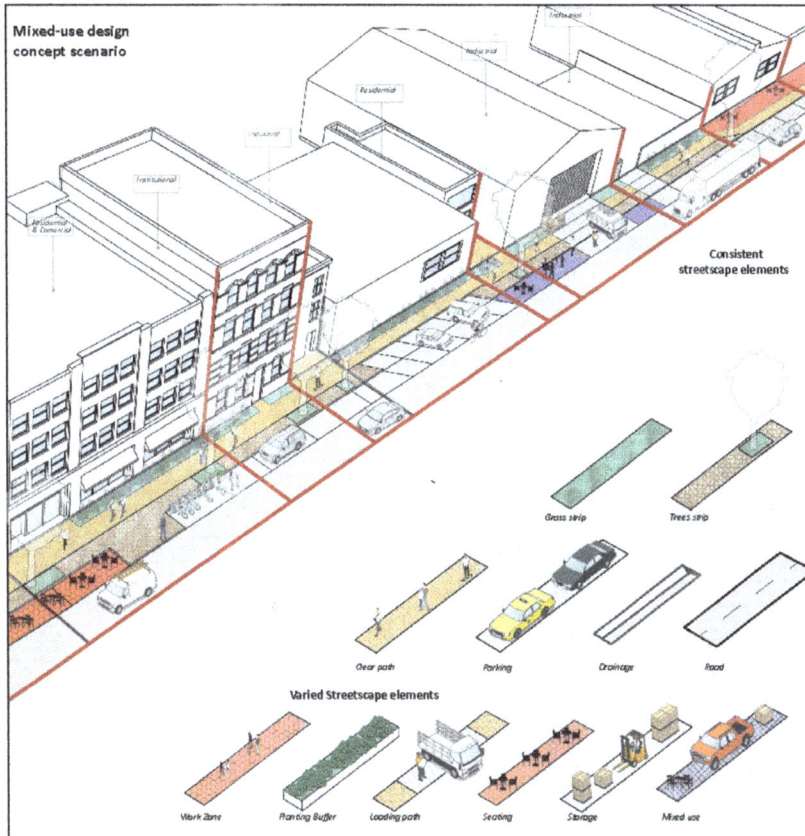

Sidewalk kit of parts

Defining the Issues and Objectives

In the study DCP found that the needs and functioning of existing industrial businesses such as loading and staging of goods are typically not accommodated within the private lot. As a result these businesses will often take over the sidewalk and road space in a variety of ways that conflict with safe pedestrian mobility. The use of the roadway and sidewalk differs greatly depending on the adjacent uses. In addition many of these streets lack basic amenities such as defined sidewalks, adequate lighting, street trees, and seating, resulting in an uninviting environment for residents, shoppers, or daily workers.

During the study, the following key objectives were identified.

1. Preserve and enhance existing businesses.
2. Create a safe, walkable pedestrian environment.
3. Maximize street plantings where possible.
4. Enhance the neighborhood character by introducing additional amenities within the public realm.

These objectives could be addressed through a planning and design strategy that caters to multiple stakeholders. DCP proposed a more flexible street prototype and design framework that would better accommodate changes over time while still meeting the needs of existing street users.

Before

Design Framework

In typical residential and commercial streets there are standard treatments, alignments, and uses and these tend to be uniform and constant along the length of the street. Standard streets typically provide sidewalks with a continuous clear path for pedestrians, street trees (and tree pits) spaced at regular intervals, and sometimes areas for planting and seating. The remaining roadway is usually dedicated to continuous movement of vehicles with delineated areas for travel lanes, parking spaces, and sometimes bicycle lanes, and is designed to accommodate drainage.

In mixed-use streets the industrial and manufacturing uses of the street have needs that often do not align with the typical street design, leading to the undesirable and often unsafe conditions described above.

For this reason DCP developed a conceptual framework to design these streets differently in order to balance the needs of the multiple stakeholder groups competing for the same space. This framework includes the continuous elements that must exist in every street, e.g., pedestrian-clear path, travel lanes, drainage, etc., but it also includes elements that are "use-dependent"—for example, loading and staging areas for industrial uses and seating

After

or planting for residential or commercial uses. This approach creates a non-uniform street design that allows for multiple users to coexist within the same space. The street is designed and delineated with a built-in flexibility that responds to adjacent uses along it. The design can always change depending on the mix of uses but it always maintains the continuous and consistent elements that are required for the street to function properly. Street furniture and green space are introduced where possible and serve both residents and workers. Reflecting the more dynamic nature of mixed-use streets, uses and needs could change over time and the design of the streets could be adapted while following a predetermined set of design guidelines.

GRAPHIC ESSAY 2

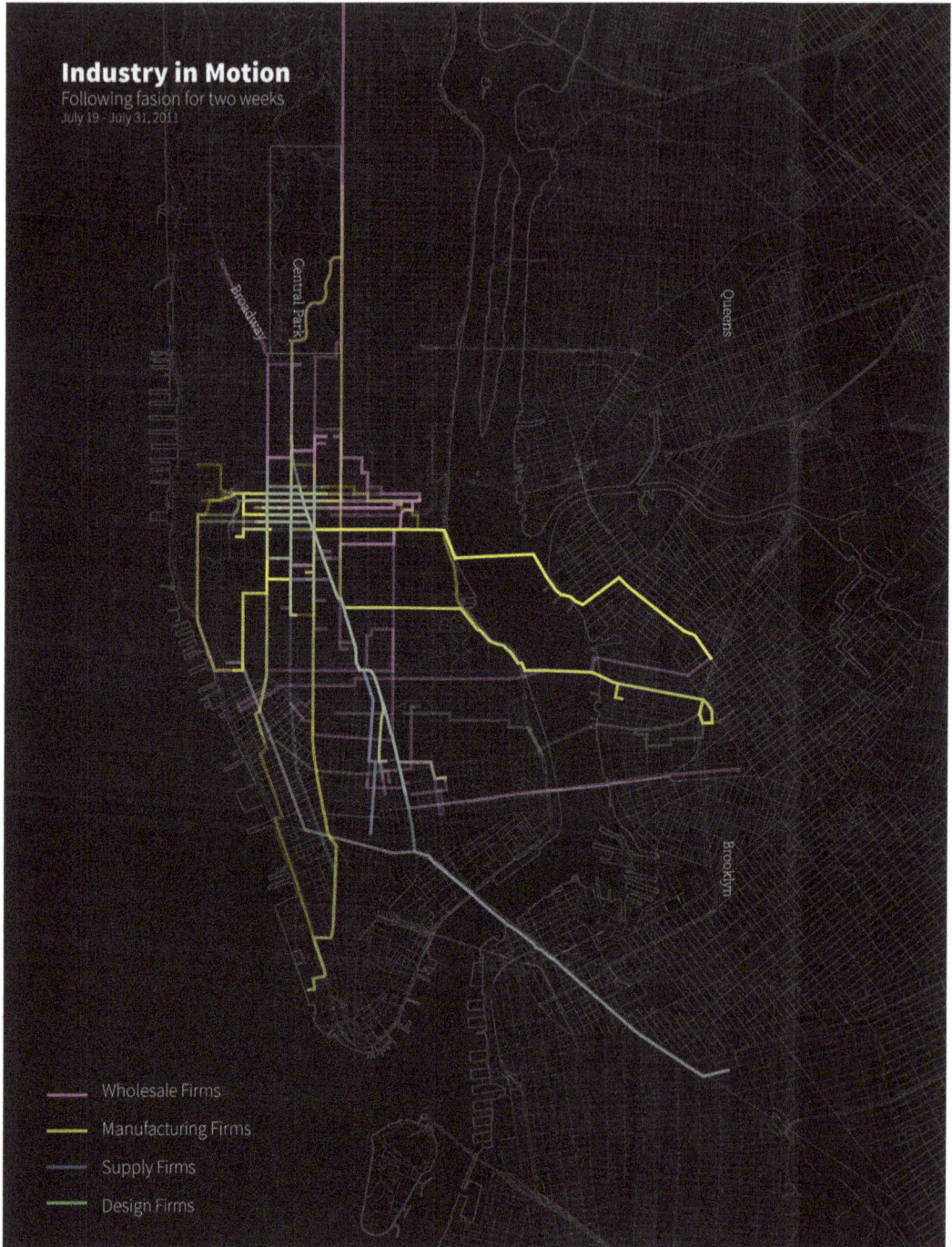

Industry in Motion
Following fasion for two weeks
July 19 - July 31, 2011

Central Park

Broadway

Queens

Brooklyn

— Wholesale Firms
— Manufacturing Firms
— Supply Firms
— Design Firms

Each trip made by fashion designers is colored by the business activity that caused the trip. The lines are semitransparent, thus darker lines mean overlapping trips were made along the route. The Garment District appears as a hub of activity in the center of the map with many dark overlapping lines.

Industry in Motion

Sarah Williams

Using Smartphones to Explore the Spatial Network of the Garment Industry in New York City

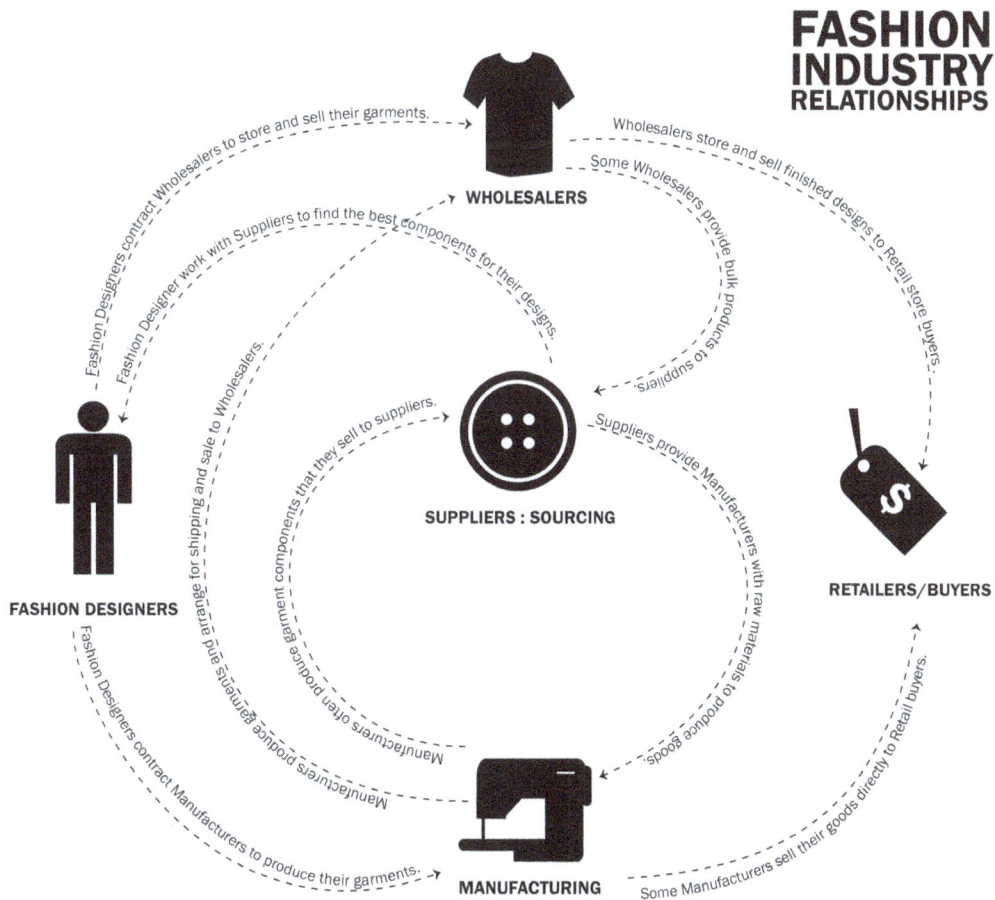

FASHION INDUSTRY RELATIONSHIPS

WHOLESALERS

Fashion Designers contract Wholesalers to store and sell their garments.

Fashion Designer work with Suppliers to find the best components for their designs.

Wholesalers store and sell finished designs to Retail store buyers.

Some Wholesalers provide bulk products to suppliers.

SUPPLIERS : SOURCING

Suppliers provide Manufacturers with raw materials to produce goods.

FASHION DESIGNERS

Fashion Designers arrange for shipping and sale to Wholesalers.

Manufacturers produce garment components that they sell to suppliers.

Manufacturers often produce garments.

RETAILERS/BUYERS

Fashion Designers contract Manufacturers to produce their garments.

MANUFACTURING

Some Manufacturers sell their goods directly to Retail buyers.

The apparel industry depends on an interconnected network of manufacturers, designers, suppliers, and wholesalers, who provide the materials for, produce, sell, and distribute their products. The Garment District is an agglomeration of those services, making the industry more efficient.

In 2010, New York City officials were interested in rezoning the Garment District, which had benefited from decades of protective rents, yet had seen an 80-percent decline in manufacturing jobs since the 1980s. Fashion designers argued that the proximity of interconnected networks of designers, manufacturers, wholesalers, and suppliers were what made the Garment District productive and were why fashion was a $31-billion industry. They argued that rezoning the District would have an adverse impact on the industry, as proximity to this network of smaller businesses was essential for their work.

Industry in Motion was a research project that set out to quantify the geo-economic dynamics of the Garment District to determine if proximity matters to the industry. The study tracked the movements of 100 fashion designers during every minute of the day for a two-week period (July 18 to 29, 2011) using their cell phones. Participants included designers and their interns from both large fashion houses and small boutiques across the city. Analysis of their business trips showed that the Garment District was essential to fashion designers across the region and rezoning efforts would affect large designers more than small firms since they use the District's services more.

Part II

The Design of Factories

The Architecture of the Places of Production

5 Making Factory Spaces

Nina Rappaport

Stuff still exists. Material goods have substance although their design and production organization can be nano, ephemeral, and digital. They require places for production that we still call factories—even within today's contemporary immaterial, and transformative, new paradigm. Although the immaterial workspace and virtual reality work experiences have fundamentally altered today's definition of manufacturing space—raising the question as to why physical spaces in factories are needed at all—we can't get around the fact that material goods must still be assembled, mixed, repaired, and resourced.

When factories are located in cities, intense local and global spatial restrictions apply because of lack of land, zoning requirements, financial and real estate machinations, building codes, trade and commerce regulations, and specific industrial processing methods dictated by a company's owner. As design projects, one could say that factories have more constraints than other building types, since the forces that make a factory direct its design *before* it becomes a physical entity and spatial commodity, require from the architect both innovative briefs and practical, efficient solutions.[1] Moreover, factories grow organically through decades of transformation in existing physical spaces often intended for earlier technologies' processing methods; or they do so in informal, and unplanned, aggregations that grow organically (see Bach and Al, Chapter 8, p. 155).

While space in this chapter does not allow for a complete history of factory architecture, key points of innovation are emphasized as opportunities for architectural design that can also serve as catalysts for the factory to return to the city as places that embody the technological power structure with layered nuances. This chapter also introduces essays focusing on spaces of production including the allocation of use (Alexander D'Hooghe et al., Graphic essay 3), design solutions (Frank Barkow, Chapter 6), sustainability (Naomi Darling, Chapter 7) informal spaces (Jonathan Bach and Stephan Al, Chapter 8), and spaces for shared production (Nina Rappaport, Chapter 9). Also highlighted here are three significant moments in the history of factory design: the experimental modernist; the "vertical urban factory"; the generic structure; and forward-looking contemporary factories.

Throughout architectural history, the factory has been a typology affording engineers and architects the means to experiment with both material and structure. The factory in general offers complex design opportunities for architects and engineers in which the function dictates the form that follows the production flow in a synergistic system.[2] Since medieval cottage industries documented in Diderot's *Encyclopédie*[3] and developing to Oliver Evans's eighteenth-century vertical production for flour mills,[4] multistoried textile plants in hillside

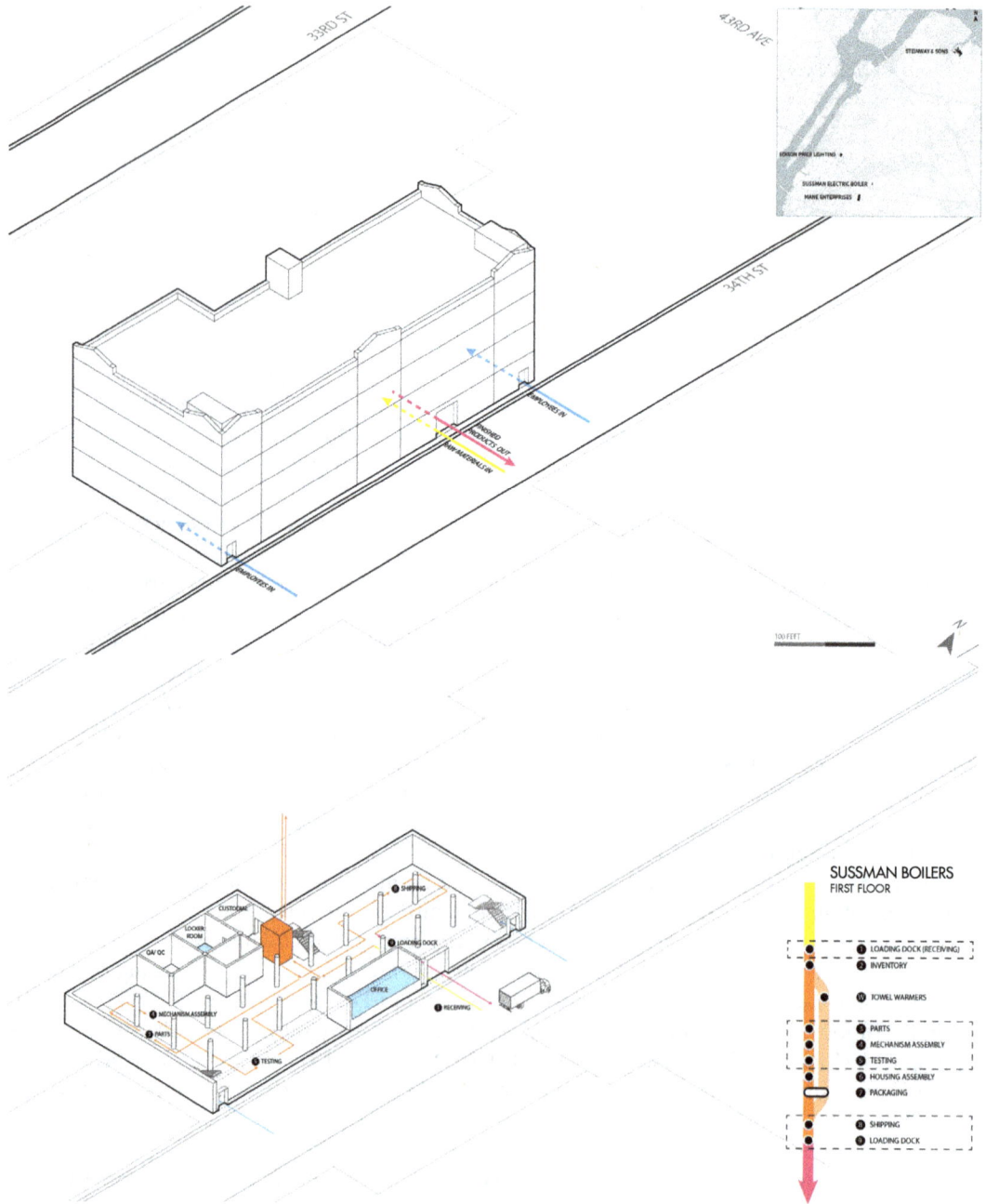

Figure 5.1 Factory flow diagram showing the flow of materials, workers, and production through a factory in Long Island City, New York. Diagrams by Henry Chan with Nina Rappaport for Vertical Urban Factory study, 2017.

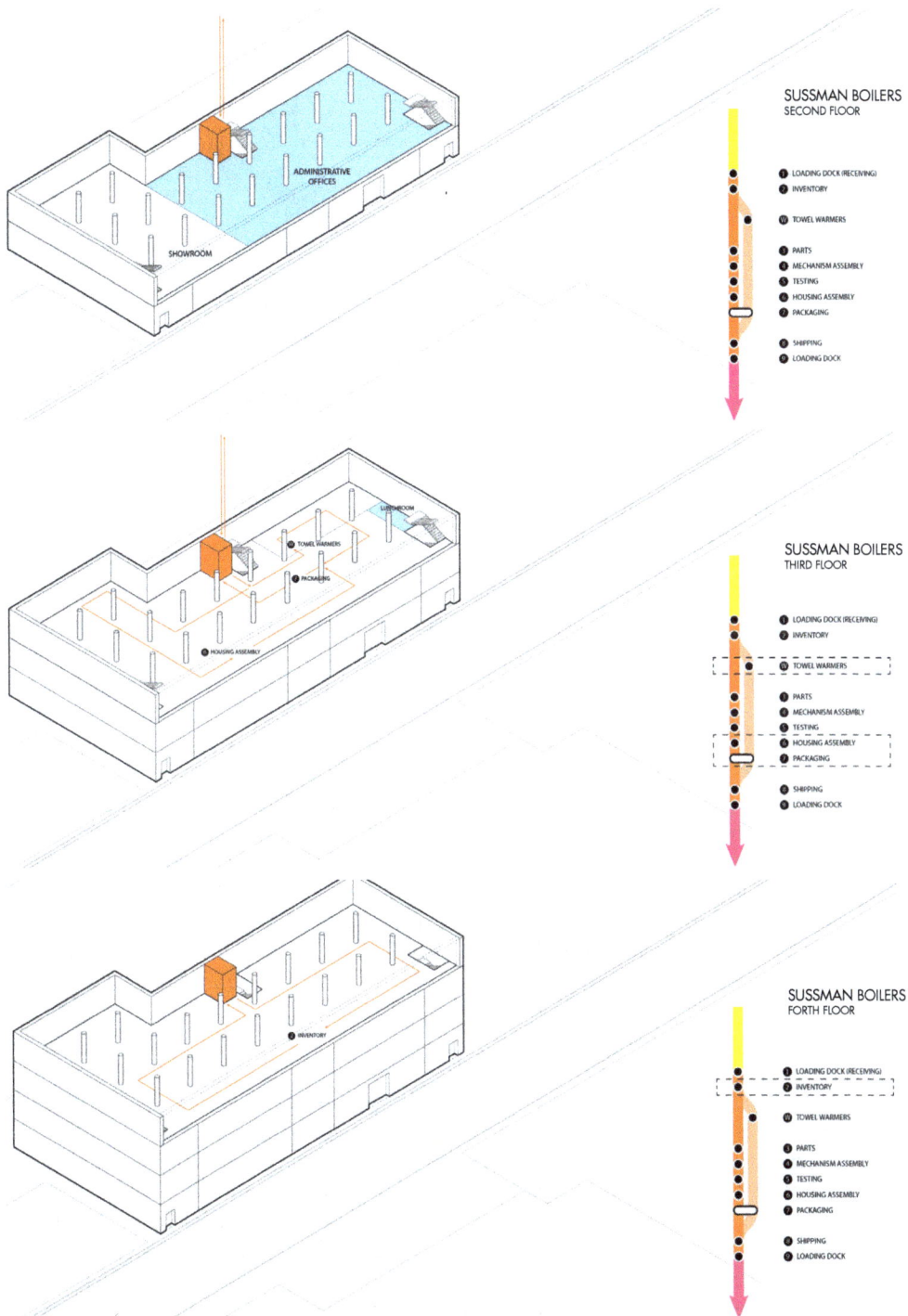

Figure 5.1 (Continued)

Figure 5.2 Frank L. Whitney, Bluebonnet Plant in Corpus Christi, Texas, 1949.

Figure 5.3 Zollverein Coal Mine Industrial Complex, Essen, Germany.

towns to "vertical urban factories"[5] and horizontal large-scale sheds—the spaces for production have been oriented according to production flow.

Robert Venturi's glove/mitten analogy for building typologies is useful for understanding factory design.[6] In the glove-type building, the concept is of a form fitting like a glove in which, metaphorically speaking, separate fingers reveal the production process that directs the building's form, especially in material and liquid processing such as waste treatment plants, breweries, and chemical plants. Elements such as stainless steel tanks are visible and sculptural, as in the Frank Whitney-designed 1949 Bluebonnet Plant in Corpus Christi, Texas, or in the Zollverein Coal Mine Industrial Complex's exposed steel piping and structures in Essen, Germany.

When the building is a mitten such as a shed—perhaps "decorated"—it encloses its perimeter to house the factory's inner workings, wrapping the mechanization and hiding the production system rather than revealing it in the building envelope. In either case the design goals for the factory typology are first and foremost efficiency and precision. The building, performing as an operating system, supports the manufacturing outcomes—with people and machines advancing the stages of production, linearly from A to Z, or cellularly as they zigzag in phased production. The wrapped factory and the articulated design provide vastly different and compelling options for the design of production spaces both historically and today.

Experimental Modernist Factory

Technological change has influenced not only the production process but also great shifts in factory design. This can be seen in the early-twentieth-century reinforced concrete systems invented by engineers such as François Hennebique, Eugène Fressyinet, and Julius Kahn, which allowed for longer spans, plenty of light and air, reduced costs, greater efficiency, and a way for the factory itself to be mass produced. During that period industrial engineers like these, in concert with their factory owner/clients, designed factories in a standardized vernacular that could be copied or exported globally, as Albert Kahn did in the late 1920s in his factories from Detroit to Russia, or as Giacomo Mattè-Trucco demonstrated in 1923 with his adaptation of the concrete-frame American factory for Fiat's Lingotto factory in Torino, Italy, then a futuristic symbol with its expansive, crowning rooftop test track.

Not only did the factory building need to be efficient, but so did the worker. As industrialists enforced worker performance, the new field of industrial engineering emerged, and—aimed at increasing both speed and profits—it affected both the organization of factory spaces and workers' physical movements.[7] The time and motion studies conducted by American industrial engineers Frank and Lillian Gilbreth radically influenced organizational structure in 1910; with Frederick Taylor's Scientific Management principles in 1911, each worker's task became more specialized, as predicted by Adam Smith in the eighteenth century. These efforts, intended to control the human production line, did so at the expense of worker well-being, yet were of great benefit to factory owners. The ensuing employee/management conflicts led to worker unrest but inspired later worker reforms focused on the betterment of the working environment with new amenities. Thus, human movement and its regulation impacted factory flow and form.

Modernist architects, in particular, had a freedom to explore the spatial and organizational systems of factory buildings, as the program itself was new. The factory was a place for experimentation, incorporating engineering innovation and creating buildings that spearheaded Modernist design, as seen in Peter Behrens's AEG Turbine Factory (Berlin, 1909), Albert Kahn's Ford Highland Park Factory (Detroit, 1909), Walter Gropius's Fagus Factory (Alfeld an der Leine, Germany, 1911), Hans Poelzig's Chemical Plant (Lubon, Poland, 1911), Erich Mendelsohn's Hat Factory (Luckenwalde, Germany, 1921), and Van der Vlugt's Van Nelle Factory (Rotterdam, The Netherlands, 1931), among others. Scale and logistics dictated the factory locations at the urban edges and in industrial districts. These historical exemplars are variously sited: occupying full city blocks; perimeters of blocks forming courtyards; hugging railroad tracks; and often with waterfront access for transportation logistics. In terms of both progress and productivity the factory was not only emblematic of the Machine Age but Modernist ideals; it represented the productive machine and, as such, was embraced by the avant-garde.[8] The Modernist factory has continuing relevance—from the organization of production tasks to the specific design parameters demanded by each project and site.

Figure 5.4 Engineers working on factory layouts, 1950s.

Vertical Urban Factory

Of particular interest for urban manufacturing is the way in which multistoried factories can house a mix of small and medium-sized companies in layers, by floor, or be owned and developed by one company as an integrated building;[9] this is possible because smaller, cleaner, and lighter manufacturing methods can make do with more compact spaces within the dense urban industrial ecosystem. The vertical urban factory, which has a long legacy dating from Robert Owen's progressive eighteenth-century New Lanark Mills in Scotland to those engineered factories such as the 1874 Menier Chocolate Factory in Noisiel, France, are themselves like complex machines. Menier, designed by Jules Saulnier (known for the first iron frame and non-load-bearing walls), had water turbines at the base of the building above the river that ran under the factory and were integrated into its structural design. The verticality of the factory was also cost-saving. As urban land became more valuable, factories expanded upward, housing vertical systems of production on multiple floors and harnessing gravity for processing, which became a necessity on condensed urban sites. The multilevels employed overhead conveyors, cranes, and transfer chutes, both straight and spiral, to convey supplies through the new "cathedrals" of commerce. Ample natural light also permeated these spaces via floor-to-ceiling windows and sawtooth roofs.

One significant Modernist vertical urban factory that was important for both its urban manufacturing process and its architectural design was the Van Nelle factory, a tea, coffee, and tobacco company founded by Kees van der Leeuw and designed by the firm Brinkman & Van der Vlugt in 1931. The Van Nelle complex, in Rotterdam, included a series of separate but connected buildings of varying heights for the processing and packaging of coffee (six stories), tea (three stories), and tobacco (eight stories). Additionally, the site included warehouses, offices, and worker amenities such as a soccer field and a library. The factory's emphasis on transparency created a new model for manufacturing spaces by exemplifying a hygienic, light-filled, airy environment, one open to both internal and external views. The curtain wall was installed from the exterior and large mushroom columns allowed for more open space between them for the ease of machinery movement. As a vertically organized factory, production flowed from the upper to the lower floors, with the raw goods delivered to the topmost floor. The final products were transferred into the glazed dispatch buildings via overhead U-shaped conveyors

Figure 5.5 Brinkman & Van der Vlugt, Van Nelle Factory, Rotterdam, The Netherlands, 1931.

circulating from the interior of the factory to the enclosed glass bridges traversing the site's internal street. The factory has an essential place in the city and has the potential to return manufacturing to urban environments with increased density and in a form that supports the new production processes.

The Factory Shed

The other volumetric orientation, large-footprint, single-story factories with production in a singular volume, was accelerated by increased requirements for efficiency on the ground-plane. Instant factories were constructed from prefabricated systems as early as 1919, seen in the Truscon Steel Company's kit-of-parts shed systems that allowed for flexible manufacturing solutions requiring large open spaces. In the 1950s, factories in the suburbs and ex-urban areas were more horizontal in their operations and volumes. In the suburban industrial districts, where there was more land, the offices and entries to the factories were often designed as separate volumes added onto the basic production shed, a continuing strategy today. Those built more cheaply for small and midsized businesses had difficulties in occupying the large spaces: a modern one-story, sub-dividable "flex factory" would be no more than 100 feet deep—not the typical 200- or even 300-foot depth of the "big box" factory. While we may regret the architectural poverty of the windowless shed, the big box has the advantage of being so generic, and of being relatively flexible to modification either for new uses or with a potential for design features to enhance the urban context. One design strategy for these flexible sheds is to modify the basic building design with additions of entry canopies, shading devices, graphic lettering, roof treatments, and systems that meet sustainability goals. The building's architectural character is expressed in details such as continuous clerestories of steel casement windows, and articulated brick and stonework. Adding or widening windows also makes production visible, which can help build support for urban manufacturing, as seen at the Markforged factory in Watertown (see Markforged interview, p. 19) and a dairy in Minneapolis. Exterior spaces can also link to the public cityscape as seen in Portland, Oregon's design guidelines for the Central Eastside manufacturing district that specify how loading docks of one-story factories can become open, active places that celebrate the movement of goods.

Another strategy is to "clip-on" volumes containing other programs, as pioneered in the "artisans villages" in the Modena region of Italy in the 1980s. In 1995, a thirty-year master plan and redesign of Bayer Inc.'s forty-five-acre campus in West Berkeley, California was designed by Lyndon Buchanan Associates with John Northmore Roberts & Associates. As Bayer changed its production process the architects reinvented its buildings and streets through a combination of carving into and adding onto the basic boxes and designing an urban plan. Not only did this enable Bayer to reuse and repurpose existing buildings, but it also made it possible to reconnect the formerly closed campus to the neighborhood by lining new streets and public spaces with the reactivated factory facades, and new landscape design as part of a comprehensive plan (see case study in Part IV).

Process Removal

One reason for the horizontal shift in manufacturing was that during World War II munitions and aircraft factories jumped scales on suburban sites, becoming massive industrial "territories" covering millions of square feet. In densely populated urban areas, factories were not only sequestered from potential air attacks but from the larger population for security reasons. Architects were encouraged to design hermetically sealed, windowless sheds with blackout panels, using Freon for air conditioning, and reliant upon fluorescent lighting instead of the operable windows. In addition, Europe and the US developed expansive infrastructure distribution networks—i.e., freeways—either removed from or expanding away from cities, so the once necessarily compact logistic systems became even more dispersed. Industrial buildings and districts are often guided by infrastructure-driven considerations, even in cases where the infrastructure itself, such as rail lines or ports, is either obsolete or repurposed for urban amenities or other new community-focused activities. The process of making things was subtracted from everyday life in what can be called "process removal."[10] The exclusion of factories from the urban realm negatively impacted urban life once they became disused through building vacancy and blight, and through the lack of blue-collar employment factories moved to greenfields. These consequences both ruined the natural environment and prompted suburban flight. Outside of the US, the trend of process removal resulted in Export Processing Zones in developing nations that ignored workers' rights and lacked humane managerial oversight.[11]

Postwar Innovations

During postwar reconstruction in Europe and also in America, architects once again found in the factory an opportunity to experiment. They worked in tandem with industrial engineers to organize the factory floor, addressing the design opportunities for the sheds of mass production, finding ways to aestheticize them, and developing innovative design ideas such as integrated mechanical systems and structures, and prefabricated and repetitive construction methods in concrete and steel. Architects also found new opportunities in designing generic buildings that have architectural character expressed in details such as innovative cladding and structural systems, articulated roofscapes and skylights, spatial organization, and material experimentation, all of which inspired variegated surfaces and innovative compositions beyond a standard form.

In particular, later Italian Modern architects who bridged industrial design and architecture embraced the factory, as had the earlier avant-garde. Italian architect-designer Marco Zanuso employed concrete to integrate structural design with mechanical systems with distinctive profiles for projects such as the Olivetti Factory (Buenos Aires, Argentina 1954) and the CEDIT factory (Palermo, Italy, 1956), for which he designed V-shaped beams and flat trusses in a prefabricated industrialized system with an organizational holism between design and industrial function. In 1962, Angelo Mangiarotti developed a concrete system for SIAG in Marcianese, Italy consisting of a concrete framework that could be expanded indefinitely to support the company's growth; in 1973, for the Snaidero factory in Majano, Italy, he innovated a metal prefabricated modular panel system.[12] Also in the 1950s, Ulrich Franzen designed the Barken, Levin & Co. apparel factory in Long Island City, New York, with its imaginative folded concrete umbrella roof structure taking on the challenge of the articulated structure.

Both Japanese Metabolists, such as Kenzo Tange, and the British "high-tech" architects of Team 4—Norman Foster, Wendy Cheesman, Richard Rogers, and Su Brumwell—experimented with kit-of-parts designs for buildings that could be erected quickly. Team 4's 1966 Reliance Controls factory in Swindon, England uses X-shaped tension rods to suspend the factory in a manner similar to a bridge, thus increasing the distance of open spans. The factory interiors were maximized with mezzanines and vertical conveyance systems to increase the usable area. These "high-tech" factory designers were instrumental in translating a factory aesthetic to all architectural typologies as in the Centre Pompidou (Paris, 1965) that was as influential as the experiments of the Modernist Movement.

As factory flows changed from linear to cellular systems the open shed was not as essential to production. Gehrad Goehl's design of the Volvo factory in Kalmar, Sweden (1973) was a groundbreaking form-follows-flow design in that its hexagonal volumes were dictated by teamwork production in "cells" rather than by a linear process. People worked in teams, each responsible for a car's assembly at a static station with a "Kalmar Carrier" mobile workstation making the car accessible from all sites as it moved in the shop floor. This influenced the building organization around a series of adjacent work-spaces forming a butterfly rather than a traditional rectilinear layout.[13]

However, each factory, whether urban or exurban, vertical or horizontal, ground-up or renovated, has similar design issues that it must solve for a future potential to transform manufacturing operations in cities. Two other dichotomies can't be ignored that also influence space: lean and automated/robotic production methods with fewer workers per factory and thus less space required; and the shift from linear assembly lines to smaller workshops like informal cottage or neo-cottage industries as places for inventing and making things, as discussed below (see Bach and Al, Chapter 8, p. 152). Both manufacturing technologies and factory workflow structure—rapidly and continually evolving—have redirected recent factory design. In manufacturing technology the shift from mass production to mass customization, on-demand production, automation, and the relationship to R&D has redirected the spatial organization in factories so that white- and blue-collar workers interact on the factory floor as an idea goes from design to creation. While factory building designs can be categorized in many ways that apply to existing and future design, the concepts—"spectacle," "flexible neo-cottage," "hybrid," and "sustainable,"—are being incorporated into factory designs that in turn support manufacturers' relocation to cities.[14]

Spectacle

The factory as "spectacle" follows Guy Debord's recognition of the consumption society,[15] both in that the architecture is a marketing tool promoting a company's brand rhetoric and that we are consuming the methods of production as participants in the capitalist process—i.e., designing and purchasing either via the web or in the factory itself, and enjoying watching people making things. Public fascination with seeing how things are made—as reflected in the craze for open-kitchen restaurants—relates to the "experience economy" that encourages consumers to bond with a product or have a meaningful encounter, thus capturing the consumer's attention and dollars.[16] Often these companies develop these factories with a focus on design as a core value, seen prominently in recent years in the furniture, fashion, and automotive sectors. To remain in cities the factories are vertical as a way to capitalize on space and costly urban land by going up, as seen in Henn Architekten's transparent multifunctional VW Gläserne Manufaktur in Dresden, Germany (2001) and Mehrdad Hadighi and Tsz Yan Ng Architects' design of a factory for the fashion house Lafayette 148 in Shantou, China (2009), with fluid concrete bands wrapping the building for natural light, as well as multitenanted buildings such

Figure 5.6 Henn Architekten, VW Gläserne Manufaktur, Dresden, Germany, 2001.

as the Noerd Building in Zurich, Switzerland by Beat Rothen Architects (2011) and the New York in Portland, Oregon, designed by DiLoreto Architects (2014).[17]

One design strategy—and marketing tool—deployed by manufacturers is to build their factories using the materials with which their products are strongly associated. Companies such as RIMOWA, a manufacturer of luggage, clad their Cologne factory with a ribbed aluminum similar to that used in their suitcases. Paolo Soleri designed the 1955 Solimene ceramic factory in Italy, using the company's ceramic pots to create the curved building facade. Projects by Barkow Leibinger for the Trumpf company also elaborate on materiality for a company image using folded metal cladding in a variety of finishes to reference the CNC machinery produced inside the factory (see Barkow, Chapter 6, p. 131). These examples show how a company can capitalize on its knowledge to promote its identity using aesthetic means reflecting their production processes or products.

Another design approach that marries building as marketing tool with urban enhancement is the transparent factory. Instead of being sequestered away from the public view, today's factories can instead capitalize on transparency, both physically and socially. A glass facade that allows the public to see and experience the working process enlivens the street in ways Jane Jacobs would have been interested in as it brings the worker into view.[18] Unlike the more normative sealed factory building, the transparent factory has the potential to heighten the public's valuation of labor.

In many cities including San Francisco, New York,[19] London, Wuppertal, and Milan, this idea of spectacle is being extended to a regional scale with the introduction of factory tours sponsored by companies or municipalities to focus on industry (see Fossa, Chapter 3, p. 76). Many companies transform their existing factories after making commitments to stay in place for reasons of convenience, workforce, knowledge-base, and existing networks of suppliers. The projects discussed below for a dairy in St. Paul, Minnesota and the Ryhove plant in Ghent, Belgium illustrate the potential for design to play a part in factories with incremental insertions that create new holistic factory schemes through their transparency and design additions.

Figure 5.7 Concept of a vertical transparent factory for New York City's Garment District. Rendering by Jessica Morris with Nina Rappaport, 2017.

A Dairy

A ninety-year-old dairy in North Minneapolis is situated across the street from houses and occupies nearly an entire city block. The company has expanded from its original 10,000-square-foot, two-story brick-and-concrete building into a mini-campus consisting of production spaces, milk tanks, a delivery area, and warehouses. Employing 150 people in a 24/7, 365-days-per-year operation, the factory daily produces 75,000 gallons of a variety of milk-related products, which are packaged and then distributed by refrigerated trucks across a five-state region. Due to a number of factors—including the consolidation demands of the regional co-op, the drive for efficiency and economic return, the market demand to drastically increase capacity, and the central location and easy freeway access of the facility—the dairy sought to remain in place. Hoping to increase capacity by 65,000 gallons per day, they looked at how they could bring in more efficient fillers and packaging lines, and increase efficiency in terms of worker flow and distribution, all while creating a modern workplace with a design that engages both the existing facility and local context.

There were substantial obstacles to overcome, including how to save and incorporate two landmarked buildings—the 1924 Odd Fellows and the 1936 White Castle, which the company owned.[20] AWH Architects discovered that Kemps could reuse and restore the Odd Fellows building

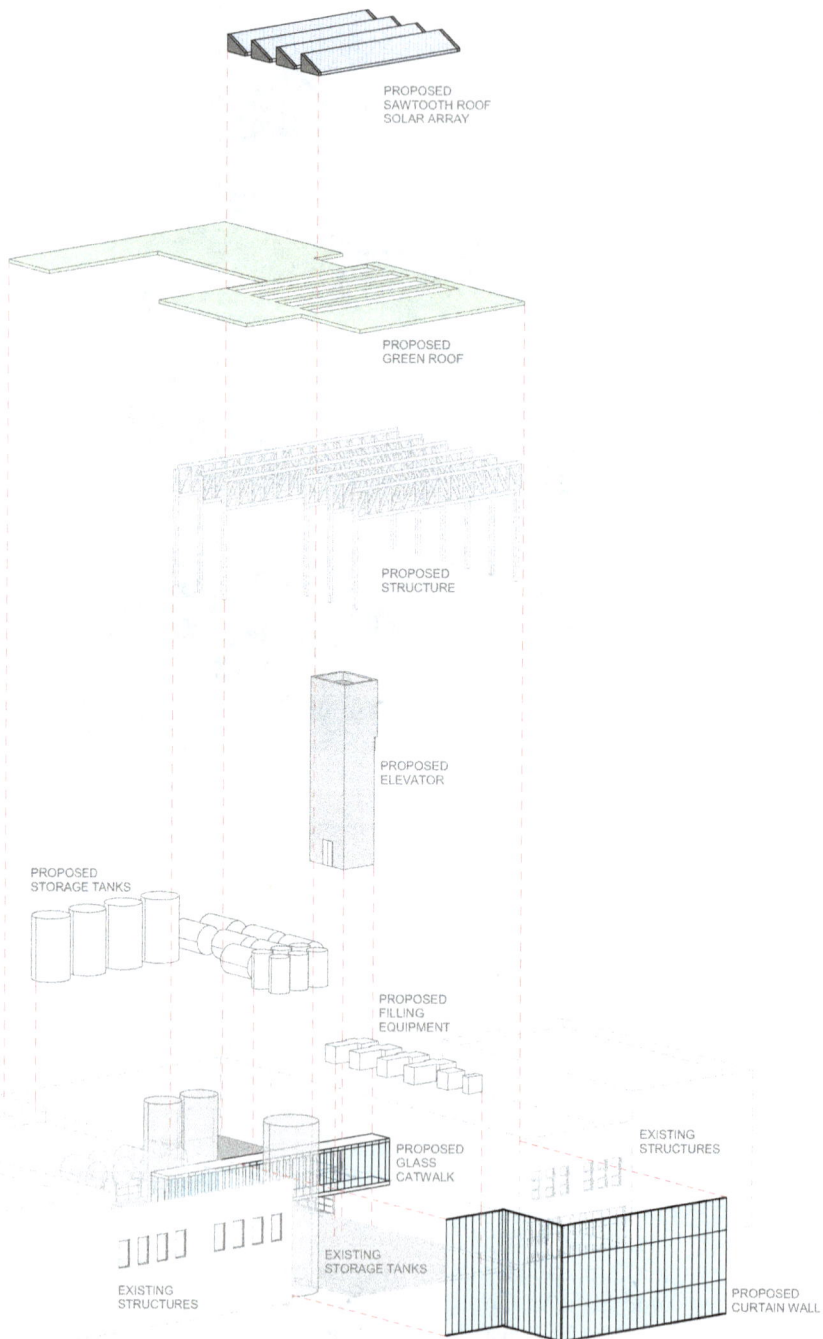

PROPOSED
SAWTOOTH ROOF
SOLAR ARRAY

PROPOSED
GREEN ROOF

PROPOSED
STRUCTURE

PROPOSED
ELEVATOR

PROPOSED
STORAGE TANKS

PROPOSED
FILLING
EQUIPMENT

EXISTING
STRUCTURES

PROPOSED
GLASS
CATWALK

EXISTING
STORAGE TANKS

EXISTING
STRUCTURES

PROPOSED
CURTAIN WALL

Figure 5.8 AWH Architects, exploded axonimetric of a dairy in St. Paul, Minnesota, 2018.

in exchange for rezoning the White Castle lot for increased industrial use. AWH designed a two-story glass addition that connects the original factory with the Odd Fellows building and features a sawtooth roof with solar panels. The new 14,000-square-foot space and 9,600-square-foot

Figure 5.9 AWH Architects, rendering of new glass volume with dairy tanks for a company in St. Paul, Minnesota, 2018.

Figure 5.10 Aerial view of Ryhove in Ghent, Belgium, designed by TRANS Architecture, 2018.

renovation are composed of a steel structure, concrete floors, and spider-glass curtain wall. The storage containers are located above new loading docks and the filling lines are integrated into existing and new automated systems. A catwalk connects the two buildings' second floors, allowing for a two-story space where the new fillers, stainless steel tanks, and other equipment are visible to passersby through the glazed curtain wall, which glows at night. The second floor houses offices that can be accessed via a new elevator core, the glass catwalk, and a stairway leading directly from the street. Kemps also focused on public outreach with an exhibition space demonstrating the company's new community engagement beyond just a physical transparency to a social one. Ryhove, a multi-product company—from food products to printing—continues to operate in their historic factory in the center of Ghent, Belgium, where it decided to stay.

It hired TRANS Architecture to design an addition and renovation of the original building rather than move to the periphery and lose their valued employees.[21] The company wanted to improve the factory organization but to still be contextual to the neighborhood. Inspired by the adjacent house typology, TRANS designed simple pitched roof profiles with half-timbered wood framework in the eaves—closer to a house typology than a normative factory with a sawtooth roof. Three peaks rise on the street facade, with one on the residential side following the adjacent house profiles. Bands of windows surrounding the building resolve in large corner windows at the entrance. The 2,000-square-meter addition is constructed of standardized prefabricated elements, including concrete columns, CLT panels, and metal sandwich panels. With the original building constructed from reinforced concrete, the architects selected steel for the addition's structure to house new machinery. The new building also reorganizes the site for improved flow by placing loading and unloading in the center court and exposing the goods handling to the public.

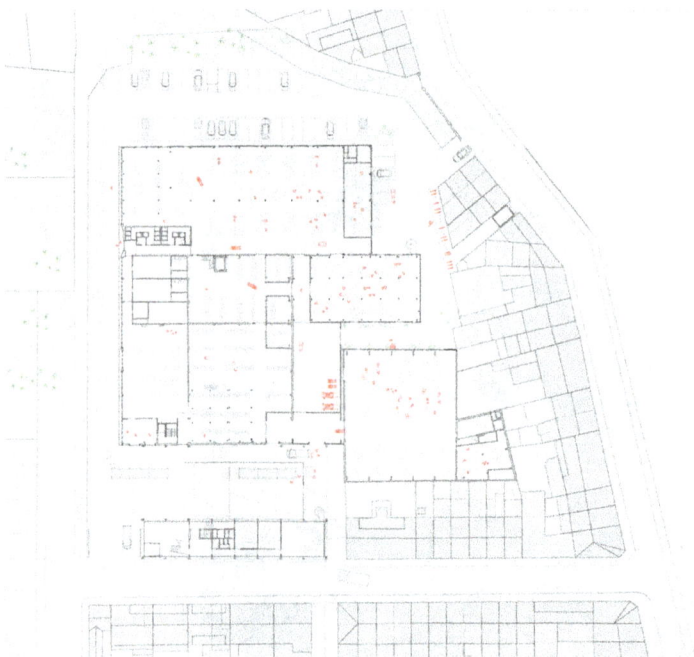

Figure 5.11 Ryhove building in in Ghent, Belgium, designed by TRANS Architecture, 2018.

Figure 5.12 Ryhove roofline in the residential neighborhood, Ghent, Belgium, designed by TRANS Architecture, 2018.

TRANS Architecture also designed flexible open space for administrative offices with a shared entrance and cafeteria. The dynamic additions realized the potential for small but significant design solutions to enhance the urban factory.

Neo-Cottage and Flexible

The smaller and flexible industries of the new economy using just-in-time and on-demand production methods can occupy neo-cottage spaces rather than entire buildings.[22] Given small-batch production and the shrinking scale of technologies, a new urban manufacturing paradigm has emerged that offers spaces in which smaller bits can be assembled to make the larger whole. There is less warehousing today because of lean production, so that urban factories with smaller, cleaner plants can produce in a more dispersed and local network. As layered factories with multiple companies—most often in existing buildings—the individual companies can often lease spaces on demand, expanding and contracting as their production increases and spaces become available.

Three models of management have helped shape the organization of many flexible vertical urban factories: government ownership, private developers, and not-for-profit developers. One model government-sponsored project is the Hôtel Industriel in Paris. In the 1980s, a series of vertical urban factories were designed by different architects to promote the development of lighter and smaller industries in cities.[23] The city of Paris built over fifteen new factory buildings for myriad production purposes in multistory buildings situated mostly on the urban edge but still in the city limits. Other cities are following the City of Paris's success. In Geneva, the new Hôtel Industriel, designed by LRS Architects, is in the planning stages (see Rappaport, Chapter 10, p. 191). The design consists of three parallel seven-story bar volumes hosting diverse light-industrial companies. The space between the two bar volumes allows for ground-floor delivery systems off-street and separate from pedestrian traffic. The high-density use for a relatively small ground plane makes the delivery systems efficient and unobtrusive. The mix also creates an industrial ecology in an individual building in which the tenants can share services and be part of a community.

Other buildings with multiple tenants are the historic multistoried factories with their solid concrete floors, gridded concrete columns, robust loading docks, and ample elevators. The City

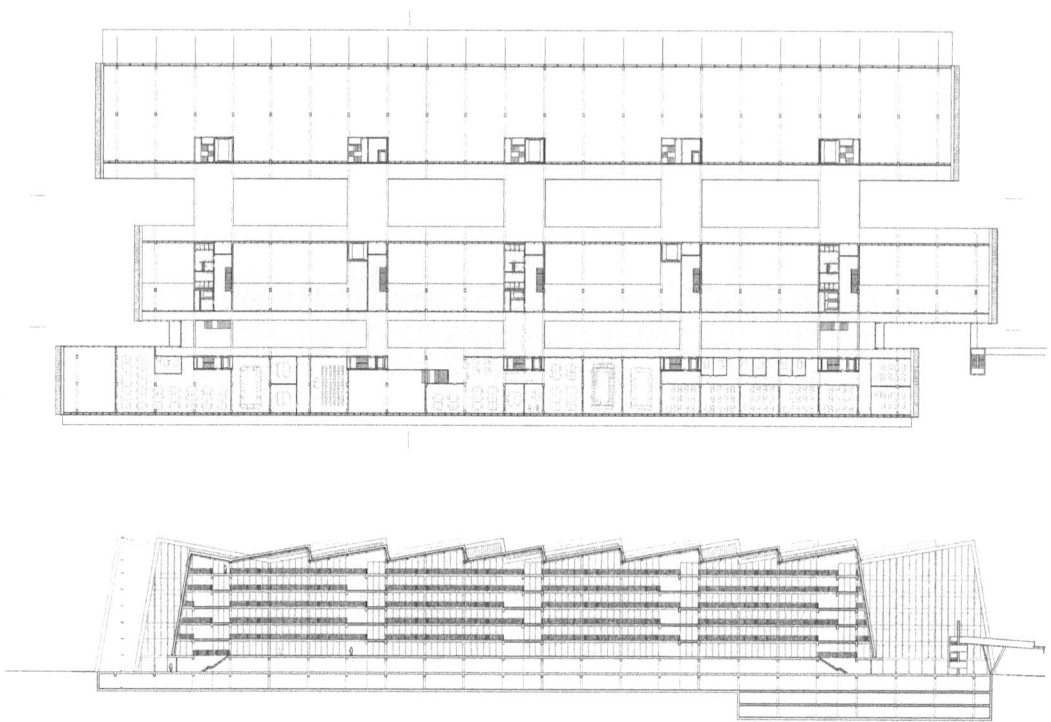

Figure 5.13 Hôtel Industriel, Geneva, Swizerland, rendering by LRS Architects, 2016.

of Brussels sponsors the Centre d'Entreprise in a former factory in the Molenbeek neighborhood. The historic building's courtyard makes it convenient for moving goods in and out and it is comprised of entrepreneurial spaces, light manufacturers, and some offices. In New York City the Greenpoint Manufacturing and Design Center (GMDC) now owns six renovated historic factory buildings. GMDC directly influenced SFMade in the nonprofit's construction of a new four-story, 56,000-square-foot building on Hooper Street in San Francisco operating under the name "PlaceMade" (see Becker and Friedman, Chapter 12, p. 215). Other strategies include private owners who manage mixed-use manufacturing spaces for profit. In North Philadelphia, the former Globe Dye Works' brick-and-concrete building houses fabricators, artisans, and small manufacturers in a variety of spaces and scales. The owners do much of the construction work themselves and focus on a strong mix of tenants—from restoration woodworkers and a boat building school, to ice cream and coffee entrepreneurs.

New ways to create shared space are also evident in cities through what is called the "Industrial Commons,"[24] where companies share facilities and expertise to reduce costs (see Rappaport, Chapter 9, p. 169). These shared fabrication spaces, which include fab labs, co-working spaces, hackerspaces, makerspaces, and collaborative workshops, are organized both formally and informally. Companies often find an existing factory space (multistoried or single-storied) in which they can establish a business based on sharing computers, high-tech machinery, woodworking tools, 3D printers, and CAD/CAM and CNC milling machines, among other costly capital investments. Examples of successes in this arena include OmniCorps in Detroit, the Parachute Factory in Las Vegas, New Mexico, and NextFab in Philadelphia (see Rappaport, Chapter 9, p. 163). Sharing of resources and knowledge is also integral to the "New" and the "Next Economy" as production becomes more democratized, with entrepreneurs making their own products.

Hybrid—Manufacturing and Living

While we are familiar with the live-work spaces that artists pioneered in New York's SoHo district and London's East End, hybrid factories that combine both living and manufacturing are rare. The mix is not easy because of the differences between residents and manufacturing needs that cause nuisances for one that are a necessity for the other, such as truck traffic, unwanted smells, and noise, but with smaller and cleaner factories a new mix is possible. As Jane Jacobs

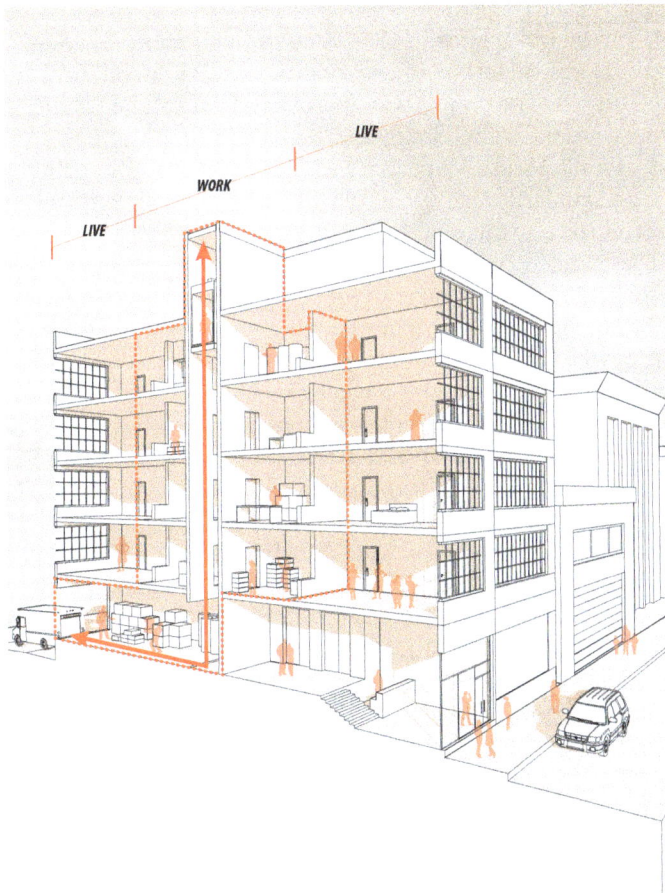

Figure 5.14 Concept for manufacturing and living spaces, rendering by Nilus Klingel with Nina Rappaport, Vertical Urban Factory, 2018.

observed, "To understand cities, we have to deal outright with combinations or mixtures of uses, not separate uses, as the essential phenomena."[25] *Vertical Urban Factory* (2015) defines potential configurations that combine manufacturing space on the first floors, commercial space in the middle floors, and residential above as a way to subsidize the high cost of manufacturing space in capital cities.[26] Uses can be mixed on each floor or staggered through parallel tower-like volumes. "Mandatory Inclusionary Manufacturing"[27] would require manufacturing use in new residential developments as part of policy and zoning regulations (see Part III). Architecturally, building infrastructure systems such as vertical access of shared or independent stairs and elevators; common or individual lobbies; common loading and services; and mechanical, fire, safety, and local building code regulations are complex design considerations that need further investigation.

One convenient way to add new programs to existing factory buildings are architectural volumes that are a kind of clip-on to the main structure, as Japanese Metabolist architects designed in the 1960s. In Modena, Italy, the "artisans villages" pioneered the addition of residential buildings in front of one-story production sheds as live-work configurations—creating a pattern of alternating residential and industrial streets.

Other integrated new hybrid multistoried projects are coming to fruition, such as Eckington Place, a complex on 3.1-acre site at the intersection of New York and Florida Avenues in Washington, DC's Ward 5 district. The project was approved as part of the Planned Unit Development (PUD) process by the developers JBG Smith and Boundary. Architect Eric Colbert & Associates designed the project as a mixed-use residential and light industrial production space that is clean and green. Rather than standard retail space, the ground floor will combine retail with artisanal industries such as distilleries, textile makers, and artists in workspaces ranging from 1,200 to 8,000 square feet. The seven-story building will have retail space rising 102 feet on the west side and 75 feet on the east side, with two connector bridges across a courtyard between buildings. The courtyard will be common outdoor space shared by tenants. The potential for a vibrant new mixed-use community with additional employment for the area adheres to the city's goals for increased job growth and industrial retention while also increasing the residential units.

In Vancouver, Strathcona Village, a multistoried project finished in 2018, is exemplary of the new mixed-use typology. Developed by Wall Financial Corp. and located at 900 Hastings Street, it combines residential condos with light-industrial spaces. The vibrant mixed-use community ranges from traditional manufacturers who make marine propellers for ships to smaller-scale innovative industries including breweries, wine distributors, and artisanal workshops. The city modeled the site's zoning based on the preexisting mix of residential and industrial uses.

The developer realized that lower land costs could make a mixed-use project feasible and that with the potential for both market-rate and lower-cost housing the variety of uses could cross-subsidize the manufacturing portion of the building. In order to entice residents, the city is limiting the size of the industrial spaces so that no single industrial tenant is allowed more than 5,000 square feet, keeping the factories small and clean.

GBL Architects orchestrated the various uses in three vertical volumes that rise from a horizontal podium fitting snugly along a major roadway a few blocks inland from the waterfront's active container port and sugar refinery. While 282 of the Strathcona housing units will be leased at market rate, 70 are designated as social housing. In a 64,000-square-feet structure, light-industrial uses are located on the ground and second floors along the Hastings Street frontage and Raymur Avenue in the rear. To be compatible with the residential uses, the industrial spaces have soundproofing, separate loading docks and elevators, and six-foot-wide

Figure 5.15 Strathcona Village view from the east, showing the various volumes, GBL Architects, Vancouver, British Columbia, 2018.

Figure 5.16 John Friedman Alice Kimm Architects designed the LACI La Kretz Innovation Campus, 2016.

corridors required for firefighting access, much larger than those in the residential sections of the building. The mechanical units exhaust odors away from the residential spaces, and an open plaza at the rear accommodates truck deliveries. Rather than negate the industrial site, the building's aesthetic mimics that of the port, with the volumes cantilevered at upper levels staggered much like stacked shipping containers. In addition, to animate the streetscape, large windows and garage-style doors provide views into the production activity. This new hybrid, both with its transparency and resolved building technology solutions for industry and residential use, contributes a significant architectural presence in the community as well as being a financially viable model in that mix.

Sustainable

New urban factories need to be sustainable both in their production processes and in their buildings. One key element to sustainable manufacturing is to build factories in cities for shorter supply chains and to reduce a company's carbon footprint, for everything from shipping and delivery to worker commutes. To build a factory that is not only sustainable but ecological in its production methods is not an easy task—a company typically focuses on one or the other outcome. However, factories are now able to achieve this balance or even produce more energy than they use; examples include Abalos & Herrara's Valdemingómez recycling plant (2001), BIG Architects' Amagerforbraeding power plant (2019), and projects by architects such as William Macdonough, who have been able to design sustainable factories with the greening of the Ford River Rouge plant and the design of the Method plant in Chicago (see Naomi Darling, Chapter 7, p. 139). In Los Angeles, John Friedman Alice Kimm Architects designed the LACI La Kretz Innovation Campus, a cleantech industry hub and incubator, which opened in 2016 in a 60,000-square-foot building on 3.2 acres, and includes a sustainable ecosystem including solar canopies and bioswales. Managed by a conglomeration of the City of Los Angeles, the Department of Water and Power, universities, and technology businesses in Los Angeles's CleanTech Corridor, it points the way toward collaborative workspaces, innovative entrepreneurs, and sustainable factory futures.

The goal of designing factories and products that are "cradle-to-cradle" or reuse waste, or create an ecosystem that satisfies the three Rs (repair, reuse, recycle), is slowly becoming a reality. In cities it is often seen as more difficult because of the existing building stock and the high cost to build new factories; however, in the future a sustainable closed-loop system can be realized with new attention.

Conclusion

With the potential for spectacle, flexible, hybrid, and sustainable factory designs, industrialists and architects can harness materials, structural concepts, and operational and production processes to offer new worker-oriented and creative spaces for production. Just as industrialists embraced design for the Modernist factory, today's architects can have an increasing role in developing innovative spatial, urban, and design solutions that also provide efficient and proactive city resources.

We must continue to ask how the design of factories can inspire new and dynamic ways of working in cities: how can their spatial organization impact the worker's comfort so that workers are no longer alienated? How can the factory environment increase well-being ergonomically, ecologically, and economically with increased equity? However, we must still grapple with the global scenario of Free Trade Zones where mass production still needs massive factories for those millions of t-shirts in areas that are neither urban nor open with their corporate practices and labor rights issues. The factory workplace is implicit in the global economy and thus needs to be revalued with a sharper focus as a space for design and social integrity in relationship to socio-economic concerns for the future of productive cities.

Notes

1 Henri LeFevbre, *The Production of Space*, trans. D. Nicholson-Smith (1974 reprint; Cambridge, MA: Blackwell Publishing, 1991).
2 Gunter Henn, "Visuelle Systemdenken fur Kommunikationsarchikturen," Degenhard Sommer ed., *Industriebau Radikale Umstrukturierung Praxisreport* (Basel: Birkhauser, 1995), 106.
3 Denis Diderot, *Encyclopédie* (1751–1772), catalogued all the trades and craftsmen in their workshops and working spaces.
4 Oliver Evans, *The Young Millwright and Miller's Guide* (Philadelphia: n.p., 1795).
5 Vertical urban factories are defined in my book *Vertical Urban Factory* (Barcelona: Actar, 2015), as multistoried factories in cities and further catagorized by different typological themes both for history and contemporary factories.
6 Robert Venturi and Denise Scott Brown, *Learning From Las Vegas* (Cambridge, MA: The MIT Press, 1977).
7 See Anson Rabinbach, *The Human Motor* (Berkeley, CA: University of California Press, 1992).
8 See Terry Smith, *Making the Modern Industry, Art and Design in America* (Chicago, IL: University of Chicago Press, 1993).
9 See *Vertical Urban Factory* (2015), definitions of layered and integrated factory, 8.
10 See *Vertical Urban Factory* (2015), 62.
11 Naomi Klein, *No Logo* (New York, NY: Picador, 2000), 196.
12 See Francesca Catano, *Angelo Mangiarotti e la Fabbrica SIAG* (Siracusa: LetteraVentidue, 2017).
13 Kenneth Frampton, "The Case of Volvo," *Lotus*, 1976, 16–41.
14 See *Vertical Urban Factory* exhibition (2011) and book (2015), sections on each of the themes.
15 See Guy Debord, *Society of the Spectacle* (New York, NY: Zone Books, 1995).
16 See B. Joseph Pine II and James H. Gilmore, *Experience Economy, Work is Theater & Every Business is a Stage* (Cambridge, MA: Harvard Business Review Press, 2007).
17 Contemporary examples as discussed in *Vertical Urban Factory* (2015).

18 Jane Jacobs promoted these types of ideas in *The Death and Life of Great American Cities* (1961) in terms of the liveliness of cities.
19 See Open House New York Factory Tours, 2016 Turnstile Tours, among many others.
20 Discussion between author and Alex Haecker of AWH Architects, February 2018.
21 Discussion between author and Bram Aerts of TRANS Architecture, November 2017.
22 See *Vertical Urban Factory* (2015) and concept of neo-cottage in contrast to large-scale factories.
23 John Loomis, "Hôtels Industriels," *Places Design Observer*, July 1995.
24 See *Vertical Urban Factory* (2015) discussion of shared manufacturing space and also Chris Anderson, *Makers, The New Industrial Revolution* (New York: Crown Publishing, 2012).
25 Jane Jacobs, *Death and Life of American Cities* (1961), 80.
26 See *Vertical Urban Factory* (2015), 446–50.
27 Concept presented in *Vertical Urban Factory* (2015) and also at Land Use Committee public hearing at New York City Council in May 2015.

6 Designing Today's Factory
Representation and Functionalism

Frank Barkow

The factory as a building typology may seem archaic in the digital global arena, but in Germany and elsewhere in Europe it remains a vital and enduring type where making products still drives export-oriented countries. Factories are never complete. Situated in "soft" master plans, growth occurs in unpredictable spurts where programming and available real estate are also unpredictable. The hierarchical factory divisions of white collar and blue collar have given way to flexible patchworks of working teams, clients, workflows, and goods movement. The urban periphery, with cheap land and easy access to infrastructure (rail and road), remains an attractive location for most modern factories. As factories expand to ever-larger dimensions (think Tesla's new Arizona plant), long distances—which become ever more problematic timewise for workers—are compensated for by an ever-more-robotic workforce, allowing gigantic factories to relocate to remote sites.

Workers

In Germany, workers' rights, including access to light and air and a maximum of 35 working hours per week, demand a satisfying response from factories.[1] This is a social mandate focused on safety that management recognizes will attract a better talent pool in a competitive marketplace. Another aspect of the German system is "Kurzarbeit," or shorter working hours.[2] Instead of laying off trained workers during recessions, funds are set aside to maintain a workforce that will remain in place once the economy recovers and orders are placed. This softening of the historically antagonistic relationship between labor and management is effective in setting up more effective and profitable companies while providing a social network for labor. In Germany, there is still a kind of social contract—what might be called social capitalism—for workers. Some companies maintained their workforces online throughout the 2008 recession by compensating them from preestablished funds for shorter working hours. An American company, on the other hand, would likely lay off many workers and thus be forced to rehire them or close the company completely; this is because there is a historical division in the US between management and labor, as well as between management and the labor unions. In Germany, that split has been avoided, as there is a more amicable working relationship—a kind of partnership—between the unions and management with workers counsels as negotiators. Other companies, such as automobile manufacturers, follow a similar model or compensate by using contract laborers on a temporary basis without commitment or benefits.

It then follows that the workplace is as important as the work produced there. Following the motto that good work can only be produced in a good building, factories should not just house worker bees but elevate the workplace to a nobler, more inspirational, and more productive environment. Manufacturers see value in designing a better workplace rather than focusing only on the bottom line.

Automobile companies such as Audi, Daimler/Mercedes-Benz, and Porsche are rethinking sprawling industrial zones as campuses, which support communication and productivity for both their workers and customers; in these new configurations, departments that are normally physically siloed overlap in their functions and workers exchange ideas. The "campus" also touches upon live-work, lifestyle, and branding issues. Former industrial zones give way to sustainable landscapes of garden and factory and even housing, where factories begin to resemble small, integrated cities. For example, when Barkow Leibinger worked with Höweler + Yoon Architecture on the Audi campus master plan in Ingolstadt in 2014, the focus was not just on the traditional factory issues of providing light and air but on developing a more progressive workplace that would in turn entice talent. Manufacturers are starting to see architecture as having a positive role in this regard; rather than being just a pragmatic tool for accommodating workers, materials, and methods, manufacturers view today's factory buildings as contributors to the products.

Toward Industry 4.0

In some ways, Germany is rather old-tech: German manufacturers make physical things, like cars and machine tools. They are also perfectionists, evolving and improving their products incrementally rather than depending—as do so many companies—on the creation of altogether new analog and digital products. Perhaps this is why the modern factory in Germany is a different paradigm than the postindustrial revolution taking place in Silicon Valley for companies such as Google, Facebook, and Amazon. The traditional factory doesn't make sense for companies such as these, which produce ideas and data rather than physical objects.

At the same time, manufacturing itself is evolving. In what is called Industry 4.0, companies are starting to think differently about what industry is and how it can be formed, embracing new technologies, and networking machines to produce more complex and flexible workflows (see Rappaport, Chapter 9, p. 161). This has not yet had a huge effect on architecture, but it is bound to. The Trumpf Smart Factory that Barkow Leibinger Architects designed in Chicago is a showroom-factory that embraces Industry 4.0; the focus is on flexibility, display, and a collaborative process with clients that allows them to both imagine and test machines to make their products. These are not so much traditional production factories with shed lighting and cranes as they are atmospheric spaces in which machines and their capabilities are showcased—spaces for display. In this way, architecture begins to recede typologically into environments in which artificial and natural lighting produce affect, rather than just efficient working places.

Another example is Barkow Leibinger Architects' unbuilt project for a Design Center for BMW in Munich, where the building is organized along split levels to accommodate closer working relationships between teams and an excavated roof that is hollowed out to produce a daylight environment to view full-size car designs. Here the product is featured for study and comparison, whereas the architecture is a kind of backdrop for visualization.

In these situations the factory is less typological and more about generating a framework that has light, and transformable conditions. It might be no more than an environment where the machines and processes are highlighted and the architecture disappears into a more nebulous

Figure 6.1 Barkow Leibinger Architects, BMW Design and Concept House Munich, competition rendering, 2007.

Figure 6.2 Barkow Leibinger Architects, BMW Design and Concept House Munich, competition rendering, 2007.

Figure 6.3 Barkow Leibinger, Trumpf Smart Factory, showroom facade facing I-90, Chicago, 2018.

internality, with less architecture and far removed from the traditional factory signified by the smokestack and the shed roof.

New Sites, New Factories

The new Trumpf 4.0 Smart Factory is prominently located on I-90 near Chicago's O'Hare International Airport, situated on the vacated corporate campus of AT&T. The context is the Great American Rust Belt—strip malls, big-box stores, tasteful corporate campuses, and marginal industrial properties. There is no spatial cohesion here, only object buildings with no relationship to each other. Land is cheaper here and clients can fly in and arrive at the site within minutes of landing at the airport.

The building is organized as an offset figure-eight unified by a sloping shed roof. The offset plan creates an entrance/parking side and a terrace side, configured as a quarter-circle facing a wetlands area. A large column-free showroom is spanned by laser-cut Vierendeel steel trusses. The lattice of the truss structure is pierced by Catwalks and viewing platforms, transforming structural depth into programmable space. A palette of Corten steel, concrete, and burnt timber siding is unpretentious. Like Eero Saarinen's John Deere Headquarters in Moline, Illinois, this building marks an industrial architecture that is about integration into a landscape and the display of machines.

Figure 6.4 Barkow Leibinger, Trumpf Smart Factory, machine hall, Chicago, 2018.

Figure 6.5 Barkow Leibinger, Trumpf Smart
Factory, exterior terrace, Chicago,
2018.

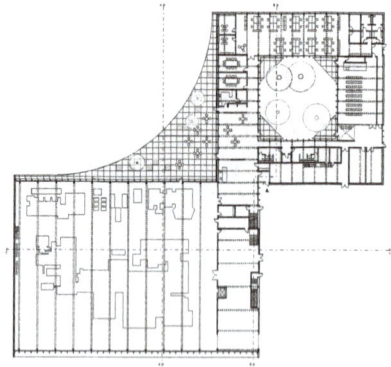

Figure 6.6 Barkow Leibinger, Trumpf Smart
Factory, ground floor plan, Chicago,
2018.

These factory projects are often infrastructural, close to highways or railroads. Together they can almost be considered an infinite factory that grows parallel to transit infrastructure. They are fragmented ex-urban sites where an old villa is juxtaposed next to an agglomeration of buildings. The site informs the building design just as Erich Mendelsohn, in designing the Hat Factory in Luckenwalde in 1922, also made an L-shaped version for a different site. The urban site in Seoul informed the design of the Trumpf building, a quasi-industrial building with an industrial showroom and offices. There, large barn doors opened up for machinery access, and cranes work inside a mid-rise industrial building.

More typically, the industrial projects that Barkow Leibinger Architects designs are in industrial zones or on campuses that grow from master plans. The plans then adapt when more land or funds are acquired for different program types, in aggregate systems that become urban in and of themselves. They are their own factory cities, such as Mercedes-Benz in Stuttgart or BMW in Munich. Many have residential uses mixed in as a hybrid, with museums, racetracks, and workshops in worlds of their own. Mercedes-Benz in Stuttgart is an aggregation of

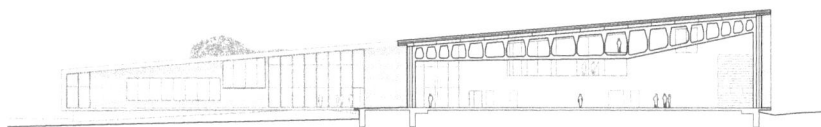

Figure 6.7 Barkow Leibinger, Trumpf Smart Factory, section through machine hall, Chicago, 2018.

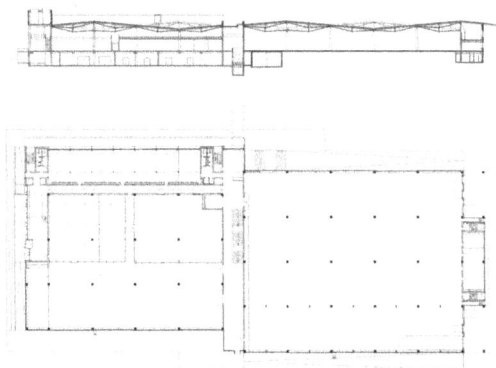

Figure 6.8 Barkow Leibinger, Section and Plan Trumpf Laser Factory, section and plan, Stuttgart/ Ditzigen, 2000.

historical structures, some of them over 100 years old; the industrial campus is a patchwork and hodgepodge of generic buildings. The ones that are specific and of better quality design—those that Americans would call brand-identity buildings—are usually limited to two or three flagship buildings, where funds are usually invested. The rest of the campus is pragmatic and matter-of-fact. The master plans are usually quite heterogeneous as, like the companies themselves, they have been in transformation over long periods of time rather than emerging whole from one design concept.

The Significance of Design

It is not always easy to convince a company—especially a publicly owned company—to include high design in a project, primarily because the general public doesn't normally see its production facilities. Often, the design of factories, as in any typology, requires a client who is a patron of architecture, like Rolf Fehlbaum, who collects architecture on his Vitra furniture campus. Fehlbaum's campus mixes pragmatic production spaces with museums, restaurants by star architects, and even historical buildings by architects such as Jean Prouvé and Buckminster Fuller. With this kind of client, architects can construct a brief about the tremendous potential of architecture.

Similarly, Barkow Leibinger Architects' work over the past decade for the Trumpf company has been about working for a patron who has an expectation of what architecture is and what it can do. Companies like Trumpf are "Mittelstand"—that is, family-owned businesses where patronage is less in the service of stockholders than owners who use architecture to house their activities but also to project their brand and improve what they produce.

With Barkow Leibinger Architects' "Cantina" project, a large leaf-like roof of steel and glu-lam timber encloses a large flexible open space and mezzanine, supporting a company cafeteria that is used for three hours per day. The roof encloses an amphitheater-like space that is excavated into the ground. This space can support open-ended programming such as events, parties, or performances, increasing the expectations of office space and communication. Companies such as Audi are increasingly intrigued about what architecture and master planning can do to transform a factoryscape into something that appeals to both workers and clients. Audi is almost as big as the adjacent city of Ingolstadt, and because it has such a huge impact on traffic and resources it is sensitive to the needs of the city. However, a more conventional company, such as Bosch, focuses only on bottom-line costs and production schedules—architecture is for accommodating space and processes, and little more. For a company that produces a specific object brand, this has little meaning or application for them. Building costs are kept to a minimum, and that is the strategy.

Another aspect of factory design is not only the way the production process influences architectural form and spatial organization, but the way architects collaborate with industrial engineers. For example, in collaboration with engineers Barkow Leibinger Architects focuses on the requirements of column grids, cranes, service, delivery, workflow, and storage. Changing demands, workflows, loading, and delivery all impact how factories are laid out and how they evolve. Industrial engineers determine which paths and systems are most efficient and how you maneuver inside. The resulting design reflects the structural requirements, vehicular planning, and loading docks so that, unfortunately, building designs are often quite constrained by set parameters. This is very different from an architectural sculpture such as Le Corbusier's Ronchamp, which has a very figurative plan and section. Instead, factory plans are guided by pragmatism in layout, lines of production, lines of goods and materials, movement, and adjacencies. Factory design is often driven by the diagrammatic exercise of laying out structural grids to accommodate different parcels of workspace with adequate fire separation, resulting in plans which are usually non-figurative—what Barkow Leibinger Architects calls non-hierarchical "patchworks" of office space and production space mixed together. Today there is less separation between ivory tower administrators and research staff and factory workers—white collar and blue collar mix together. This trend toward more flexibility, quickness, lightness, and adaptability will continue.

While often the factory infrastructure and services are more prescribed, the roofscapes and the cladding allow for more design experimentation. The roof, which I call the section of the building, becomes more figural. Barkow Leibinger Architects designs a shape in section that focuses on daylighting and also animates the form of the building, which would otherwise be just a flat box. There is more freedom in the sectional description of the project and a more diagrammatic pragmatism in terms of plan-making.

The factory skin is another building element that can give a factory project character and architectural interest. This envelope is a material and form that the firm can control even as other parts of the project are left to efficiency or the economy. Whereas the interiors of Barkow Leibinger Architects' factory in Barr, Switzerland are straightforward and laid out on simple grids, the folded facades are articulated to condition light and provide a volumetric passage along the facade. The facade itself works like a scissors constructed of steel and clad in standing-seam copper, with transparent and translucent glass inserts. The facade here mediates between the pragmatic internal factory spaces and the surrounding agricultural landscape. Facade as an architectural site in its own right can be articulated more ambitiously in contrast to pragmatic interior production spaces.

Architectural expression does not need to be expensive. For a recent project in Connecticut with the metal fabrication company Kammetal, we are modifying a Butler building—the cheapest and most economical industrial building type. It is a pragmatic off-the-shelf system for agriculture or industry that Barkow Leibinger Architects is designing with custom fabricated inserts, an interface that lies somewhere between an off-the-shelf and bespoke design solution. However, architects have to find a manufacturing client interested in architecture or who sees architecture as an instrument for transformation, change, or improvement. Most manufacturers focus on the economics of building costs, but if industrialists can demonstrate that, through communication and invention, the factory can be an investment for the future, then industrial architecture can be elevated as a building typology.

Factories continue to evolve as a viable building typology and will do so in far more radical ways and scales as robotic, drone, and automated processes slowly replace the worker in the workspace. Consider Tesla's new Gigafactory in Arizona; an impossibly large building for humans to even be able to get around, it marks an example of this new orientation where the old problems of daylighting, ventilation, or even amenities are now rendered meaningless. Here the factory is reduced to its most economical and pragmatic essence as the machine slowly replaces the human. Hyperfunction will replace the old paradigms of representation and image. Here industrial architecture can finally be reduced (or elevated) to machine product when they are no longer inhabited by human beings. This is simply a fact, but one where perhaps architecture begins to resemble infrastructure and not an essential space of occupation. It is also one that will begin to remap and become situated in both our cities and countrysides.

The urban factory as a type could be a way of resisting homogeneity as a response to new forms of production that is of a scale between a factory and a "werkstatt." The culture of the German "Mittelstand," or family-owned small-scale enterprise, is in line with this thinking. Berlin as city that in its pre-war state was very industrial and could see a resurgence of smaller-scaled, start-up, infill industries as hybrids. In a way the enormous artistic output in Berlin in the last twenty-five years has paved the way. Artist studios in Berlin act as de-facto factories where art is conceived and produced in existing and purpose-built factories that cater to both the local and international art scene. While in competition with commercial development, artists (as well as industry) become ever more resourceful in generating spaces within the existing fabric of the city. Younger artists find spaces that are cheaper in the ex-urbs, closer to the periphery. This serves as a model for industry in a country that still produces in-country.

In Berlin, the conditions of work-live-conceive can exist in close proximity to one and other and begin to "infill" urban sites with the goal of producing housing density but also new forms of programmatic intensity, resisting uniform uses, like on Friederickstrasse, which was historically programmatically polyphonic and vital. Hybrid projects combining work and living can respond to the urgency of housing needs with a deployable scale that can include both start-ups and industrial typology, not just on the industrial perimeter but more central in the city as an urban condition, either repurposing existing industrial buildings like Albert Kahn's in Detroit or making new projects.

In terms of the challenges of urban factory design, Barkow Leibinger Architects has been focusing on engineering applications, as with the aforementioned Chicago building, where the firm employed a digitally cut steel structure and long-span structures that one could imagine could carry residential space over the top in a city. A potential for structural engineering is how to embed this architecture in more of a dance on a complex urban site. For example, Rafael Moneo's laboratory building at Columbia University, which uses complex structures to make the project work on a dense urban site

Figure 6.9 Barkow Leibinger, model of Cantenary Infill Project, Berlin, 2010.

with steel truss to span over the ground-floor basketball court, makes a new condition. Berlin has numerous interstitial sites near the S-bahn and railroad tracks that could profit from engineering structures to place the housing program over column-free span.

One direction that Barkow Leibinger is exploring is seen in the Catenary Infill Project, research for a party wall condition in which timber boxes would expand as according to space, with off-set cantilevers that generate column-free spaces in between. By hanging a chain of extruded volumes between the two party walls, the natural force of gravity pulls them downwards, thus applying tension to the two walls and assuming structural stability. This is a work-live prototype and the column-free spaces could be a light and vertical industry in the city, as they are also flexible to variously sized sites and adjustable according to need, especially with the spaces generated by the World War II-era historic buildings and their party walls.

In the shift from industrial projects at the periphery of cities to the center, we are looking for new models that are agile and hybrid programmatically, and that are structurally inventive, in the search to rethink how we work and live in emerging cities.

Notes

1 Arbeitsrechtslinien, Sektion 5, paragraf, 8. Deutsches Bau Ordung/Fabrikbau, 2012.
2 A form of government work subsidy in which employees get about 80 percent of their salary for working half-time (wwwww.ezonomics.com/whatis/kurzarbeit/).

7 The Potential for the Sustainable Urban Factory

Naomi Darling

Factories, traditionally one of the major polluters in the world, both in terms of their processes and their building efficiencies, are transforming to become positive contributors to the environment. In this era of climate change, factory buildings have an important role to play by operating with renewable energy, recapturing and reusing their waste, and contributing to the vitality of our cities by providing spaces for work and building social networks and capital. To do so requires that architects and factory owners extend their time horizon to be inclusive of building component life cycles and apply a circular economy framework to all aspects of the design, construction, operations, and afterlife of factories so that they can become carbon-negative, long-term contributors to their local ecologies. As the earth's climate continues to warm at an alarming rate, the speed at which these changes are implemented is critical. Concepts from sustainability metrics, new industrial urban farming, and material reuse projects demonstrate pathways forward for the sustainable urban factory.

William McDonough and Michael Braungart's work in the 1990s[1] highlighted problems with standard linear models of production, or cradle-to-grave, in which resources ultimately follow a linear path to become waste. For example, a disposable plastic pen is purchased, used, and then thrown away. Left to nature, this pen would take between 450 and 1,000 years to decompose.[2] Imagine the afterlife of a refrigerator, a computer, or a car. These products all follow a linear path from extraction of resources to production, use, and waste. While prior to industrial production our resources were part of the earth's natural biological system or biosphere, our ability to chemically change material properties lead to the creation of materials that do not decompose and return to the earth in a timely and safe manner. These alloys, compounds, plastics, and composites together form the technosphere. A recent study suggests that the mass of the earth's technosphere—including roads, houses, computers, phones, landfills—may be on the order of 30 trillion tons.[3] In a million years, a paleontologist excavating through the strata of earth's history will find a clear marker of the Anthropocene[4] in the sheer mass of the detritus remaining. To minimize the depth of the Anthropocene strata, the manufacturing sector must transition from a linear model of production to a circular model, with materials in the technosphere being infinitely recycled without losing their quality or value. This is the cradle-to-cradle model, in which the technical nutrients—the products of our industrial processes—can be endlessly recycled, emulating nature's efficiencies of zero waste. This requires that technical and biological nutrients are kept separate so that they do not degrade one another, maintaining optimal value.[5]

A circular economy builds upon this cradle-to-cradle model synthesizing related ideas from other frameworks, such as biomimicry, industrial ecology, natural capitalism, and the blue

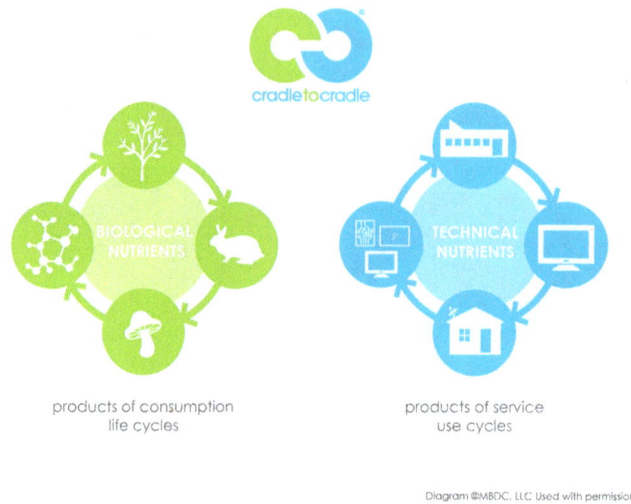

products of consumption
life cycles

products of service
use cycles

Diagram ©MBDC. LLC Used with permission.

Figure 7.1 Cradle-to-cradle diagram showing biological and technical nutrients.

economy.[6] A circular economy model ties the two cycles of biological and technical nutrients into an economic model that is powered by renewable energy with the goals of designing out all waste and pollution while building social capital and regenerating ecological systems. Technical nutrients can be recaptured through maintenance, reuse, and disassembly, striving toward a closed-loop system.

The ultimate goal is to eliminate waste altogether. As products, and some buildings, are designed and manufactured with shorter and shorter life expectancies, this becomes paramount in maintaining and restoring ecological health. How can the ideas of circular economies be realized not only in the manufacture of products but also in the design and construction of the very places where this manufacturing occurs? A few examples will highlight the current research and developments in this new field.

The Danish shipping company Maersk Line has developed an innovative Cradle to Cradle® Passport documenting approximately 95 percent, by weight, of the materials used to build their new Triple-E ships.[7] Triple-E stands for "Economy of scale, Energy efficient and Environmentally improved."[8] Currently, at the end of a ship's life the steel is recycled with steel of different grades to a uniform, lowest-common-denominator, low-grade steel. With the "material passport," Maersk can impact the entire steel recycling industry by tracking different grades of steel through their life cycles and recycling the high-grade steel as a higher-quality scrap metal from which new ships can be made. Daewoo Shipbuilding and Marine Engineering in South Korea built the new vessels and approximately seventy-five ship-component suppliers are actively involved to maintain the "material passport."[9] This model keeps the technical nutrients cycling through the economic system without losing value, benefiting both the financial profitability of Maersk as well as the environment. This model of "material passports" is in the early stages of development for the building sector and further described below. An early example can be found in Thailand, where a 1989 ban

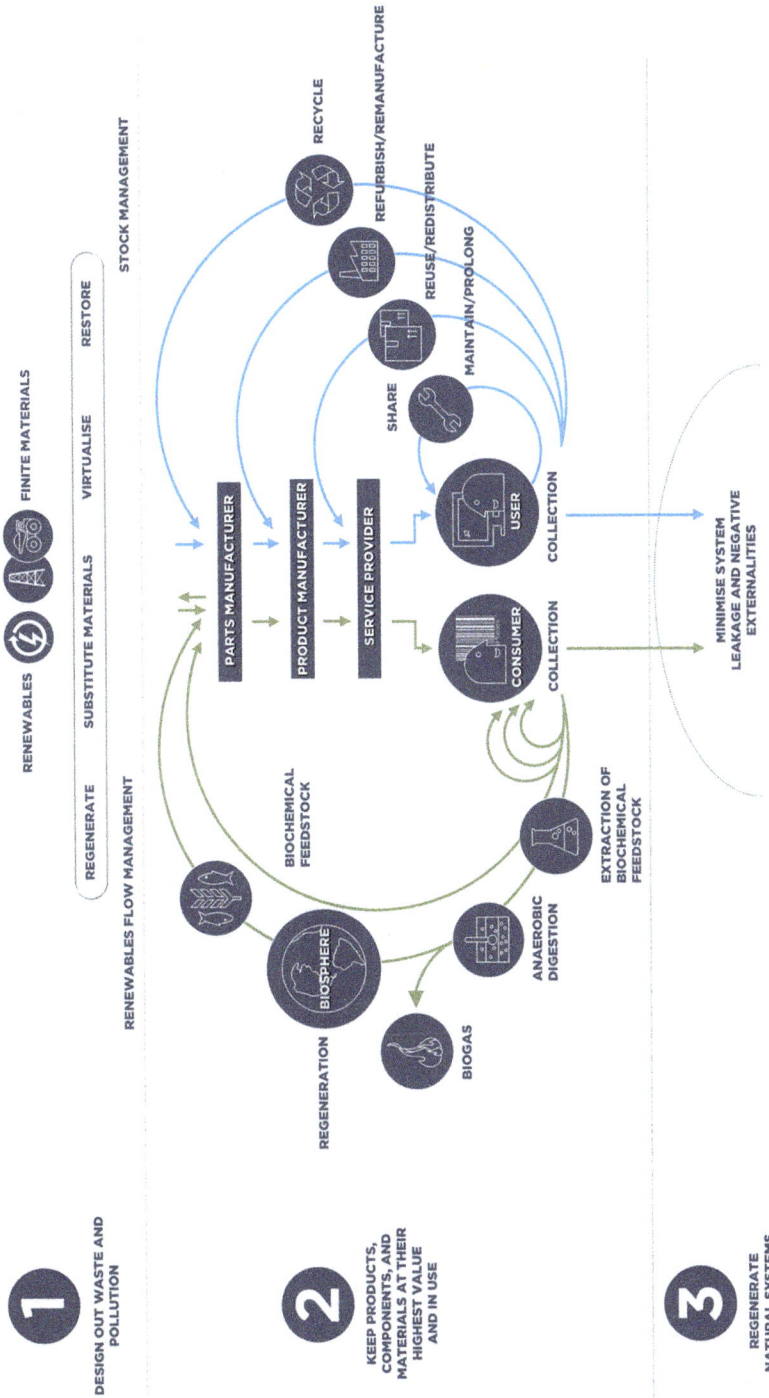

Figure 7.2 Circular economy diagram, as envisioned by the Ellen MacArthur Foundation.

on timber harvesting and logging drove up prices so much that a similar "passport" system was implemented for teak. When a traditional wooden teak house is disassembled, the government tracks the movement of the teak, collecting taxes on its sale if it moves out of its village of origin.[10]

How do buildings mimic natural systems not only in their life-cycle materiality but also in their daily operation? The Living Building Challenge is a sustainability metric that provides a biomimetic model comparing a building to a flower.[11] For a project to achieve Living Building Certification it must be self-sufficient, operating within the resources of its site by producing all of its energy, and collecting and treating all of its water, on-site. A Living Building creates a positive impact on its local community through sourcing materials locally, being conscious of sustainable business practices, and providing educational opportunities to the public. In addition, a Living Building connects occupants to light, air, nature, and community. To date, seventeen projects have achieved Living Building status, with 440 more projects registered to seek certification.[12] While it may not make sense for each building in an urban context to become self-sufficient in terms of utilities, all of these projects demonstrate that net-zero energy and water are possible while contributing to the vitality of local material markets and communities. While a factory has not yet achieved Living Building status, the challenge is there for a factory to pursue this aspirational sustainability metric.

How are these conceptual models, taken together, changing the architecture of the factory? Many companies are embracing aspects of sustainability—from water recycling, to recapture and recycling of materials, to closed-loop processing flows, and use of alternative energy systems, but few are able to do this as a total building or complete manufacturing retrofit. For those companies in an existing building, the parameters of the physical environment need to accommodate new technologies for manufacturing flows in an economical way. An early notable example is the Ford River Rouge plant, designed by Albert Kahn in the early 1900s and renovated by William McDonough + Partners in the 1990s to achieve LEED Gold status, becoming the first LEED-certified factory.[13] Other companies are building new buildings in suburban industrial parks, such as Frito Lay and Sabra Hummus, both subsidiaries of Pepsico.[14] Nestlé, despite the company's controversial groundwater extraction practices,[15] has innovated with a "zero-water" factory in Mexico[16] and designs for a sustainable modular factory to expand its operations globally.[17] In Switzerland, Nestlé and General Mills have joint-ventured in a 50/50 company, Cereal Partners Worldwide (CPW), to develop the CPW Innovation Centre—the first LEED Platinum factory in Switzerland—with Concept-Consult Architectes.[18] Completed in 2011, the Innovation Centre, located at the edge of the small Swiss town of Orbe, is comprehensive in its approach, with sustainable strategies for site location and planning, water efficiency, day lighting, energy strategies, local material usage, waste management strategies, and indoor environmental quality.

Although the technology exists for centers of manufacturing to be sustainable in cities, very few sustainable urban factories exist. A small workshop production facility was completed in Berlin in 2012 by Roswag Architekten[19] and in 2016 the Brooklyn Navy Yard Building 128, the New Lab, envisioned as a multi-disciplinary design, prototyping, and advanced manufacturing hub, converted a 51,000-square-foot machine shop into 84,000 square feet of entrepreneurial space working to be a green industrial complex (see Rappaport, Chapter 9, p. 164).[20] This essay will focus on a few key examples: a new building in Chicago with a rooftop hydroponics farm; an adaptive reuse project closer to the urban core, also in Chicago; a new factory in Philadelphia; and a concept demonstration project to be discussed as a model for designing for disassembly and circular material flows.

Method Soap Factory and Gotham Greens

Pullman, a neighborhood in Chicago's South Side, was established in the 1880s as a manufacturing center and company town by the Pullman Palace Car Company.[21] Over 100 years later Pullman is an industrial development site as the home of the first LEED Platinum factory and the largest urban rooftop garden within the city limits of a major urban center in the United States. Method Soap's[22] founders wanted their factory to reflect their biodegradable, nontoxic, cradle-to-cradle-certified soaps and cleaning supplies, which are part of the earth's biological cycles. William McDonough + Partners designed the new factory on a capped brownfield site, formerly the Pullman lumberyard. Sited in the Pullman Park mixed-use development, the new factory creates green jobs at the edge of a dense metropolis, a short commute from the original Pullman row houses in this vital Chicago neighborhood, a transit stop on the Chicago commuter rail line. The community benefits and the historical narrative were both important factors in the site selection.[23]

The new Method Soap Manufacturing Facility is 157,600 square feet of colorful, bright, and airy space constructed with a tight budget that focused the design team on prioritizing where to make an impact. The building is an insulated concrete box made of tilt-up panels mechanically fastened for future disassembly and adaptive reuse.

McDonough's office developed a schematic housing proposal for future conversion in the eventual case that Method outgrows the factory. Skylights and sidewall daylighting provide the factory with natural daylight while the offices are located on the south side with operable windows. A large transparent front window wall provides openness and transparency, making the inside of the factory visually accessible to the community.

Colorful graphics of Method's soap bottles enliven the space while also publicizing the factory's products.[24] Renewable energy provides 50 percent of the energy for the factory through a 230-foot, 600-kW wind turbine on-site, as well as three solar-panel "trees" that track the sun and solar thermal collectors on the roof, which provide hot water for sinks and showers.[25]

Figure 7.3 William McDonough + Partners, Method Soap Manufacturing Facility, showing the bioswale, wind turbine, solar trees, and roof-top greenhouses, Chicago, 2015.

Figure 7.4 William McDonough + Partners, Method Soap Manufacturing Facility, showing the daylight from large front window providing visual access to the factory, Chicago, 2015.

Figure 7.5 William McDonough + Partners, Method Soap Manufacturing Facility, with colorful graphics highlighting the factory's soaps, Chicago, 2015.

As a soap factory, thematically, the water story is the biggest narrative of the project. The twenty-two-acre site infiltrates rainwater back into the ground through plantings and permeable surfaces and a bioswale removes pollutants from the storm water runoff on the paved surfaces.[26]

Figure 7.6 Gotham Greens Greenhouse interior on the roof of the Method Soap factory by William McDonough + Partners, Chicago, 2015.

The green landscape continues on the roof with a 75,000-square-foot hydroponic greenhouse built by Gotham Greens, the largest rooftop greenhouse in the world and the feature of the project of which the architects are most proud.[27] The idea of having greenhouses on the roof growing food was an important part of the factory's conceptual design and ecological goals, but it wasn't until the factory construction was well underway that Gotham Greens, an independent company, was selected to build and operate the greenhouses on Method's roof. Finding a grower meant that the roof needed to be reinforced and bracing needed to be added to support the additional weight.[28] Gotham Greens expanded their operation from the New York Tri-State area into the Chicagoland markets, where they now grow approximately 8 million heads of leafy greens, lettuces, and herbs in their rooftop greenhouses atop Method.

Although commercial-scale greenhouses are capital-intensive to build, they are thirty times more productive than conventional farms while using 90 percent less water, which enables the company to be financially viable. Growing locally within the urban regions that they serve means that transport fees can be reduced, enabling their greens to be competitively priced with other organic products. Additionally, there are reciprocal benefits to both Gotham Greens and Method by having the greenhouses located on the factory roof. The greenhouses capture the passive heat from the building below while providing an additional layer of insulation for the factory, thus reducing energy demands. Furthermore, Gotham Greens has created fifty full-time jobs on the roof of Method Soap's Manufacturing Facility, hiring employees from the South Side of Chicago and Pullman. Jobs with living wages and benefits contribute to neighborhood revitalization. As this area is a food desert, Gotham Greens has also partnered with local food rescue organizations to increase access to locally grown fresh produce in the immediate neighborhood.[29]

There are additional environmental benefits to urban rooftop farming: there is no need for harmful pesticides or fertilizers, one of the main contributors to river and ocean pollution through agricultural runoff. Agriculture consumes about 70 percent of the world's freshwater. By 2025, an estimated 1.8 billion people will live in areas of water scarcity while a full two-thirds of the world's population will live in water-stressed regions.[30] These two facts together make an agricultural alternative that can grow food with only 10 percent of the current water demands and none of the negative consequences of runoff, an important contributor to a distributed food security framework, especially for urban areas with the infrastructure for adaptive reuse projects and the financial markets to support organic, locally grown produce.

The Plant

Eight miles north of the Method Soap Manufacturing Facility and Gotham Greens is The Plant, established in 2010 in a former 93,500-square-foot brick pork-packing facility by Bubbly Dynamics, a social enterprise dedicated to creating replicable models for sustainable urban development in vacant industrial buildings located in disinvested neighborhoods.[31] The site is at the transition between residential and industrial uses with linkages to the surrounding neighborhood via West 46th Street and South Bishop Street. Directly to the east is the potential for a greenway on a former freight rail corridor. As the city expands these factors place the site in the pathway of growth. Bubbly founder John Edel believes that "factories need to be reimagined as centers of creativity and imagination through local businesses."[32]

The first project undertaken by Bubbly Dynamics was the Chicago Sustainable Manufacturing Center, an adaptive reuse project of a 24,000-square-foot, brick paint warehouse targeting

Figure 7.7 The Plant by Bubbly Dynamics: exterior during an open market, Chicago.

small and emerging manufacturers. Like the Greenpoint Manufacturing and Design Center in New York City (see Rappaport, p. 161, and Friedman, p. 216), the building is meant to replicate at the scale of a single building the kind of diverse, mixed-use, and interactive ecology of the traditional manufacturing neighborhood. The building hosts among others a bicycle shop, a small-scale furniture studio, and a community makerspace. Building upon the successes and lessons of their first project, Bubbly Dynamics purchased the Plant facility in 2010 for $525,000, recognizing immediately that the value of the site is for food production. Today, the net-zero closed-loop food production space located in Chicago's Back of the Yards neighborhood takes advantage of the existing floors sloped to drain, a concrete frame that was used to conduct daily steam cleanings, and an abundance of built-in power and stainless-steel food processing equipment. Following the strategies employed at the Chicago Sustainable Manufacturing Center, and to ensure a profitable business model and maintain control, Bubbly Dynamics has renovated slowly as funds and materials became available, capitalizing on diverting building goods from the waste stream. For example, a local drywall distributor donated cases of sheetrock with damaged corners to the Plant to save on waste transfer fees. This ethos has allowed Bubbly Dynamics to keep material costs low, instead investing the funds into a dedicated workforce. By maximizing what already exists, The Plant has embraced an aesthetics driven by adaptive reuse and contrasting the old with the new.[33]

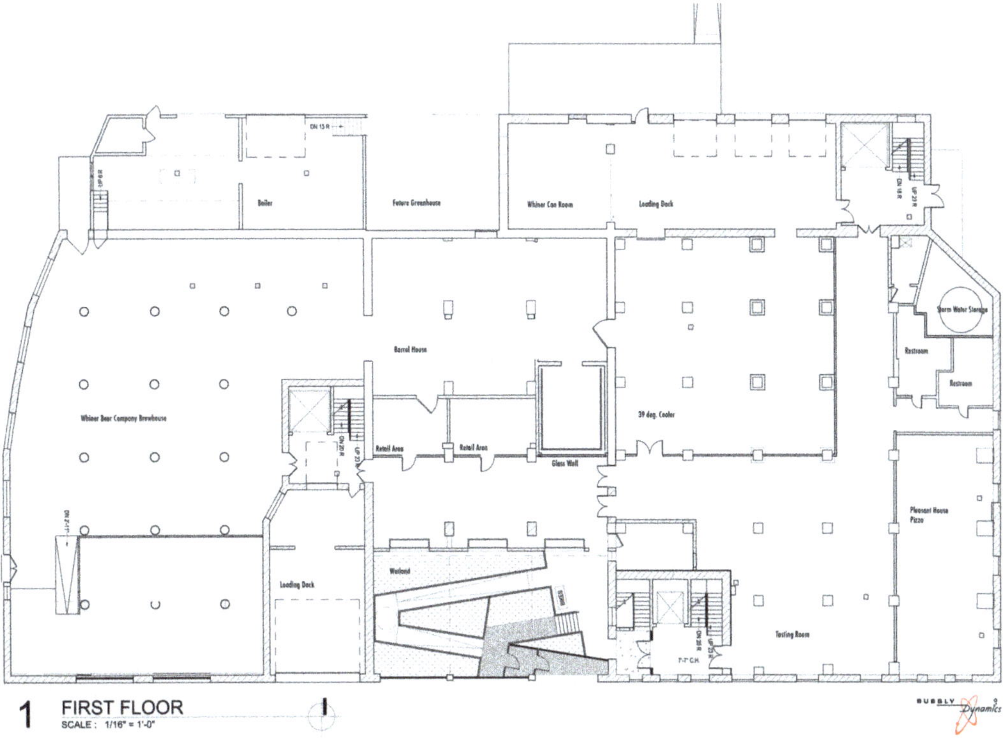

1 FIRST FLOOR
SCALE : 1/16" = 1'-0"

Figure 7.8 The Plant by Bubbly Dynamics: first-floor plan, Chicago.

The three-story brick-and-concrete factory building was built with structural concrete columns on a grid with large open spaces for pork packing. On the ground floor, these expansive spaces were maintained, with only a few partition walls added to separate the different businesses. The ground floor is now occupied by a beer company and brewhouse, a large tasting space, and a pizza house, all businesses that welcome the public to gather and dine. Loading docks, elevators, and stairs are all used in their original configuration with a celebratory entry ramp added. On the upper two floors, the spaces are divided into smaller spaces with non-load-bearing partition walls to accommodate over a dozen interdependent food production businesses, which produce vegetables, bread, beer, honey, spices, and kombucha, among other food products. The small food-based businesses create a closed-loop system, as waste from one process is used as nutrients for another. For example, the spent distiller's grains and yeast from the brewery is used on-site by the bakery for making bread and as a growing medium for mushrooms, which can then be made into compost and used by the farms operating in the building.[34] Waste heat from the bakery, brewery, and farm grow lights is redirected with fans to where it is needed and also captured through hydronic loops. Storm water is captured from the roof surface, stored in a former pork brine tank, pressurized, and distributed to the farming operations on-site. A current project is to develop a method to capture the carbon dioxide emissions from the brewery and kombucha operations and pump it into the water for irrigating the farms, where it will be absorbed by the growing greens.[35]

Currently, The Plant is connected to the power grid operated by Con Edison, which sets all prices for power purchase and sale with a hefty two- to fourfold mark-up. In Illinois, Con Edison has established that a landowner cannot make and sell power to a third party, meaning that The Plant and Bubbly Dynamics cannot sell the power that is generated on-site directly to the building users or tenants. These laws have delayed plans to bring online an anaerobic digester designed to divert over 10,000 tons of citywide food waste from landfills to produce biogas not only to sell but to use on-site to generate electricity and provide heating.[36] The set purchase price for power and waste disposal fees have made it challenging to make the project financially viable, highlighting the important role of policy and regulation in transitioning to a green circular economy.

Socially, The Plant has focused on community building, supporting small businesses and job creation. As of early 2018, The Plant has ninety full-time employees working in companies ranging in size from one or two people to twenty to twenty-four. As build-out continues, this number is expected to grow. An affiliated nonprofit organization, Plant Chicago, operates on-site, leading educational programming and outreach activities and partnering with four public schools to provide science programming for students in grades 4 to 12 as well as workshops in topics such as aquaponics and pickling.[37] To make the greatest change, Bubbly Dynamics has started consulting to help similar projects in disinvested urban neighborhoods get off the ground.[38]

Tasty Baking Company

In the Philadelphia Navy Yard, on the periphery of the city, is a new food production and distribution center for Tasty Baking, the company behind the longtime Philadelphia classic, Tastykake. Founded in 1914, the Tasty Baking Company had the innovative idea for individually wrapped snack cakes that remain their primary product today.[39] After almost ninety years, their Hunting Park Avenue bakery was not able to accommodate contemporary baking processes and the company moved from North Philadelphia into new facilities in South

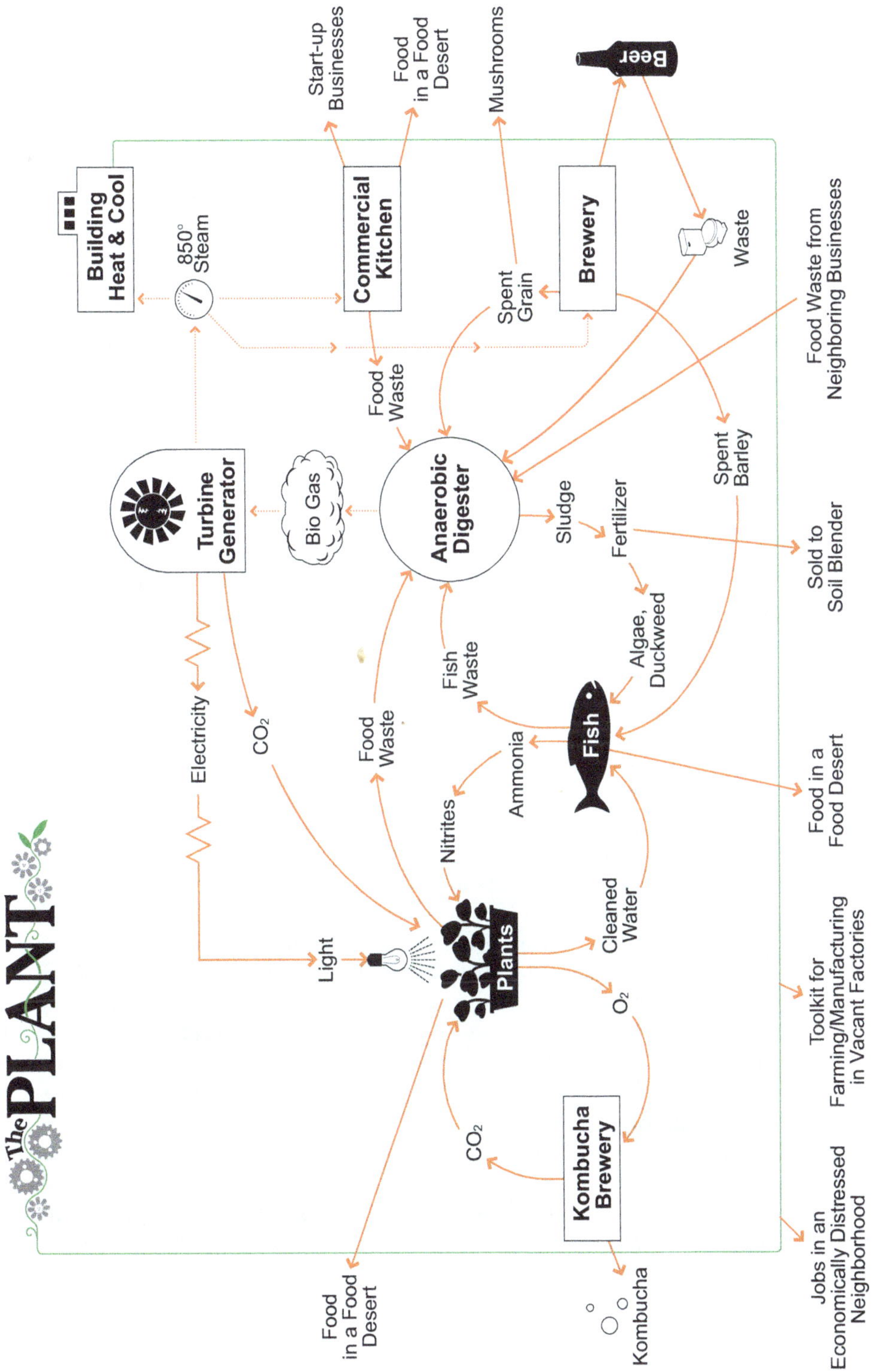

Figure 7.9 Circularity Lab Pavilion concept diagram.

Philadelphia in 2010. Developed as a partnership between Liberty Property Trust and Synterra Partners, the new 345,500-square-foot building was developed on a postindustrial brownfield site, reusing the existing buildings as foundation material for the new facility, which achieved LEED Silver rating.[40] By staying in Philadelphia the company is maintaining its broader social networks within the city as well as bringing vitality to the Navy Yard, which is also undergoing a transformation. With the move of the factory from the far north to the far south of the city, one factor to consider is the impact of location to the many employees who work in the factory. While the two locations are only about twelve miles apart, this translates to a thirty-minute commute by car or a one-hour commute via two city buses and walking.[41] It would be interesting to learn whether this distance has posed a challenge to any of the workers and how this move impacted the social culture of the factory. In addition to site selection and location, other sustainability measures include a reflective white roof to minimize heat absorption and decrease energy usage, drought-resistant landscaping to minimize water usage, a rainwater collection system, and the use of local materials in the building. Public spaces include a historical display from the archives of the company, a theater, and a mezzanine that overlooks the baking and manufacturing facility.[42]

Circularity Lab

The Circularity Lab Design Scheme, currently under development in a partnership between Google, Arup, Turner Construction, the City of New York, and the architecture firm 3XN Architect and its green research branch GXN Innovation, develops upon the closed-loop operational and production systems seen at the Plant with a prototype for full material circularity. Building upon cradle-to-cradle and circular economy ideas, Kasper Guldager Jensen of GXN Innovation and John Sommers of the contracting firm MT Højgaard published "Building a Circular Future" in 2016.[43] The three recommendations—to design for disassembly, to create a material passport for all buildings, and to engage in a circular economy, are all being tested in the Circularity Lab Pavilion prototype that was launched in the summer of 2018 in New York and San Francisco.

The Circularity Lab Pavilion prototype has an overall footprint of about 36 feet by 36 feet with an enclosed dimension of about 10 feet by 40 feet. The space itself is a multifunctional space that can be used for meetings, work, or lectures.[44] The innovation is in the attempt to fully close the material and manufacturing loops in all of the components and to fully test the idea of design for disassembly, rentable utility units, and modular finishes and materials that fall into either the biosphere or the technosphere. The goal of the project is to inspire with a 1:1 built prototype that looks good and demonstrates eliminating waste through full reuse of building components with existing technology and materials that are already on the market.[45] The prototype is circular in form as well as name, giving clear shape to the idea.

The most interesting aspect of this project is to look at the materials specification list. For example, the flooring system is from a C2C (cradle-to-cradle) supplier who rents and reclaims all parts of their flooring system, making the foundation 100-percent circular on a component level. The skin is made from a cork that can be recycled by the manufacturer without a loss in grade or quality. The floors and interior surfaces are made from a compressed board of tomato stems or straw developed by GXN Innovation. The insulation is a biological seagrass that can be returned to the biosphere after use.[46] Ultimately, making such changes to the building industry on a large scale would transition our economy from a purchase-and-dispose model

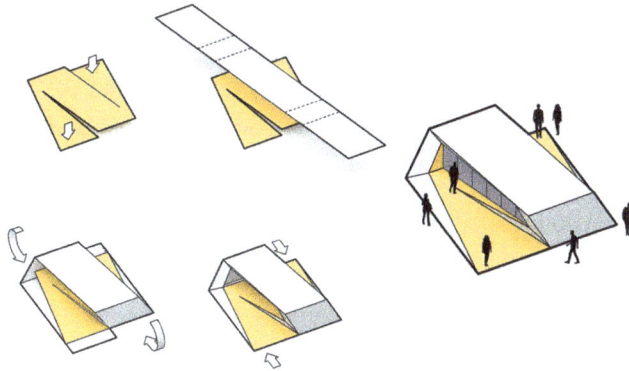

Figure 7.10 Circularity Lab Pavilion concept diagram.

Figure 7.11 Designing for Disassembly with concrete. Developed by Martin Ravnsvbaek and Hans
       Nicolai Sondergaard at VIA University College.

to a rent-and-return model, putting the responsibility on the manufacturers to design all of
their products for easy disassembly into components that can economically—both in terms of
time and energy input—be reincorporated into new products. As in the aforementioned case
of Maersk shipping, material passports for the prototype will ultimately allow disassembled
building components to be reused at the highest grade of biological or technical nutrient.

Jensen and Sommers, in their book *Building a Circular Future*, make further recommendations, including: making all joints visible for a new circular aesthetic; using easily disassembled components such as steel and wood; and new reinforced concrete building standards
that would prefabricate reinforced concrete units that could be easily assembled with bolts,
threaded rod, and washers that would fasten into an embedded anchor box precast into the
concrete unit.[47] Such changes to our global building industry would enable disassembly to
happen economically on a large scale and reimagine our cities as material banks for future
projects.

Conclusion

The case studies cited above demonstrate the potential for the future sustainable urban factory. Method Soap Manufacturing Facility is a factory that cleanses water on-site and operates with renewable energy, while its collaboration with Gotham Greens shows the reciprocal benefits for greenhouses on factory roofs for energy reduction, water reuse, and activating community. The Plant demonstrates closed-loop benefits of multiple food processes occurring together to eliminate waste while also highlighting the potential impact of governmental policy and regulation structures to incentivize clean energy production for a carbon-neutral future. The new TastyKake factory highlights the importance of location within a city to maintain and nurture the social and cultural networks of a company and its employees. Although the Circularity Lab Pavilion project is small, its strategies for full material circularity, including material passports for building components and designing for disassembly and material reuse, are all ideas that can be applied to the design and construction of new factories. Imagine entire cities and regions with closed-loop energy, water, and material systems where all waste is eliminated. As natural resources become increasingly scarce and more expensive to extract, a rent-and-return model for all goods, including building components, makes economic and environmental sense. Buildings can have longer life expectancies, and designing for long life, loose fit, and to be well suited to local climate and cultures must still be a priority, alongside allowances for easy adaptability for changing technology. When buildings must come down, if the components are designed for ease of disassembly, reuse, and recycling with clearly differentiated biosphere and technosphere material loops, they can become the inputs for future buildings as cities become repositories for materials. In this landscape, vertical urban factories[48] can operate within the richness of material supplies available in cities, transforming the waste of millions of people into new products, operating using renewable energy, and becoming vital centers for jobs, community building, and capital. These are measures that will reduce and ideally eliminate the future contributions to the Anthropocene strata on our earth's crust, while slowing the warming of our planet.

Notes

1   William McDonough Architects, *The Hannover Principles: Design for Sustainability* (Charlottesville, VA: William McDonough + Partners); William McDonough and Michael Braungart, *Cradle to Cradle—Remaking the Way We Make Things* (New York, NY: North Point Press, 2002).

2   www.postconsumers.com/2011/10/31/how-long-does-it-take-a-plastic-bottle-to-biodegrade/.

3   https://phys.org/news/2016-11-earth-technosphere-trillion-tons.html.

4   A proposed geological epoch characterized by the impacts of human activity including climate change. https://en.wikipedia.org/wiki/Anthropocene.

5   McDonough and Braungart, *Cradle to Cradle*, 92–117. www.c2ccertified.org/. In addition, McDonough and Braungart have developed a cradle-to-cradle certification system through the Cradle to Cradle Products Innovation Institute, with hundreds of certified products.

6   Janine M. Benyus, *Biomimicry: Inspired by Nature* (New York, NY: Harper Perennial, 2002), c1997; Thomas Graedel and Braden R. Allenby, *Industrial Ecology* (2nd edn) (New York: Prentice Hall, 2002); Paul Hawken, Amory Lovins, and L. Hunter Lovins, *Natural Capitalism: Creating the Next Industrial Revolution* (Boston, MA: Little, Brown and Company, 1999); Gunter Pauli, *The Blue Economy 3.0: The Marriage of Science, Innovation and Entrepreneurship Creates a New Business Model that Transforms Society* (Bloomington, IN: Xlibris, 2017).

7   www.maersk.com/en/explore/fleet/triple-e/the-hard-facts/cradle-to-cradle.

8 www.maersk.com/en/explore/fleet/triple-e. In addition to material innovations, the Triple-E vessels are more energy-efficient with larger, slower propellers and have the capacity to transport 18,000 TEU (twenty-foot equivalent), making them the largest transportation vessels in operation. Triple-E vessels have reduced CO2 emissions by 35 percent per container transported between Europe and Asia.

9 www.maersk.com/en/explore/fleet/triple-e/the-hard-facts/cradle-to-cradle.

10 Personal conversation with builder in Nan Province, Thailand, January 2018. Unfortunately, this has not stopped all illegal logging, which has still continued, contributing to Thailand's deforestation problems.

11 https://living-future.org/lbc/.

12 Email correspondence with Hannah Johnson, Living Community Challenge Coordinator, Living Future Institute, March 22, 2018.

13 www.thehenryford.org/visit/ford-rouge-factory-tour/history-and-timeline/reinventing/. Also McDonough and Braungart, *Cradle to Cradle*, 157–65.

14 http://sabra.com/sabra-story/sustainability; www.fritolay.com/making-a-positive-impact/environment; www.pepsico.com/live/pressrelease/sabra-dipping-company-opens-the-doors-to-new-manufacturing-plant-and-new-opportu05262010.

15 www.npr.org/sections/thetwo-way/2018/04/03/599207550/michigan-oks-nestl-water-extraction-despite-over-80k-public-comments-against-it; www.bloomberg.com/news/features/2017-09-21/nestl-makes-billions-bottling-water-it-pays-nearly-nothing-for; https://canadians.org/media/nestle-has-extracted-one-billion-litres-water-expired-permits.

16 www.nestle.com/stories/zero-water-factory.

17 www.nestle-ea.com/en/media/newsandfeatures/flexible-fast-and-functional-nestl-to-adopt-modular-factories.

18 https://concept-consult.ch/en/architecture/cereal-partners-worldwide-cpw-innovation-centre-en/. Personal correspondence with David Linford, Director at Concept-Consult Architectes, February 28–March 14, 2018.

19 www.zrs-berlin.de/en/architektur-en/betriebsgebaeude-artis-berlin-en.

20 https://newlab.com/new-lab-history/.

21 John W. Reps, *The Making of Urban America. A History of City Planning in the United States* (Princeton, NJ: Princeton University Press, 1992), 422–424.

22 Method was purchased by Ecover in 2012 and the merged company was acquired by SC Johnson in 2017.

23 Telephone conversation with William McDonough and Roger Schickedantz, March 1, 2018.

24 *Ibid*.

25 www.usgbc.org/projects/method-products-pbc/; https://chicago.curbed.com/2015/4/29/9966136/method-factory-tour/.

26 https://methodhome.com/beyond-the-bottle/soap-factory/; http://plus.usgbc.org/made-in-the-city/.

27 Phone conversation with William McDonough and Roger Schickedantz, March 1, 2018.

28 *Ibid*.

29 Email correspondence with Viraj Puri, cofounder and CEO of Gotham Greens, March 5–16, 2018.

30 www.seametrics.com/blog/global-water-crisis-facts/.

31 www.bubblydynamics.com/the-plant/.

32 Telephone conversation with John Edel, Bubbly Dynamics founder, March 2, 2018.

33 *Ibid*.

34 www.bubblydynamics.com/the-plant/.

35 Telephone conversation with John Edel, March 2, 2018.

36 *Ibid*.

37 www.plantchicago.org/who-we-are/.

38 Telephone conversation with John Edel, March 2, 2018.

39 www.tastykake.com/history.

40 www.architectmagazine.com/project-gallery/tasty-baking-company-bakery-distribution-facility.

41 Calculated using Google Maps, April 10, 2018.

42 www.tastykake.com/aboutus; www.architectmagazine.com/project-gallery/tasty-baking-company-bakery-distribution-facility.

43 Kasper Guldager Jensen and John Sommers, *Building a Circular Future* (Hvidovre, Denmark: KLS PurePrint, 2016). www.buildingacircularfuture.com.
44 3XN Architects and GXN Innovation, "Circularity Lab—New York-Bay Area 2018 Design Scheme Project," design progress document shared with author, January 2, 2018.
45 Telephone conversation with Kasper Guldager Jensen, March 1, 2018.
46 3XN Architects and GXN Innovation, "Circularity Lab—New York-Bay Area 2018 Design Scheme Project," 39–45.
47 Jensen and Sommers, *Building a Circular Future*, 98–101.
48 See Nina Rappaport, *Vertical Urban Factory* (Barcelona: Actar, 2016).

8 Spaces of Informal Production in China

Jonathan Bach and Stefan Al

Introduction

When dealing with the formal and informal in the world of manufacturing and urban space, things are seldom what they appear. In the 1980s a friend recounted how, as a buyer in Hong Kong for a major Western clothing brand, she would go at midnight to the border with Shenzhen where women would come with carts full of garments and hand them over to be labeled "Made in Hong Kong." The question of informal production in China, as elsewhere, entails judgments about the contours of formality and informality. Formal production conjures up images of clearly defined public and private sectors regulated by law and cleanly delineated in time and space. Yet China's economic rise could not be explained without forms of informal production, from the piecemeal garment work that led to China's textile boom to the family business model of "shop in the front, factory in the back" (*qián diàn hòu chǎng*), to the larger-scale quasi-legal factories set up by former village collectives.

Informal production, of course, is inseparable from informal employment, even though they are not necessarily identical phenomena. Informal employment encompasses the wide world of workers without a contract, usually "off the books," who are to be found everywhere from providing services to working in manufacturing. It also includes entrepreneurs who don't work for others but are not necessarily registered as a formal business, who are self-employed, who set up small workshops, or who turn their homes into production sites. Informal workers in their many guises are rapidly becoming the norm; a recent study found that "formal employees" declined sharply to only 43 percent of the Chinese workforce in 2013, while "casual workers" made up 42 percent.[1]

This chapter considers the spatial and architectural dimensions of informal production. By definition the informal is not standardized or regularized but that doesn't mean it doesn't follow rules when it comes to production. Informal production sites are premised on a combination of proximity, collaboration, and flexibility that exists symbiotically within their environments. Thus, for example, the "shop in the front, factory in the back" model allows manufacturers to also act as wholesalers, giving them constant access to feedback on demand, the ability to make quick modifications, and cultivate direct lines to buyers. Similarly, the location of many informal production sites in China's "urban villages," especially in the Pearl River Delta region, draws on the flow of migrant workers, the density of the quasi-legal buildings and factories erected on village-owned land, and the incentives of collective profit-sharing that build on diaspora ties for investment, distribution, and knowledge transfer.[2]

Yet the very conditions for informal manufacturing are often also those that fall afoul of concerted efforts to bring economic production more firmly within state control. The state wants control for the standard reasons of health and safety, to bring such enterprises inside the fold of taxation and statistics, and to enable intellectual property rights and targeted growth of selected industries. This means that informal production is increasingly relegated to those spaces that exist in the gray areas and at the smaller end of the scale. The Shenzhen municipal government, for example, defines manufacturing as informal when it occurs in "three kinds of small places" (*sān xiǎo chǎngsuǒ*), by which is meant: 1) small shops with an area of less than 300 square meters; 2) small workshops with a building height of less than 24 meters; and 3) small recreation sites with area of less than 200 square meters.[3]

The Urban Village as Production Space

These "three kinds of small places" are often located in urban villages with significant autonomy over their land. These form what the government refers to as "three-in-one" places (*sān hé yī*) where, like the "shop in the front, factory in the back" of yore, residence has been mixed up with production, storage, or marketing.[4] The layout of a typical urban village consists of a dense core of illegally constructed housing where the original village once stood, often with shops and workspaces on the first floor of exceedingly narrow streets and light-industrial areas either on earlier agricultural land or the site of early township and village enterprises. These spaces were often used for production, manufacturing, and machining as well as warehousing and offices.

Urban villages exist in a symbiotic relationship with adjacent industrial development as the villages grow and change according to the flow of migrants, many of whom work in nearby factories. Villages thus both compete with and augment existing industrial clusters. Yidong Yang points out that in the Dalang district of Shenzhen, alongside the 268 industrial parks that form the core of the district's fashion industry, there are 20,000 small stalls that extend and amplify the industry.[5] It is hard to call these factories in the traditional sense but they are often creative uses of available space that add value to the garments they produce. Wu Ling details how at night the urban village she studied became an extended factory shift as workers put buttons on clothes and embroidered garments sewn during the day in the formal factories. The town she studied had over 30,000 informal workshops providing 200,000 jobs in the informal economy.[6]

Electronics and garments are the most common forms of informal production, and Shipai Village in Guangzhou is an example of the symbiotic relation between the formal IT sector and the thousands of people working in the gray areas of the informal economy. As Guangzhou's largest and densest urban village, it established itself in the 1990s as the city's center for all kinds of electronic equipment. The village's businesses even set prices for some components at the national level.

Municipal governments seek to crack down on informal spaces yet they have also come to recognize the potential of informal spaces of urban villages for generating new ideas, rapid prototyping, and that ephemeral objective of desire, creativity. Village-owned factories, which are often less competitive than large corporations, are being reimagined as "creative incubation centers" and the Shenzhen government has supported the location of "makerspaces" in villages. They hope to capitalize on the raw talent of the many migrants—blue- and white-collar alike—to generate the next major innovation or brand by connecting designers with technically skilled

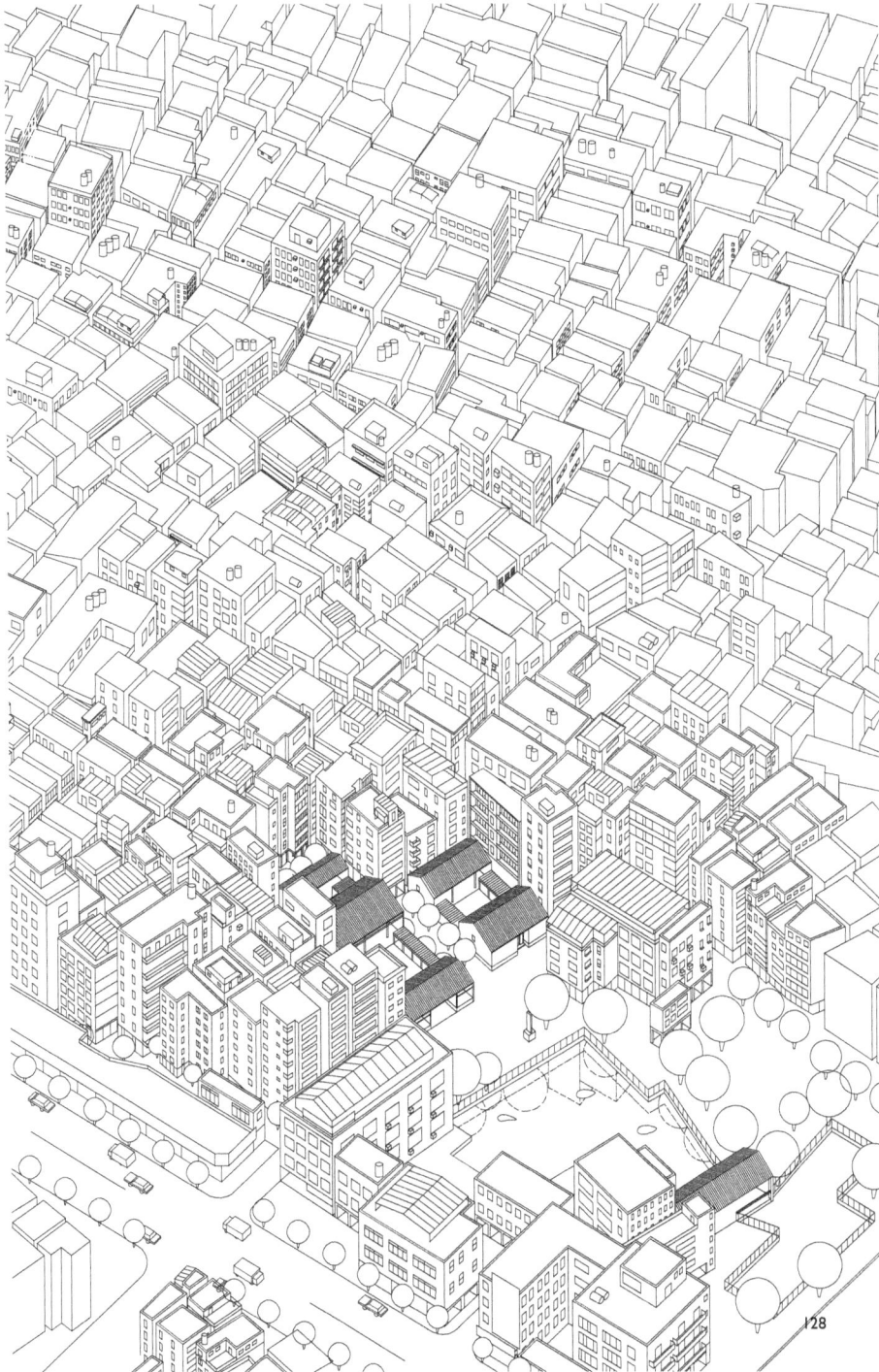

Figure 8.1 Shipai Urban Village, Guangzhou, China.

Figure 8.2 Inside Huaqiangbei, Shenzhen, China.

workers. Many residents of urban villages work, or have worked, for major electronics or consumer-goods manufacturing firms and, as jobs dry up due to increasing wage costs, many turn to informal or start-up companies, bringing their skills and often access to materials and prototypes with them.

Production Ecosystems

While the expression "shop in the front, factory in the back" might give the impression of self-sufficient production sites, the hallmark of contemporary informal production is its distributed nature where a collaborative network of smaller workshops, factories, and makeshift spaces work together to make products for the market.

For example, the well-known electronics manufacturing district of Huaqiangbei in Shenzhen became the epicenter of copycat (*shānzhài*) electronics, notably cell phones but also virtually every sort of electronic item, from cameras to security systems and their accessories. Millions of units of phones and other electronics are produced in a gray market, mainly in a series of large buildings with wholesale on the lower floors and manufacturing on the upper floors, a modern-day variation on "shop in the front, factory in the back." The manufacturing often takes place in small windowless workshops with sometimes only a half-dozen people hunched over soldering irons, busy reverse-engineering the latest cell phone models and adapting them to new uses.

Yet as Sylvia Lindtner writes, this form of production "is comprised of a horizontal web of component producers, traders, design solution houses, vendors, and assembly lines."[7] The Taiwanese firm World Peace International, she notes, will make circuit boards available for free to the tens of thousands of small companies, making money off of components. Thus, what might appear as a small stall tucked away on the seventh floor of an electronics wholesaler, or in the back room of an illegally constructed village apartment building, is effectively part of a formal-informal ecosystem.[8]

This raises the question of how to design for distributed systems that are constantly evolving and that rely on shifting networks rather than hierarchically organized workspaces. The key lies in some form of spatial organization of the network. One increasingly popular spatial response has been the growth of co-working spaces, which, while not the site of production per se, can serve as types of nerve centers or nodes for collaboration. They potentially provide both international and local connections as well as sociality, which is also one of the qualities of urban villages.[9]

Dafen Village

A different model is Dafen Village, an urban village in Shenzhen, internationally infamous for its "fake" paintings, ranging from Da Vincis to Warhols, exhibited in its countless exhibition alleys and about 800 galleries that make the village a popular tourist attraction. However, it is also an example of informal manufacturing. Currently there are over 6,000 artists in the village, even some painting "original" art that is exhibited in the Dafen Art Museum. Although Dafen's economy relies mainly on painting of replicas, the village also produces and sells calligraphy, arts and crafts, sculptures, picture frames, and paint.

This impressive industry arose organically. In 1989, Huang Jiang, a Hong Kong painter and businessman, brought about twenty artists to Dafen to paint replicas of well-known masters such as Van Gogh and Picasso. They were sold at relatively low prices worldwide. Within a decade, thousands of painters moved to Dafen to make a living in the village's flourishing new industry. Today "Dafen Oil Painting" has become a well-known cultural brand in China and abroad.[10]

The manufacturing of paintings occurs in factories but also in informal spaces such as residential buildings and alleyways. Residential buildings are typically six stories tall, with the ground floor accommodating a gallery and upper floors containing apartments used for painting or living, or both. Even the two-to-three-meter-wide alleyways become spaces for production. They are used as "wall galleries" where artists can display and sell their work. Since these galleries are cheap to rent, some artists use the space for producing paintings.

Why did this industry flourish in an urban village instead of the formal city? Some of the reasons point to the informal conditions of the village, including its low-cost small lots and flexibility of use—all of which create opportunities for small business owners. One Beijing survey of villages revealed that rents are up to ten times cheaper in the village compared to adjacent formal housing, with the per-square-meter cost about 25 percent lower.[11] These lower costs can be explained though the informal status of the village, the inexpensive and relatively low-quality housing, and the small units. It makes housing affordable for a migrant population and others looking for cheap rents, including students and business owners. At the same time the villages are not constrained by the city's formal and rigid land use plan that segregates uses such as commercial, industrial, and residential. Business can benefit from a land use pattern where live, work, and play are mixed. The small businesses of the mixed-use villages that provide services to the local population and tourists provide opportunity for small business owners and entrepreneurs and employment for residents. Moreover, it is quite common to find a business owner living above his business in the villages.[12]

In Dafen, novice painters can get their start by renting out a few square meters of wall space. Wang Wei, for instance, graduated from Sichuan Music and Art College and moved to Dafen to launch his career. He initially worked as a factory worker in an electronics factory, hoping he could make it as a painter on the side.

> In my spare time I started to paint, but my landlord disliked the smell of oil painting. I resigned from the factory and rented a small exhibition area in Dafen. It is about two square meters and costs 500 RMB each month [about $75]. Since then, I have started painting again. So now I am a painter in Dafen.[13]

Dafen is not only a unique example of informal manufacturing; it also represents hope for urban villages in general because its success is recognized by the government. The village

Figure 8.3 Dafen Village, in China, marked by colorful buildings and narrow streets, has become an international center of replica paintings.

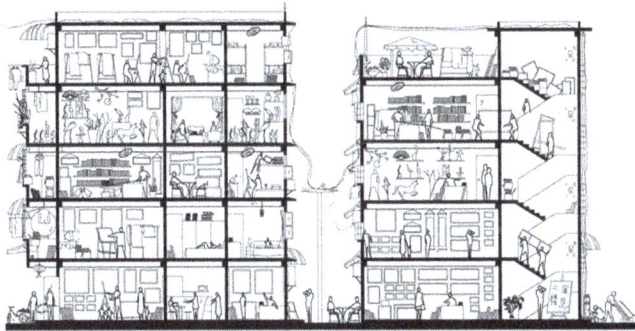

Figure 8.4 Dafen Village has a mixed-use land use pattern, with galleries on ground floors as well as on exterior walls, taking advantage of passing tourists. The stores also sell to retailers in large quantities.

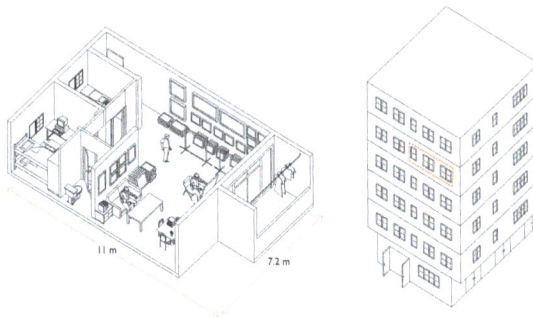

Figure 8.5 In Dafen Village the buildings originally for residential use today also accommodate the manufacturing and selling of paintings.

Figure 8.6 Wang Wei paints in this "wall gallery," within one of Dafen's countless exhibition alleys.

is recognized as a model by city officials who agreed to feature Dafen in the Shenzhen Pavilion of the 2010 World Expo in Shanghai. Today Dafen is a cultural landmark with a thriving industrial ecosystem around painting, providing jobs for artists, teachers, art dealers, and students.[14]

Conclusion

The architectural contours of informal manufacturing in China draw primarily on the larger topography of informality. The urban village, with its unauthorized buildings, relative autonomy, and high concentration of migrant labor, becomes the site of concentrated government intervention to "upgrade" the urban infrastructure, which also encompasses the "quality" (*suzhi*) of the workers and, hence, shaping their larger living and working environments. The urban village needs to be seen as evolving together with the larger industrial infrastructure. This means not only the demolition of villages, as has been common, but their transformation. In southern China, a renewed focus is on creative and IT industries in the villages, working in concert with the more formal factories beyond. This in turn requires a renewed emphasis on rethinking the urban village as a mixed-use area, one of the few remaining urban environs in China where people can live, work, and consume goods and services in a diverse neighborhood.[15]

China's urban villages were fertile ground for manufacturing because they allowed manufacturing to occur from the bottom up, rather than planned from the top. Their small lots gave opportunities to small businesses and entrepreneurs, unlike the formal factory towns, which require large upfront investments or large sums of rent. Moreover, the many small businesses clustered together benefit from agglomeration economies. In addition, the flexible use of buildings allowed for different industries to develop organically, and the lack of regulation allowed for unique factory expansions, including shipping containers that were added to buildings. Moreover, the fact that the villages were integrated in the city, rather than removed from the city in master-planned peri-urban industrial clusters, enabled a steady supply of foot traffic and potential customers.

Because of the poor reputation of the villages as scars on the city landscape, they remain a conundrum for city planning departments, despite increasing attention paid to them in recent years by designers, architects, and progressive planners. It has proven difficult to design for the urban village in a context where property rights are contested, developers are eager to strike deals for big projects, and the narrow streets and small plots seem like obstacles for the rationality of modern urban planning. Yet the villages play a key role in the manufacturing ecosystem where informal and formal practices co-evolve with contemporary efforts to cultivate innovation, entrepreneurship, and creativity. Is it possible to design for distributed production in informal settings without throwing the baby out with the bathwater?

This is a key question for planners and architects in the West as well, since the blurring of informal and formal in Western cities today comes in the context of the double challenge of gentrification (especially where creative economies and IT dominate), and shrinking cities (for many provincial cities who are especially challenged to find new uses for their former industrial heritage). In Shenzhen, the small informal electronics companies toiling over transistors and reverse-engineering the latest technology have colloquially been compared to the legendary garages where tinkering gave rise to today's computer and software giants. The line between informality and entrepreneurship is a blurry one, and their relation is symbiotic. Thus many postindustrial Western cities aim today to create an atmosphere of informality through co-working spaces, the re-use of industrial zones such as Industry City in Brooklyn, where artisans making chocolate and spirits work alongside workshops and commercial spaces of varying kinds and sizes in a new type of village environment (see Kimball, Chapter 14).

Yet the informal, by definition, is unplanned, so every attempt to harness its power will be met with unintended consequences. This does not mean, however, that serendipitous intersections and adaptive reuse cannot be built into the process more than is commonly the case. While unplanned, informality is also path-dependent, so it is possible to plan and build in ways that encourage the kinds of interactions produced by informality, in particular the characteristics of proximity, collaboration, and flexibility that are often to be found and enabled by mixed-use and mixed-income settings. To harness the self-organizing processes that stem from the informal, designers could create clusters to nurture agglomeration effects, allow the flexible use of buildings, and exploit the clustering and serendipitous effects of being in the city as opposed to new industrial districts on the outskirts. These are a few lessons that connect the challenges in China's growing cities and the postindustrial settings of the West.

Notes

1 Zhe Liang, Simon Appleton, and Lina Song, "Informal Employment in China: Trends, Patterns and Determinants of Entry," discussion paper, no. 10139, (Bonn: Institute for the Study of Labor, August 2016), 8. Looking at the period from 2007 to 2013, they found a decrease in formal employees from 65 percent to 43 percent, and an increase in casual workers from 24 percent to 42 percent. On the informal economy in China, see Phillip C.C. Huang, "China's Neglected Informal Economy: Reality and Theory," *Modern China*, v.1, n.4 (2009), 405–438.

2 These processes are discussed in more detail for the case of Shenzhen in Mary Ann O'Donnell, Winnie Wong, and Jonathan Bach, eds., *Learning from Shenzhen: China's Post-Mao Experiment from Special Zone to Model City* (Chicago, IL: University of Chicago Press, 2016).

3 Personal communication with Ye Liu, May 11, 2017.

4 *Ibid.*

5 Yidong Yang, "Enhance the Profound Vitality of Urban Villages," Presentation at the Technical University of Delft, Faculty of Architecture and the Built Environment, November 3, 2016.

6 Ling Wu, *Migrant Workers and Informal Economy in Urban China: An Ethnographic Study of a Migrant Enclave in Guangzhou*, Doctoral Dissertation, (Hong Kong SAR: University of Hong Kong), 92. Retrieved from http://dx.doi.org/10.5353/th_b5089967.

7 Sylvia Lindnter, Anna Greenspan, and David Li, "Designed in Shenzhen: Shanzhai Manufacturers and Maker Entrepreneurs," (Aarhus: Aarhus Series on Human Centered Computing, v.1, n.1, 2015), 10. See also Valérie Fernandez, Gilles Puel, and Clément Renaud, "The Open Innovation Paradigm: from Outsourcing to Open-sourcing in Shenzhen, China," *International Review for Spatial Planning and Sustainable Development*, v.4, n.4 (2016), 27–41.

8 See Michael Keane and Elaine Jing Zhao, "Renegades on the Frontier: The Shanzhai Grassroots Communities of Shenzhen in China's Creative Economy," *Eurasian Geography and Economics*, v.53 (2013), 216–230.

9 See Sylvia Lindtner, "Laboratory of the Precarious: Prototyping Entrepreneurial Living in Shenzhen," *Women's Studies Quarterly*, v.45, n.3&4 (2017), 287–305.

10 For a comprehensive treatment of Dafen Village, including a discussion of its origins, see Winnie Won Yin Wong, *Van Gogh on Demand: China and the Readymade* (Chicago, IL: University of Chicago Press, 2014).

11 Siqi Zheng, Fenjie Long, C. Cindy Fan, and Yizhen Gu, "Urban Villages in China: A 2008 Survey of Migrant Settlements in Beijing," *Eurasian Geography and Economics*, v.50, n.4 (Columbia, MD: Bellwether Publishing, 2009), 425–446.

12 For a detailed discussion of the organization and history of urban villages in Shenzhen, see Mary Ann O'Donnell, "Laying Siege to the Villages: The Vernacular Geography of Shenzhen," and Jonathan Bach, "'They Come in Peasants and Leave Citizens': Urban Villages and the Making of Shenzhen," in O'Donnell et al., *Learning from Shenzhen*, op. cit.

13 Stefan Al, ed., *Villages in the City: A Guide to South China's Informal Settlements* (Hong Kong: Hong Kong University Press, 2014), 89.

14 Despite Dafen Village's international status as a copy-painting village, as of this writing, it is slated to be redeveloped in the near future, and it is unclear what, if any, accommodations will be made in the redevelopment to maintain its current identity.

15 While urban villages are a kind of naturally occurring space that combines living and working, new developments are striving to replicate some of this sociality through top-down designed "incubators" such as the "Middle Space" complex in Shenzhen. See Jun Deng, "Middle Space: Four Incubators in Shenzhen," Architizer.com (2018), https://architizer.com/projects/middle-space-4-incubators-in-shenzhen/.

9 Production Spaces for Industry 4.0

Nina Rappaport

The Fourth Industrial Revolution in which we are now operating is developing a new paradigm. "Industry 4.0" encompasses digital and advanced fabrication technologies, artificial intelligence, additive manufacturing, and smart and green machines, among other innovations.[1] In this paradigm, advanced manufacturing often finds itself well-suited to the city, where highly skilled talent and synergies among creative fields facilitate rapid prototyping and the creation of customized high-value products. This paradigm is also marked by a hybrid approach to space-making: architectural spaces in which new products are designed, tested, produced, and introduced into the marketplace are transforming factory architecture away from the traditional one-factory-per-company model toward neo-cottage industries set within "industrial commons." New manufacturing hubs are being realized through a mix of financial, real estate, technological, and managerial strategies never before practiced by industrialists. Common among them is the renovation of former multistoried urban loft factories to accommodate small-batch production and prototyping—an urban transformation within the former spaces of urban mass production and, unlike the industries of old, these new uses are well-suited to the modern city: clean, quiet, and highly networked. This model has emboldened entrepreneurs to spearhead new approaches to urban industry, creating higher-paying manufacturing jobs and training in the fields of automation and computer engineering.

Many of these spaces are membership-based (like health clubs) and others are leased, similar to a speculative office building. Some utilize a more cooperative structure in an industrial commons—but they all share the goals of job creation and innovative product development, especially in advanced manufacturing. The four scenarios described in this essay—not-for-profit (Greenpoint Manufacturing and Design Center), for-profit (NextFab), private with public support (New Lab), and public with nonprofit management and private support (UI Labs)—characterize the dominant models that are shaping the productive city of the next economy.

Greenpoint Manufacturing and Design Center

The model nonprofit, Greenpoint Manufacturing and Design Center (GMDC), in Brooklyn continues to expand from its original space and industrial audience since its founding in 1993. In its original 360,000-square-foot brick complex at the confluence of Newtown Creek and the East River—which in 1868 was a marine rope factory—entrepreneurs developed a working hub for the woodworking industry. The maze of hallways leads to entrances to individual tenant spaces; large wooden light monitors project above the varied roof levels; solar panels are arrayed on a lower wing of the building; and tall ceilings and ample loading docks attract a

Figure 9.1 One of the renovated factories on Humboldt Street, owned by Greenpoint Manufacturing Design Center, Brooklyn, New York, 2016.

vibrant mix of industrial tenants. This industrial mini-district is occupied by furniture manufacturers, a mattress company, stage-set fabricators, traditional metal spinners, jewelry designers and producers—but also accommodates digitally savvy companies using advanced manufacturing technologies. The building management provides basic services and divides workshops into spatially viable units in which a company can fit-out according to their needs. In each of their six buildings in Brooklyn and Queens, which together total over 700,000 square feet, an organic synergy has developed between the industrial tenants so that when a furniture maker who works in wood requires a metal joint system, the adjacent metal fabricator can supply it in an exchange of expertise. These synergies and collaborations are enhanced by the unique characteristics of the former factories GMDC repurposes—buildings that are becoming increasingly scarce in cities such as New York, as they have been converted to other non-manufacturing uses.

As a not-for-profit, GMDC offers spaces at below-market rates and leases them for a minimum of five years, reducing the uncertainty a small manufacturer would ordinarily face on the traditional market with regard to annual leases. However, as real estate prices escalate across the boroughs, the biggest challenges to GMDC are increasing acquisition prices and construction costs. Having completed their seventh building renovation, a 90,000-square-foot factory in Ozone Park, Queens, GMDC is benefiting from a network of financing from local and state capital funds, New Market Tax Credit Program, and historic-preservation tax credits. The factory, which was designed by Shook and Sons in 1906 and was renovated to plans by architects Beyer Blinder and Belle, was one of the earliest poured concrete buildings in the region. GMDC also provides expertise to other industrial groups who want to venture into the real estate arena, such as SFMade in San Francisco. GMDC thrives on its mission of job creation, supporting over 100 businesses, which employ over 600 people. As director Brian Coleman notes, "manufacturing is still an entry into the middle class, as the jobs pay $50,000 a year, a far cry from the $20,000 in service jobs in a fast-food chain."[2] Many of these jobs require new workforce training in digital literacy and advanced fabrication skill sets, a hallmark of Industry 4.0.

Figure 9.2 Metal spinning work at Greenpoint Manufacturing Design Center's original building in North Greenpoint, Brooklyn, New York, 2017.

Figure 9.3 Works manufacturing at Greenpoint Manufacturing Design Center, Brooklyn, New York, 2018.

Figure 9.4 Woodshop, NextFab, Philadelphia, 2017.

NextFab

One way to foster entrepreneurship and new industrial skill sets is through the laboratory model. Evan Malone started Philadelphia's NextFab in 2009 as a for-profit incubator that educates entrepreneurs in Industry 4.0 and gives them the space and tools to make things. The idea was born from the Fab Lab movement that sprang up from MIT's first fabrication labs, which were founded around 2001 to assist technologically underserved communities. The movement has grown in the intervening time, Malone notes, with the "disruption in employment and the lack of job stability [serving] as a catalyst for the maker movement." Because long-term employment is becoming increasingly rare, those "who always had an idea that they had wanted to pursue"[3] are in need of the support that NextFab enables.

These fab labs have grown to a formal typology around the world closely aligned with the DIY movement and open-source facilities and "makerspaces." Some of the spaces are more informal hackerspaces, expanded garages, or cooperative clubs like OmniCorpDetroit, established to share space and equipment too expensive for any one person to buy alone, as well as to make products for personal use, or prototype them for the marketplace. NextFab quickly grew, thanks to the popularity that Malone predicted, and in 2013 moved from its first facility into a 21,000-square-foot space on Washington Street designed by architect Jackie Gusic of inHabit. The modest entrance leads to a lobby and a glass-enclosed space where the milling machines, 3D printers, and metalworking spaces are all on display. Along with a paint room, all of these resources are open to NextFab's 700 members to use until 10 p.m. One membership tier is a business incubation component of the RAPID Hardware Accelerator program, which provides venture services to help start-ups grow their companies. Inventors such as Jesse Garcia, an alum of the program who is developing a concussion detector for football helmets, can take advantage of NextFab's infrastructure and services to prototype a design, gain acumen in product development, and finally bring the product to market. NextFab's membership is similar to a gym—space and equipment are shared and classes provided. Four types of membership are available: general membership in which members pay monthly fees to use a space and equipment and classes are free; a second lower rate of $19 per month and a charge for classes; and a third, highly discounted, tier for veterans, seniors, and organizations using the space for nonprofit purposes. Finally, a separate membership tier is the business incubation component where a venture services group helps start-ups get off the ground as small-batch manufacturers, to grow their company in the RAPID hardware accelerator program. There inventors can bring a product to reality with prototyping and gain acumen in product development. Malone notes that when he came to Philadelphia in the 1980s, "its history of cottage manufacturing as the 'workshop of the world' still had that energy." There is still "a lot of scrappy can-do attitude and a lot of diamonds in the rough"[4] that he wants to enhance and contribute to.

Riding on their continued success, NextFab recently leased the 10,000-square-foot adjacent garage for individual workspaces while also setting up a 4,000-square-foot project in North Philadelphia, oriented more towards craft, where there is a textile room for digital embroidery, a wood shop, and a jewelry studio. NextFab has opened a new space in Wilmington, Delaware, with large workshop spaces and shared office space, demonstrating that the spaces to innovate and the tools to create are in great demand. In growing the network of incubators, Malone says he is pursuing "ideas to adjust attitudes about manufacturing since the US, with its immigrants and diversity of perspectives, is still a 'wild frontier.' We have a lot of opportunity now to compete in advanced manufacturing for customized high-value products rather than commodities." He is filling the void not only in the US but also in joint ventures in Australia and in a program for Syrian refugees in Jordan.

New Lab

Entering the bustling gates of the Brooklyn Navy Yard, now filled with 7,000 workers in a variety of industrial buildings, transformations are continuous. Building 128, a 160,000-square-foot historic ship machine shop, which had sat vacant for over twenty years, was

Figsure 9.5 Metal shop, NextFab, Philadelphia, 2017.

transformed into New Labs, an inspiring urban manufacturing center in the model of Industry 4.0. The renovation was designed by Marvel Architects, and is marked by a historically sensitive approach that maintains the original overhead cranes and includes a circuit of interior second-floor mezzanines and an open catwalk corridor bridging the common spaces that free up the upper floors for individual spaces and allowing natural light to pour in from clerestory windows. The project qualified for a historic preservation tax credit project as the entire Navy Yard site is designated on the National Register of Historic Places.

The 70-foot-high space opened in September 2016 and now houses 400 people from 70 companies working in rented studios and workshops, having web conferences in glass-enclosed private meeting rooms, and commingling in colorful lounges and cafes. Launched from a beta group of entrepreneurial designers and engineers, New Lab has blossomed into an incubator hive of hybrid advanced manufacturing in spaces ranging from 300 to 8,000 square feet based on but expanding beyond the model set by FabLab.

David Belt, co-founder and CEO of New Lab, is the owner of development company Macro Sea and its sister company DBI, with which he has built or coordinated numerous projects, including St. Ann's Warehouse in Dumbo, Brooklyn. In 2011 he conceived of the idea to realize, with artist and entrepreneur Scott Cohen, a "passion project." Belt researched new manufacturing models and envisioned an entrepreneurial space for robust companies that already had a product concept underway. He was also acquainted with the Brooklyn collective Dark

Figure 9.6 New Lab, Brooklyn Navy Yard, New York, second-floor view, 2017.

Matter Manufacturing, which included the nonprofit Terreform ONE, a design collaborative that had created an "unfeasibility study" that envisioned the Brooklyn Navy Yard as a massive retrofitted "maker village." Belt took them on as a beta group, housed temporarily in Building 280 while he and Cohen raised $30 million from the city, state, nonprofit urban investment groups, and Historic Preservation Tax Credits, to fund the restoration of the building, which he leases from the Brooklyn Navy Yard.

With the beta group in place to help attract additional collaborators, Belt and Cohen conceived of a closely controlled tenant composition of "optimistic" tech entrepreneurs developing technology for social good, such as clean energy and medical advancement. Others use robotics, artificial intelligence, 3D printing, and nanotechnologies, and all are often found assisting each other with product development. Some examples of companies include Honeybee, a thirty-three-year-old robotics company and NASA contractor exploring new robotics systems for use in surgery; StrongArm, which makes ErgoSkeleton braces to improve body mechanics for safer movement; furniture company MODO; and Unreasonable Women, which designs and produces bathing suits for all body types. Belt calls the innovation hub "hyper-localized manufacturing," as it enhances and catalyzes a symbiotic ecosystem between people, products, and companies.

As with NextFab, members are provided with benefits according to their needs, through membership levels ranging from paying for access to common space and the shop, up to rental of a 6,000-square-foot studio with use of meeting rooms and event space. However, as some products under development are proprietary, privacy must also be honored as much as collaboration, resulting in an interesting mix of public and private space—not dissimilar to a typical research laboratory. Members also have access to the Navy Yard's extensive employment services.

We are thinking about what we need to do now to make it meaningful also in terms of job creation. It is a research laboratory for machinery in a symbiotic relationship that is an ambitious project narrative that we know is not an easy model.[5]

– David Belt

Corporate collaborators have supplied $3 million in advanced prototyping tools and software in exchange for user feedback. Another collaborator, Haas, a CNC machinery company, provides training classes for members who it sees as ideal future customers of their milling technologies. Software companies, including Autodesk and Solid Works, have donated software to New Lab similar to the relationships of machine suppliers to the UI Labs described below.

Thus the former heavy-duty workshop atmosphere has been transformed into a space for a clean and modern form of manufacturing, and while there is a bit too much luxurious shared open space and some tenants complain that they don't have enough messy, garagelike creative space, few places like this exist: a professional, advanced manufacturing facility with the potential for deep experimentation within a supportive networked environment.

UI Labs

On the northern end of the former industrial district of Goose Island in Chicago, a steel bridge leads to a glowing warehouse. Passing markers for a digital water infrastructure monitoring

Figure 9.7 UI Labs Manufacturing Machinery.

project, one enters through twenty-five-foot-high industrial shed doors into an expansive lobby featuring exhibitions and a donor wall of collaborators. A glass enclosure offers glimpses into a vast space containing the latest industrial machinery.

Designed by SOM Chicago, the 64,000-square-foot former window and door factory now houses the umbrella UI Labs with its Digital Manufacturing and Design Innovation Institute (DMDII) and City Tech innovation platforms. As a public–private partnership, UI Labs is part of a network of thirteen institutes around the country under the umbrella of Manufacturing USA, co-sponsored by the US Department of Commerce, the US Department of Defense, and the US Department of Energy, among others—each with a specific area of expertise and focus to "secure America's future through manufacturing innovation, education, and collaboration."[6] A brainchild of the Obama administration, the network is set up to increase knowledge capacity and advance manufacturing expertise, and disseminate digital manufacturing in the US.

Established in 2014, UI Labs is a membership-based organization like New Lab, but here the membership consists of established Original Equipment Manufacturers (OEMs) looking to solve big problems in R&D, through access to smaller start-ups and a variety of new supply chains, even to those of competitors. The idea, says Colette Buscemi, a senior director, is to "create unnatural alliances where the government, large and small corporations, academics in advanced digital manufacturing can rub shoulders."[7] Of UI Labs' current 307-company membership, 75 percent are from industry and 25 percent from academia or nonprofit research organizations, with three membership tiers at different costs. Members, Buscemi adds, "can

Figure 9.8 UI Labs, Metrology Lab, Chicago, Illinois, 2018.

be confident that they are working on the most pressing and promising issues in digital manufacturing because of the strategic planning that we do with all these experts at the table."[8] In fact, one company that was developing a software tool assisted a start-up for novices to develop wind turbines using a simple integrated technology. Besides offices and co-working areas, the shared space includes conference rooms with white boards, chat and call rooms, and co-working spaces.

Within the glass-enclosed 25,000-square-foot Future Factory is $6 million-worth of equipment, including twelve-axis machines and a microbiology lab in a controlled room. At one side of the space, a model conveyor belt tests assembly line flow and a start-up demonstrates an augmented reality program to train factory workers. The UI Lab is also aspiring to increase workforce development, including digital skills, through a new 1,000-jobs campaign in Chicago just as the Brooklyn Navy Yard does internally. It also started an online digital workforce development program with Costar and SUNY Buffalo and is working with the job placement company Manpower to prepare for the positions one will find in the future job taxonomy.

One idea for the future of these co-working industrial spaces is the concept of an "industrial commons." This would be a combination of a FabLab with a New Lab but with a messier atmosphere—more like a garage with super-advanced amenities. The spaces required must be large enough to house at least two large-scale milling machines and common workspaces. Even

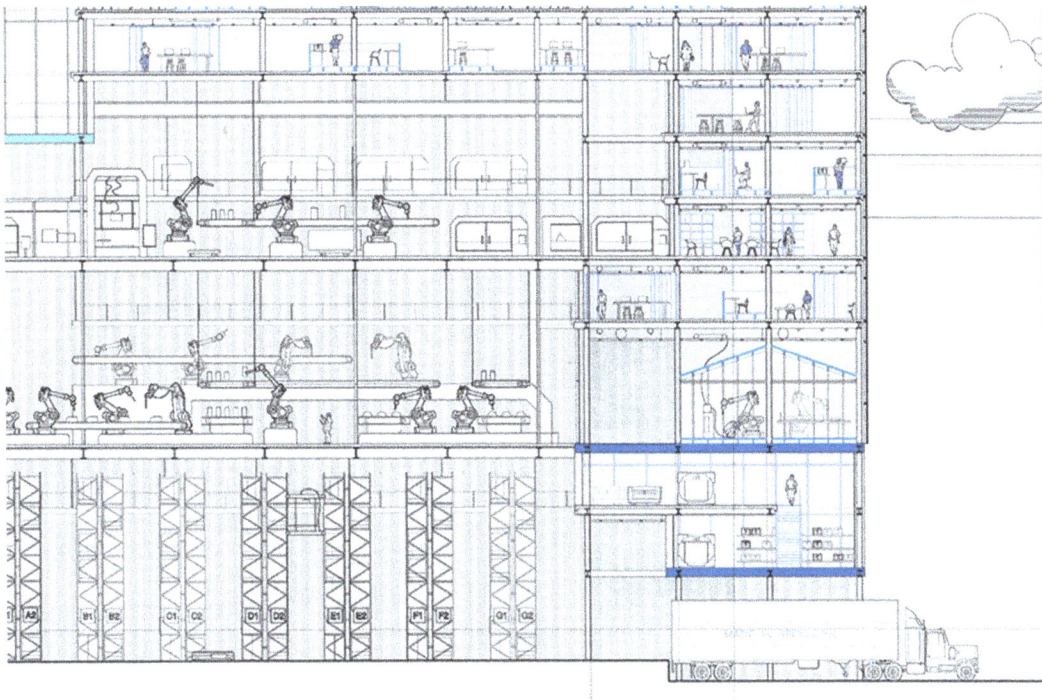

Figure 9.9 Concept for a new industrial commons.

the smallest facility at 1,000 square feet could have space enough for an enterprise as seen in the Afrilabs in Nairobi, Kenya, or the makerspace Omnicorps in Detroit, which occupies 2,000 square feet in an informal industrial space.

A mixed-use and mixed-tenanted former factory building is ideal for these new collaborations because—as with GMDC—a company can grow into adjacent flexible spaces when the space is available and additional machinery can be purchased. In contributing to the Fourth Industrial Revolution—spatially, organizationally, financially, and, perhaps most important of all, collaboratively—these new laboratories and institutes can inspire the next generation of entrepreneurial advanced manufacturing and incubate both projects and urban jobs. Perhaps those spaces that are a bit rougher at the edges and more like a garage might have an even greater impact; most inventions, as has been proven, are created in more random situations, odd combinations of spaces, and spontaneous encounters not in a forced march confined to one's computer station or laboratory. These new or renewed shared spaces must be as nimble and flexible as the entrepreneurs whom they house so they can self-organize and thrive with ingenuity for the public good.

Notes

1 This essay is adapted from an essay by Nina Rappaport in *Metropolis* magazine, April 2017.
2 Discussion between author and Brian Coleman, February 2017.
3 Discussion between author and Evan Malone, February 2017.
4 *Ibid.*
5 Discussion between author and David Belt, February 2017.
6 UI Labs brochure, 2017.
7 Discussion between author and Colette Buscemi, December 2016.
8 *Ibid.*

Changing Spaces in Urban Manufacturing

Alexander D'Hooghe and Kobi Ruthenberg,
Adam Lubinsky and Paul van der Grient

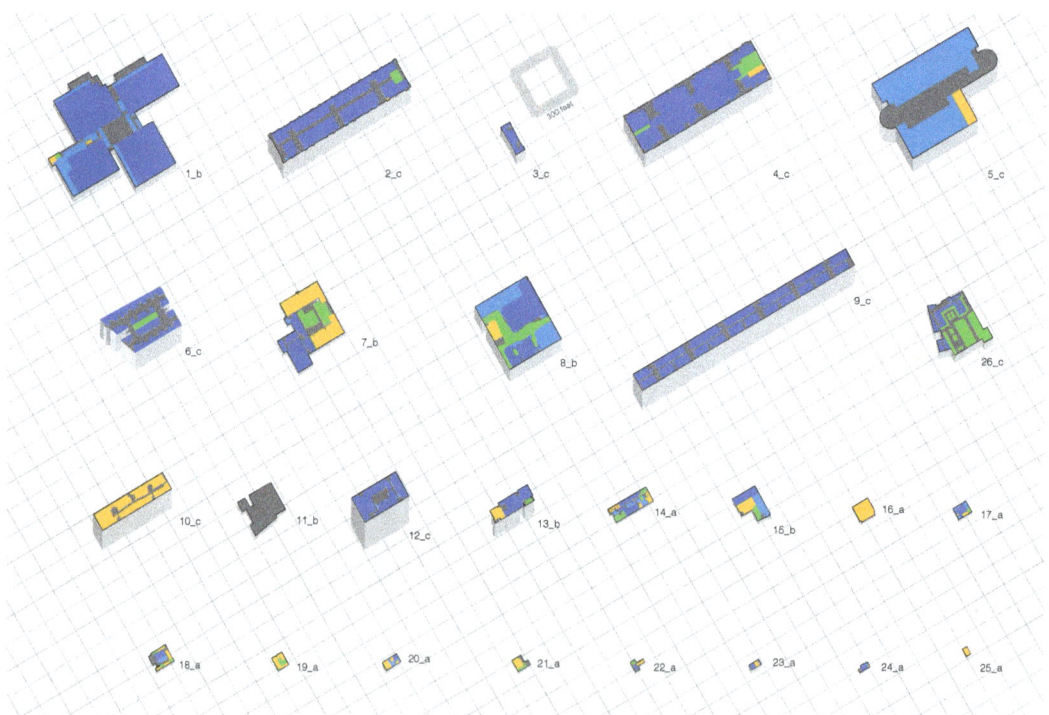

1. Production Plant for Hydraulic Components
2. Brooklyn Army Terminal, Building A
3. Brooklyn Army Terminal, Annex Building
4. Brooklyn Army Terminal, Building C
5. Prologis Ichikawa
6. Tagore 8
7. Emerson Processing
8. Aimer
9. Innovation and Design Building
10. Boston Design Center
11. Zahner
12. Building 77, Brooklyn Navy Yard
13. Sunray
14. LabCentral
15. Greentown Labs
16. 908 Devices
17. Brooklyn Foodworks
18. Gingko Bioworks
19. Formlabs
20. Nano-C Labs
21. Blade
22. Empire Robotics
23. Radlab
24. New Valence Robotics
25. EyeNetra
26. Abattoir

Advances in manufacturing technologies as well as the need for increased integration among high-tech industries have increased the importance of research, development, and complex prototyping as well as the need for a workforce skilled in 3D modeling, coding, and the operation of automated machinery. New businesses, which are no longer focused on the whole production process and its substantial logistics, materials, and cheaper labor needs, are proliferating in urban areas in proximity to creative industries. As a result, emerging incubators

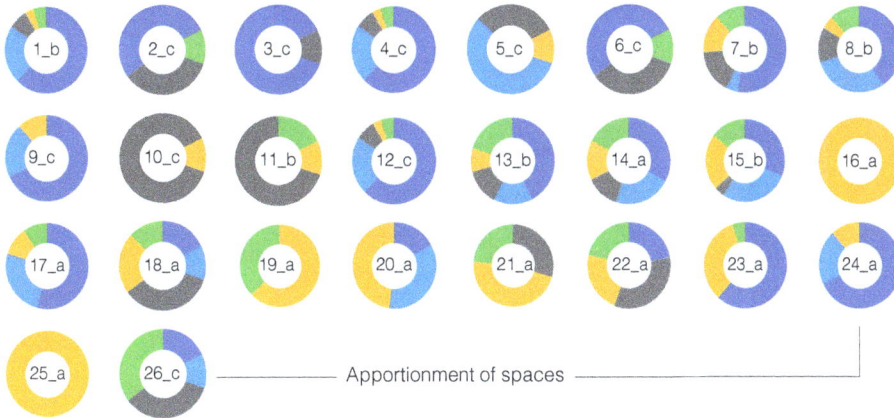

Apportionment of spaces

	Overall Averages	Excluding Traditional Manufacturing	Excluding firms over 100k sqft	Excluding Non US-Based & Single Tenant Buildings
Manufacturing	37%	31%	30%	29%
Storage/Manufacturing Support	12%	10%	11%	11%
Circulation/Mechanical	9%	10%	9%	11%
Office	34%	40%	42%	42%
Amenities	8%	8%	7%	8%
Average Total Area	88,927 SF	36,357 SF	10,361 SF	11,112 SF
Average # of Employees	78	43	42	46
Average Area per User	376 SF	288 SF	292 SF	270 SF

a - Single Tenant in Multi Tenant Building
b - Single Tenant Building
c - Multi Tenant Building

Manufacturing
Support / Storage
Circulation / Mechanical
Office
Amenities

and accelerators accommodate a mix of "production" businesses, which behave more like tech start-ups than artisan workshops or mass-production factories.

This paper examines these new manufacturing trends and their implications for building programs and systems. Based on ORG and WXY's recent research, this chapter puts forward the following observations on contemporary practices in urban manufacturing.[1]

Program

Office and Manufacturing Spaces

Administration, design, and fabrication activities are increasingly interlinked as these "production" businesses internalize more of the product development process. We identify a trend toward an increasing need for "office" use among contemporary manufacturing tenants. This increase indicates the spatial integration and co-location of managerial, creative product

	S	**M**
Height *	12'-0" - 18'-0"	18'-0"
no. of floors/ mezzanines	1 (w/ mezzanine option)	1 - 2
Square footage *	625 - 25,000	25,000 - 100,000
Footprint	multi-tenant	multi-tenant to single tenant
Structure	adaptable to structural grid	adaptable to structural grid
Program	Shared resources (i.e., production, storage, office, and/ or amenities)	Shared resources
Circulation	Shared shipping & receiving	Shared shipping & receiving

Notes:

* Heights shown indicate a system of high bay space able to be broken into 2 or 3 levels/ mezzanines. Heights also are determined by size of product manufactured and storageheight requirements.

** SMALL and MEDIUM sized businesses often need space flexibility to grow, as shown in range of square footage and also the ability to add mezzanines (height).

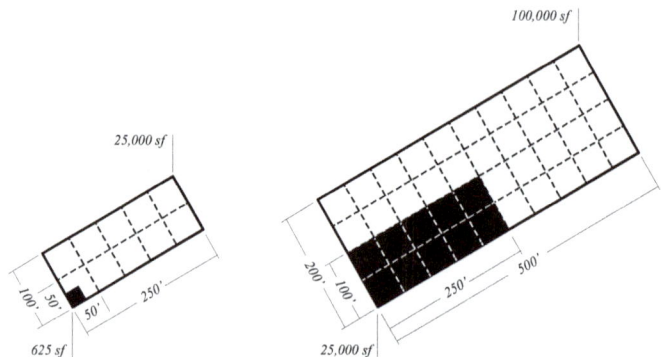

development, and fabrication or prototyping. On average we identify that contemporary manufacturers allocate about one-third of their space to what traditionally has been classified as office space, where personnel are sitting at desks and computer workstations rather than on the prototyping and fabrication machines themselves. This generally is a consequence of the increasing role of the computer in the manufacturing process.

Public and Shared Amenities

We identify an increasing prevalence of "mixing" spaces such as lobbies, event spaces, common areas, and recreational amenities in urban factories. This trend is due in part to the mentoring and management acceleration programs that lead to greater interdependency between manufacturers who might share space within a building or are within proximity to one another. We also see a correlation between business size and inclination to share, with small businesses tending to share more as they cannot afford to internalize many operational processes.

	L	XL
Height *	18'-0" - 40'-0"	40' and higher
no. of floors/ mezzanines	2 - 3	3 +
Square footage **	100,000 - 300,000	300,000 +
Footprint	single tenant	regular structural grid or long single tenant
Structure	regular structural grid preferred	span structure (free from columns)
Program	Resources included (i.e., prod., storage, office, and/ or amenities)	Resources included
Circulation	Shared shipping & receiving	Direct shipping & receiving; direct access to ground floor

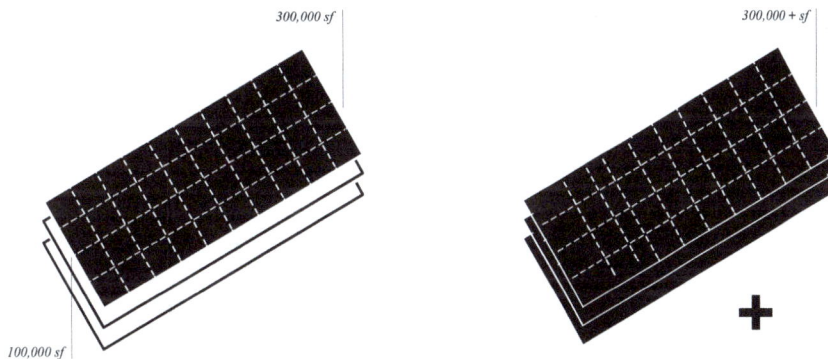

300,000 sf

100,000 sf

300,000 + sf

+

Parking

The proliferation of advanced manufacturing in urban areas has created less reliance on transportation by cars than is found in exurban areas. Still, much of the existing urban industrial space is located in more peripheral locations where land values are lower and public transportation is more distant. As a result, the need for parking remains. Many of these peripheral industrial locations are on former port and waterfront land, where "flood-able" ground-floor space can be used for parking.

Fragmentation of Operations

Outsourcing and co-manufacturing are increasingly common for manufacturing companies of all scales that cannot afford to internalize the entire production process. This trend is highly related to the cost of material sourcing and economies of cheaper labor found outside the developed world. Offsite storage and distribution is another aspect that allows for reduction of manufacturing footprints in urban settings, especially with just-in-time and on-demand production.

Manufacturing Districts

Co-location of uses provides a healthy ecosystem for small businesses with affinity to R&D to grow and stabilize with proximities to consultants, accelerators, larger institutions, and consultants.

Building Systems

Environmental Conditions

What was traditionally thought of as a binary condition of served and servant spaces[2] appears to be giving way to a more complex condition. As manufacturing processes are gradually automated, the concept of calibrating a space for humans becomes progressively ambiguous. The environmental needs of workers and machines can occasionally conflict, resulting in a design and management dilemma of optimization. Provisions of air and daylight are often hampered by the need of machines for extreme climate control. As a result, deep floor plates enjoy a renewed appreciation as possibilities for uses (such as 3D printing farms) that don't require intensive human presence to develop.

Flexibility

As a way to allow for rapid growth with minimal disturbance to operations, we identify that tenants prefer to be able to grow vertically within their space. This means that generous floor-to-ceiling heights are typically appreciated by tenants even while their manufacturing processes may not immediately require them. To accommodate for vertical expansion, we suggest a robust structural system of floor-to-ceiling heights of up to 40 feet, which allows for lighter construction partitioning and mezzanine alternatives to be managed internally and to accommodate for smaller uses.

Logistical Spaces

Loading, staging, and storage seem to be increasingly internalized as tenants scale up. It appears that over a certain scale of operation (normally above 100,000 square feet) a tenant will require access to its own loading bay due to frequent loading needs throughout the day. Similarly, larger firms often cannot tolerate the need to share freight elevators in multitenanted buildings. When direct access to loading bays cannot be achieved, we identify opportunities to partially offset disruptions to material flow with trailer truck parking or generous spaces for shared storage amenities adjacent to the loading bays.

Structural Repetition

Typical dimensions of equipment and building elements often dictate structural modules in plan. While the requirements for car parking are often used as the basis for grid size determination, we increasingly see that in manufacturing and logistical facilities, grids align to loading bay dimensions, which in turn dictate facade openings. These vary around 48 to 52 feet with the ability to accommodate four bays in each span.

Floor-Plate Dimensions

The divergent environmental needs of workers and machines may open up possibilities for larger and deeper floor plates (over 120 feet), provided that the interior spaces not receiving natural light are occupied by the automated forms of production, such as 3D printer farms. Critical to the circulation layout and cores distribution is an understanding of current typical business size, ensuring that in multitenanted buildings circulation both maximizes tenant space while minimizing distances from cores and circulation corridors.

Tenant Scalar Categories

In an attempt to classify the set of manufacturing tenants we studied with an interest in forming tools for the design of multitenant manufacturing facilities or zones, we propose a simple four-category system based on S, M, L, and XL sizes. Small tenants are typically under 25,000 square feet with a very flexible operation and often requirements for rapid growth. Of medium size are established businesses with about 25,000 to 100,000 square feet who might be able to share portions of their operations and facilities and perhaps still aspire to grow more. Large tenants are those that might be too autonomous to allow for sharing and often present very rigid demands for the previously described building systems. Finally, extra-large refers to those businesses that have achieved a scale potentially allowing them to share portions of their own facilities with small tenants who will be hosted by or sublease from them.

Notes

1 The findings in the below sections are largely merged from two studies—the first, led by Prof. Alexander D'Hooghe at the MIT Center for Advanced Urbanism in 2015, had a focus on the Boston metro area advanced-manufacturing sector. The second was a global survey of multistory manufacturing facilities performed for the Brooklyn Navy Yard in 2016 by ORG in conjunction with WXY as part of the Brooklyn Navy Yard Master Plan. WXY utilized ORG's primary research to further analyze interior layout data and configurations to draw conclusions on the breakdown of typical current internal spatial configurations.
2 Dean Hawkes, "Space for Services: The Architectural Dimension," *The Environmental Tradition: Studies in the Architecture of Environment* (London: E & FN Spon, 1996), 72.

GRAPHIC ESSAY ④

Re-Urbanizing the Box

Robert N. Lane

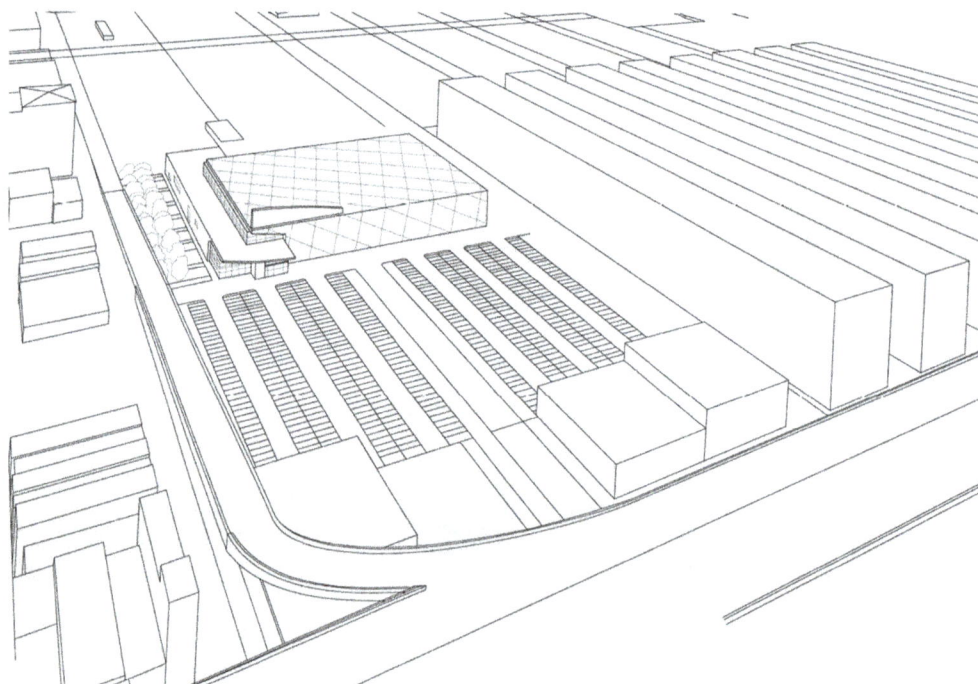

Short term: the superstore site, in keeping with the big-box program, is a superblock with a large, open parking lot. The context is largely undeveloped waterfront. A major connecting corridor is as yet undeveloped.

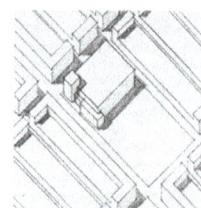

This design study focuses on the issues and opportunities associated with the industrial shed and the capacity of these kinds of structures to accommodate multiple programs over time.

Funded by individual project grants from the National Endowment for the Arts and the New York State Council for the Arts, this design study emerged from the larger *Beyond the Box* research initiative conducted in partnership with Michael Conard and Ann Kaufman Webster.

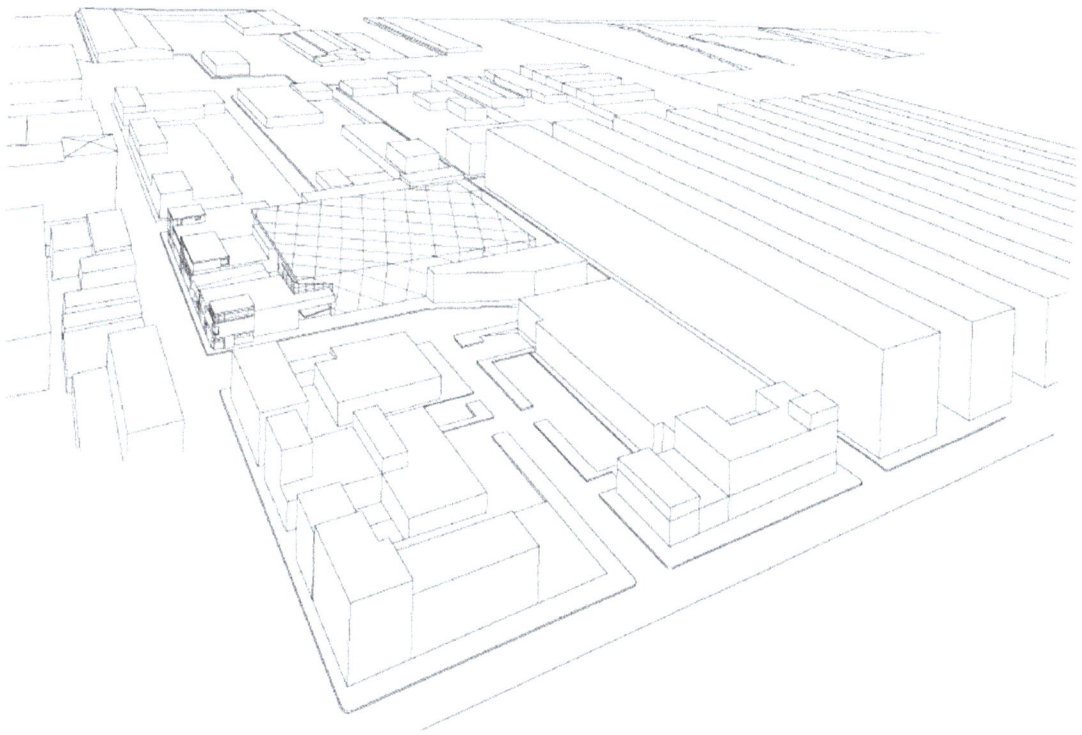

Intermediate term: the "big box" is now a warehousing and distribution facility for a variety of small and medium-sized manufacturers. The block-and-street pattern is re-imposed as other medium-sized manufacturers begin to fill in the parking lot. The waterfront context and the major street corridor are starting to be redeveloped.

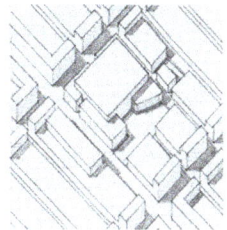

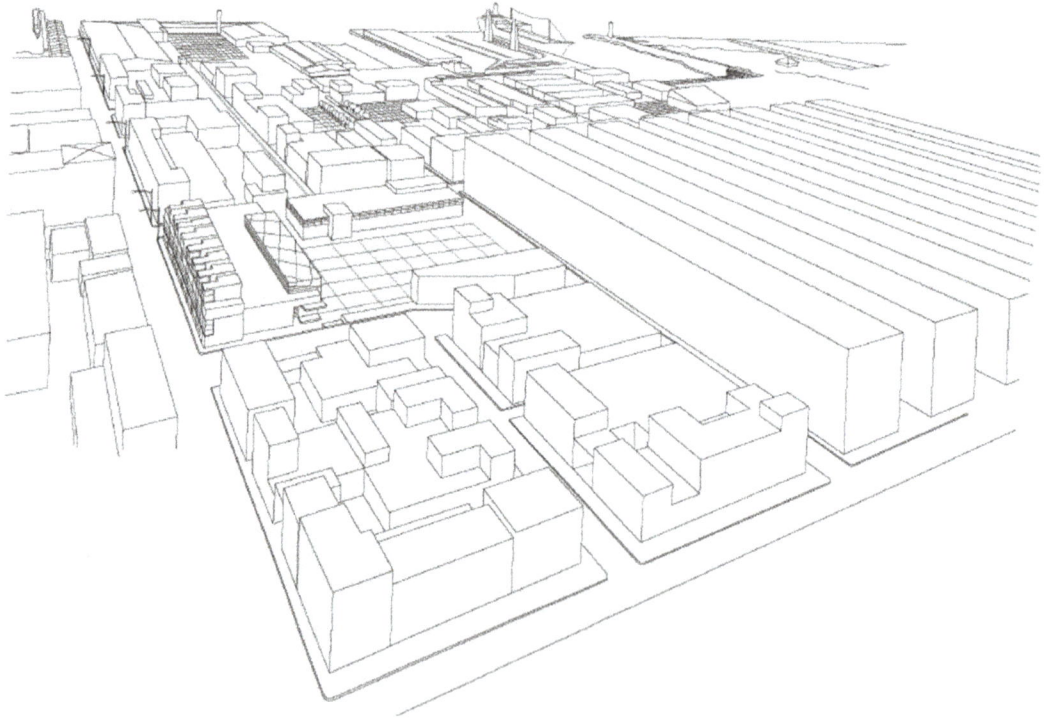

Long term: the "big box" is repossessed as
open space. The rest of the superblock has
been filled in with small-scale mixed-use
development. The open space of the former big
box is now a place for creative interaction and
is part of a system of open spaces in a redeveloped waterfront.

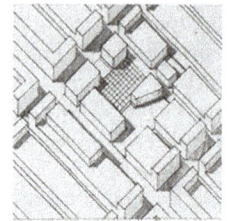

Part III
The Design of Policy
Making it Happen

10 Considering Industry as Infrastructure

Policy to Support Spaces for Urban Manufacturing

Nina Rappaport

Why an Urban Industrial Policy

Throughout history, cities have been magnets for entrepreneurs and inventors, where workers are plentiful, energy resources are often close at hand, transit options are fluid, consumers are nearby, and marketplaces are abundant. This synergy between resources, suppliers, and consumers is symbiotic, reinforcing urban dynamism and energy, and capable of being harnessed for worker well-being and equity. Today, as industrial production is being redefined for advanced manufacturing, robotics, lean production, and just-in-time manufacturing impact the design of both the factory and the urban industrial landscape; to keep up, the policies that shape our urban landscape need to change. Consistently, and perhaps paradoxically to some, economies contain two types of industry simultaneously: the mass production of global supply chains populated by low-skilled workers and with increasing automation, alongside the small-batch production of highly skilled engineers and technology operators, craftspeople, and entrepreneurs. The latter new manufacturing is cleaner, smaller, and lighter, and its urban footprint shares little in common with the more widespread form of industry, allowing it to inhabit dense urban manufacturing sites. However, zoning laws, building codes, and economic development polices designed to segregate dirty manufacturing from the rest of the city have not kept up with these technological revolutions.[1] Public agencies, private developers, locally based non-governmental organizations, and manufacturers have the potential to establish initiatives for mixed-use projects that, by reintroducing manufacturing to the site of consumption, are more sustainable than the developments of the past. This section of the book describes some innovative policy initiatives that are underexplored in terms of their application to industrial land use; among them are performance zoning, land banking, and transfer of development rights. Other approaches include up-zoning industrial areas to enable dense vertical urban factories; encouraging or requiring a mix of uses within both buildings and designated districts; new "craft manufacturing" zones; and a relaxation of outdated limitations on certain industries and their locations within the city. All represent new experimental proposals with strong precedents from the historic city. For urban industry to thrive, economic incentives alone will be insufficient—the space of physical production must be envisioned as an urban infrastructure as vital to cities as water, energy, and transit systems.

First, we need to recognize that the design of both urban manufacturing districts and manufacturing buildings themselves result from soft and hard infrastructures that interact in a web of policies that are ultimately not spearheaded by designers, planners, or architects; rather, they are orchestrated by economic, social, and public agents whose policies are political at the global, regional, and local levels. All of these soft infrastructures that underpin the physical space of production are part of what Henri Lefebvre calls "spatial practice"—a practice that challenges architects and urbanists to acquire agency over such issues in order to be engaged.[2] Thus, urbanists gain their agency by instigating ideas and interacting with policy makers in order to direct change. Specifically, manufacturing, economic, and land-use policies as well as other regulatory and urban design processes guide development potentials in every dynamic: from the programmatic use to the bulk allowed on a building site; the invested financial capabilities as direct funds or loans for construction; the taxes and incentives for businesses to grow; the development and permissions processes; and access to a robust material supply chain, logistics, and transportation flow.

The chapters in this book present an ideology: an interest in stimulating *local* urban manufacturing and thus more productive and sustainable cities—yet most manufacturing is *global*. Both local production and globalization reinforce each other in a necessary synergy. Local and regional government agencies must pay significant attention to local initiatives that support a socially equitable city and combine economic stimulation with social concerns for jobs, education, and sustainable environments. We continue to ask: what is the shape of economic and land-use policies that will be able to serve as catalysts for industrial job creation in the next economy, and how do the policies influence a city's design for manufacturing spaces as a basis for industry to be considered infrastructure?

In this section of the book, chapters by those in the fields of urban planning and real estate tackle various industrial policies to unveil the mysteries of what happens inside the space of manufacturing, to help guard against the marginalization of production through "process removal,"[3] in which manufacturing processes are removed from public view and everyday life. The concepts and configurations highlighted here are not comprehensive, but represent a selective overview of inventive models and prototypes for how land-use and building and zoning regulations can enhance, in a proactive way, the potential for diverse manufacturing sectors to thrive—both traditional or legacy companies, as well as newly minted advanced manufacturers.

Who Makes Policy

A few general industrial policy approaches are worth reviewing—"top-down," "bottom-up," "laissez-faire," and combinations thereof. In top-down control, governments often initiate industrial development in new districts, as seen in Abu Dhabi's industrial parks; Russia (with its Monotowns); China, the Philippines, and Singapore (with their free trade zones); and Mexico (with its *maquiladoras*). By designating districts as Export Processing Zones these nations set policies that entice companies (primarily large multinational ones) whose arrival increases local employment. Many of the players have vested interests in the issues they are addressing as well as their own perspectives and ideologies. In these far-flung centers of production clustered around ports and international borders, acres of hermetically sealed sheds contain workers treated as little more than cogs in machines, furthering manufacturing goals in conditions analogous to what Karl Marx and Friedrich Engels observed in mid-nineteenth-century Manchester. To jump-start emerging economies, trade regulations are often loosened through Free Trade policies so that transnational corporations can more easily trade with each other.[4] But local economic growth is better encouraged with subsidies for start-ups or research initiatives and capacity-building grants so companies can stay put or relocate locally by providing funding for energy-savings assistance, job training, and technology and digital upgrades.

In bottom-up organizations, localized business development corporations often take the lead with industrial networks that initiate policies, as in Antwerp, Philadelphia, Portland, and San Francisco, where industrial improvement has led to benefits for industrial retention. In some cities in emerging nations such as Vietnam (Hanoi), India (Dharavi), or Colombia (Medellín), an "informal" economy of local entrepreneurs thrives through internal networks. Economist Robert Neuwirth calls these resilient operations "System D," in reference to the do-it-yourself (DIY) economy of self-reliance.[5] Over half of the 1.8 billion workers in the world were working in System D in 2009, contributing to a market economy of $10 trillion.[6] In these self-initiated enterprises workers use resources on hand, jerry-rig tools and machinery, and occupy space in an ad-hoc way to make new products, as seen in how, ten years ago, Nigerian curtain makers occupied a former office space in Johannesburg.[7] A fascinating physical space is in Seoul, South Korea, where small businesses, artisans, and restaurants inhabit a rabbit warren of spaces in the Sewoon Sangga building, a horizontal 1.2-km-long concrete megastructure designed by Kim SooGuen in the late 1960s; it is a linear, mixed-use labyrinthine city, where entrepreneurs make, assemble, and sell electric components (not unlike Huaqiangbei in Shenzhen) but where there is also a new community maker space and rooftop garden.

Figure 10.1 Kim SooGuen Architecture, Sewoon Sanga megastructure, Seoul, South Korea, built in the late 1960s as a mixed-use manufacturing center.

Figure 10.2 Globe Dye Works, a mixed manufacturing building, Philadelphia, 2017.

The below-the-radar businesses become part of the industrial ecology in which the mix of uses and exchange networks become an unexpected engine for economic growth and a model for the more formal economies.

A third, more prevalent, mode of policy initiative involves some combination of all of the above. As Laura Wolf-Powers identifies in this book (Chapter 13), the potential in aligning federal, metropolitan, regional, and local policies into engaging nongovernmental intermediary organizations in this process points one way to the future. Ultimately, no matter the approach city officials take, the crucial challenge is coordinating the disparate city departments of economic development and city planning to consider a community's spatial needs in terms of its relationship to economic equity.

Oversight at different levels of public/private involvement can catalyze industrial growth. These include government sponsorship for industrial zones, ground-up nonprofit projects beyond the capacities of local Business Improvement Districts, and private developers, as seen in Strathcona Village in Vancouver, Industry City in Brooklyn, and Globe Dye Works in Philadelphia. In Brussels and Antwerp it has taken a combination of all three policy initiators, from top-down to bottom-up, to develop industries that are productive and beneficial to the community.

The Zoning Challenge

Land, as our base, is constantly with us, but space is often neglected in terms of its relationship to a local economy and becomes all about economic development as a commodity. Economic geography is the field that correlates economic value and land use, wherein economists evaluate and place a monetary value on industrial location. As a commodity, land acquires value relative to its resources, location, and potential for development and use. Natural resources such as coal, marble, iron ore, gold, wheat, and fish are extracted and processed as commodities nearby or shipped to widespread factories outside the community. Transit nodes, such as maritime ports, then later railroads and highways, and now airports or even drone-launching facilities, connect goods to marketplaces—the transit cost, along with labor power (that of the added value of the worker), must be accounted for in a company's bottom line. As logistics costs increase, reducing transit costs by relocating production to the marketplace is of increasing importance.

When an industry chooses to locate in a city as opposed to near essential natural resources, zoning and land-use controls (developed in the late nineteenth century to separate residential areas from noxious uses) guide the outcome of industrial developments. We sometimes forget that Modern European architects further reinforced the division of urban programs in their ideas for the Functional City, segregating residential, transportation, work, and recreation uses from each other.[8] The legalization of land-use separation in the US came to the fore in the 1926 Supreme Court case of *Euclid vs. Amber*, which enforced zoning to protect residential landowners' investments from undesirable uses, including industry. The idea that urban manufacturing was undesirable (sometimes described as the "pig in the parlor instead of the barnyard") became standard; each use had its own place. As Leonardo Benevolo explores, the suitable location of industrial uses so as not to damage the health and welfare of residents began to define a new profession of Modern urban planning, but in a response to an existing condition rather than anticipating or directing a future vision.[9]

These reactive rather than proactive policies that separate uses result in monotonous neighborhoods in the US, and are now considered outdated in their deterministic approach. As discussed here (and in Bingham and Shapiro, Chapter 11), some efforts toward mixed-use manufacturing districts are visible in New York, Philadelphia, Washington, DC, Berkeley, Portland, Chicago, and San Francisco, among other cities around the globe. For example, some cities try to manage the economic impacts in terms of the numbers and kinds of jobs and the economic viability of different kinds of businesses. In San Francisco, the project sponsor needs to submit a Production, Distribution, and Repair (PDR) Business Plan that explains the kinds of businesses being targeted for the site, including a plan for keeping PDR space affordable, and a detailed overview of the workforce and hiring strategy as well as how various city, state, and federal hiring programs will be utilized. In Chicago, a Planned Manufacturing District review includes consideration of the size of the district, the number of existing firms and employees that would be affected, recent and planned public and private investments within the district, and the potential of the district to support additional industrial uses and increased manufacturing employment. Finally, in Berkeley, the project sponsor needs to "encourage the creation and continuation of well paid jobs which do not require advanced degrees."

On the other hand, many European countries such as Belgium, England, France, and Germany don't use zoning to plan a district holistically but instead use case-by-case projections. In Germany, the land-use plan allows for non-disturbing industries (those that don't pollute or make too much noise) and artisanal workshops in residential areas after city planning review. In England, live-work units are okay as long as they don't change the physical character of the residential building. In the "general urban zone" in France, mixed housing and industrial employment can exist side-by-side. Thus it is worthwhile to inspire planners and economists to reevaluate the potential for mixed uses both at the district and the individual building scale, fostering both industrial retention and rebirth.

Making Space

Building Scale

Imagine a dense vertical city of factories functioning as machines—a rich and energetic cityscape woven with interconnections of skybridges and conveyors—and evoking the sublime futuristic vision similar to designer Hugh Ferriss' renderings of the 1920s.

Providing a space and place for urban manufacturing is essential for equitable jobs, sustainable economies, and diverse vital cities. Zoning policies and building codes have a place in this organization as they can spark new directions in the spatial use decisions at the building, district, and thus urban scale—enabling new factory types, including the construction and rehabilitation of "vertical urban factories."[10] This typology, a multistoried factory (often just four to eight stories tall), has roots in eighteenth-century cotton mills that integrated the processing mechanisms into their building volumes as the function follows flow (see Rappaport, p. 105), harnessing the power of gravity. If policies based on floor-area ratio (FAR) could enable larger

Figure 10.3 Futuristic concept of vertical urban factories.

buildings to be built that are also more flexible in their interior layouts, new factory types might be designed, including taller factories that could create a more dense and compact urbanism and thereby reduce a company's carbon footprint and employees' transit costs as they can live near work, in addition to encouraging a tighter supplier network and consumer base.

However, in most US cities this vision is not enabled by zoning, which tends to favor low-rise factories because of lack of urban vision. In New York City, for example, the M1-1 zones that house light-manufacturing restrict development to a one- to two-FAR maximum with required off-street parking and loading, reducing manufacturing uses to low-slung, one-story buildings. In some cities the industrial use is specified with zoning qualifications such as "enclosed light industry," "low-impact manufacturing," or "warehousing or distribution." Cities designate heavier manufacturing, such as concrete blending and mixing and sanitation facilities, to specifically defined M areas. In New York's historic manufacturing neighborhoods, home to much of the city's stock of original "vertical urban factories"—the loft factories—M1-4, M1-5, and M1-6 zoning allow for taller and bulkier buildings of up to twelve FAR, but often developers don't employ the full allocation of potential space. Often, the higher costs involved in the construction of additional parking, building code requirements such as duplicate elevators, or fire and safety regulations make the development of new factories at these densities unfeasible. However, in locations with higher real estate value for some manufacturers the additional space could increase the viability of new multistory construction, thereby increasing the property value in the long term.[11] Reimagining the multistory factory also corresponds to directions in new manufacturing processes, which can further encourage policies for a new urban industrial ecosystem.

At the building scale some cities are experimenting with their zoning policies to enable denser and taller manufacturing spaces. The city of Geneva, recognizing a shortage of industrial space, held a competition in 2015 with a developer to design a new Hôtel Industriel based on the 1980s-era government-sponsored multitenanted industrial buildings in France.[12] The new zoning policy allowed for a mix of industrial uses in a commercial district. LRS Architects' project consists of three parallel seven-story bars hosting different activities and integrating manufacturing within the city fabric. Located in between the two main building volumes, the off-street loading and receiving areas are separated from pedestrians and the main sidewalk.

Figure 10.4 LRS Architects, rendering of the view from the main street of a proposed Hôtel Industriel, Geneva, Switzerland, 2015.

Figure 10.5 LRS Architects, rendering of the view from the shared courtyard of a proposed Hôtel Industriel, Geneva, Switzerland, 2015.

In Singapore's urban escalation, economic development and city planning agencies have designated industrial land in Jurong City so as not to displace manufacturing with residential. The city is promoting higher FAR in vertical urban factories with thematic industrial zones—airport logistics, clean technology, scientific research, food production, and business incubator space—rather than contributing to urban sprawl.[13] Similar to 1960s Hong Kong's "flatted" factories, the industrial flats (or layered factories) share passenger and freight elevators, loading bays, lobbies, and delivery services to cut costs. For example, the Seletar Aerospace Park houses forty-five aerospace companies in a 320-hectare district dedicated to related activities including the maintenance, repair, and overhaul of aircraft and components; manufacturing and assembly of aircraft engines; business and general aviation; as well as training, research, and development.

Hybrid Spaces

As development pressures on urban industrial spaces continue to intensify, some cities coordinate policies that have to react to change by mandating industrial uses before such pressures cause industrial sites to be overtaken by more lucrative uses. Traditional Euclidian zoning encourages single-use buildings. However, requiring industrial uses in buildings at a specific percentage could reduce the total residential conversion of urban manufacturing spaces. Additionally, to amortize the cost of constructing new industrial space and to provide lower industrial rents necessary for emerging manufacturers, high-density residential development could be used as a subsidy tool in concert with Historic Preservation Tax Credits and New Market Tax Credits, as well as other municipal financial incentives. The mixed-industrial/residential typology faces unique challenges in most building and safety codes that would have to be reevaluated to comply with each of the different uses, along with elevators, fire, safety controls, and loading docks that would satisfy both residential and industrial uses. However, in recognizing the potential for mixed-use spaces, cities can adopt new zoning codes in what can be called "mandatory inclusionary manufacturing,"[14] serving as a catalyst for incubating new urban production methods. Manufacturing, residential, commercial, or even hotel uses can be catalysts to cross-subsidize industrial rent in a new hybrid.

Figure 10.6 Rendering of Seletar Aerospace Park, an urban industrial park, Singapore, 2017.

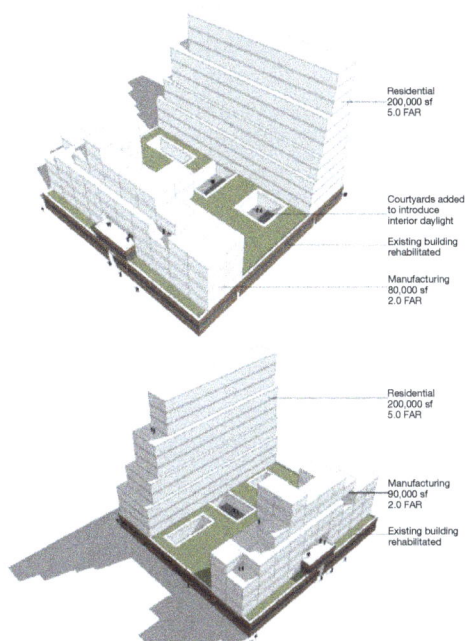

Figure 10.7 Study of potential for manufacturing and residential spaces on one site, and shared common areas, by Andy Urbany and Peter Horan/NYU/Vertical Urban Factory.

A recent study on the potential for this mixed-use typology,[15] the question of whether or not residential uses in a building can help to subsidize manufacturing spaces in that same building in the current high-valued real estate climate was evaluated for a site in Brooklyn. If on average in New York's more industrial neighborhoods industrial space rents for $15–20 per square foot (as of 2017), in order to maintain this threshold residential rentals would be required at $65–75 per square foot for a one-bedroom unit. However, there could be separate equity and debt sources so that each space would be funded separately using New Market Tax Credits for the building's manufacturing portion. The residential-portion income could pay for site acquisition or improvement, which also subsidizes the manufacturing to reduce development costs. The difference between this mixed-use development project and that of a purely manufacturing use is the cross-subsidy to finance the hybrid project and enforce the provision of industrial space; however, in a city such as New York, enforcement continues to be difficult.

In north Crown Heights, Brooklyn, Community Board 8 (CB8) is proposing a similar idea to that of mandatory inclusionary industry.[16] In a six-block area that is zoned M1-1, where industrial uses of parking lots, machinists, and car mechanics are directly across the street from low-rise residential buildings, industrial site owners, who are among the community stakeholders, are sitting on their properties because it is too expensive to build just a one-story building. The community's new concept for the zone—known as "M-CROWN"—is to mandate 1.5 FAR for industrial uses, after which an owner has the option to build up to an additional 4.1 FAR for either industrial or residential use. Residential development will be required to set aside 20 percent of the resulting apartments as affordable housing. While CB8 expects that most new development occurring under the M-CROWN plan would locate industrial uses on the lower floors with residential above, it also proposes allowing the transfer of both development rights and development obligations for additional market flexibility in maximizing the potential for both manufacturing space and residential units in the M-CROWN zone. CB8 calculates that the M-CROWN plan would allow for 845,000 square feet of new manufacturing space in the district. As the CB8 Chair Nizjoni Granville notes,

> During the ten years that the Community Board has studied development options for the M-CROWN zone, residential and retail interest in western Crown Heights has soared. The flip side is that the neighborhood is in even greater need of living-wage jobs for families and affordable apartments. With the proper mixed-use zoning, the M-CROWN district represents an opportunity to unlock tremendous value for the community from an area that is now a development desert.[17]

This neighborhood makes for a perfect case study to model in other fragile industrial districts being pressured by residential development. Other cities are experimenting with similar strategies, such as Portland, with a 3,000-square-foot requirement of industrial floor area use within all buildings in the city's former industrial employment zone.

Developers in some cities have received government support and even encouragement for experimenting with this new combination. In Vancouver, the Wall Financial Corporation completed an innovative mixed-use building complex called Strathcona Village that combines residential condos with light-industrial spaces. The city changed the zoning in order to mix light manufacturing with housing. The neighborhood, which sits alongside an active container port and sugar refinery, includes companies that make marine propellers for ships, as well

Figure 10.8 Proposal for M-CROWN plan, showing residential and non-residential uses as built, Crown Heights, Brooklyn, New York, 2017. Current zoning above. Proposed zoning below.

Figure 10.9 GBL Architects: Strathcona Village and mixed-use volumes made visible through design and massing concepts, Vancouver, British Columbia, 2018.

as breweries, wine distributors, and a residential area. While the site was zoned as low-rise industrial, the city changed the zoning to allow the developer to build a taller mixed-use project. The composition of the building is mixed both in terms of income levels and programs, with both housing and 64,000 square feet of light-industrial space. GBL Architects designed a horizontal podium for commercial and industrial uses that features three integrated, vertical but independent volumes so that light-industrial space with all the functional requirements for manufacturing, including easy truck access, is in the rear lower floors along Hastings Street and Raymur Avenue. The city policy required that large windows and garage-style doors be installed to activate the streetscape with production.

District Scale

A number of cities are experimenting with innovative regulations and policies that can retain or grow manufacturing at the district scale. Somerville, Massachusetts, in 2017, proposed a new "Fabrication" zoning area to preserve existing workspace and provide smaller incubator space for both arts-related uses and other creative businesses that focus primarily on production. The zoning would require five percent of the floor area of any new building to be set aside for artisans, which, by increasing the availability of spaces, would keep the space affordable. The zoning allows for mixed-use and multitenanted buildings of up to four stories but would prohibit residential use. The proposed basic loft buildings for all types of production would encourage large floor plates with a facade at the street wall rather than setbacks to create an urban district supporting pedestrian life. Other districts would be restricted to industrial commercial uses only. This new zoning overlay has the potential to be a model for small and light industries in other cities.

The city of Washington, D.C. is promoting economic growth and light industry, focusing on Ward 5, an industrial-zoned 1,000-acre area on east New York Avenue. This area, with numerous low-rise brick and metal factory sheds and vacant lots, has seen recent strong employment growth in the emergence of over 500 businesses. Both the mayor and the economic development

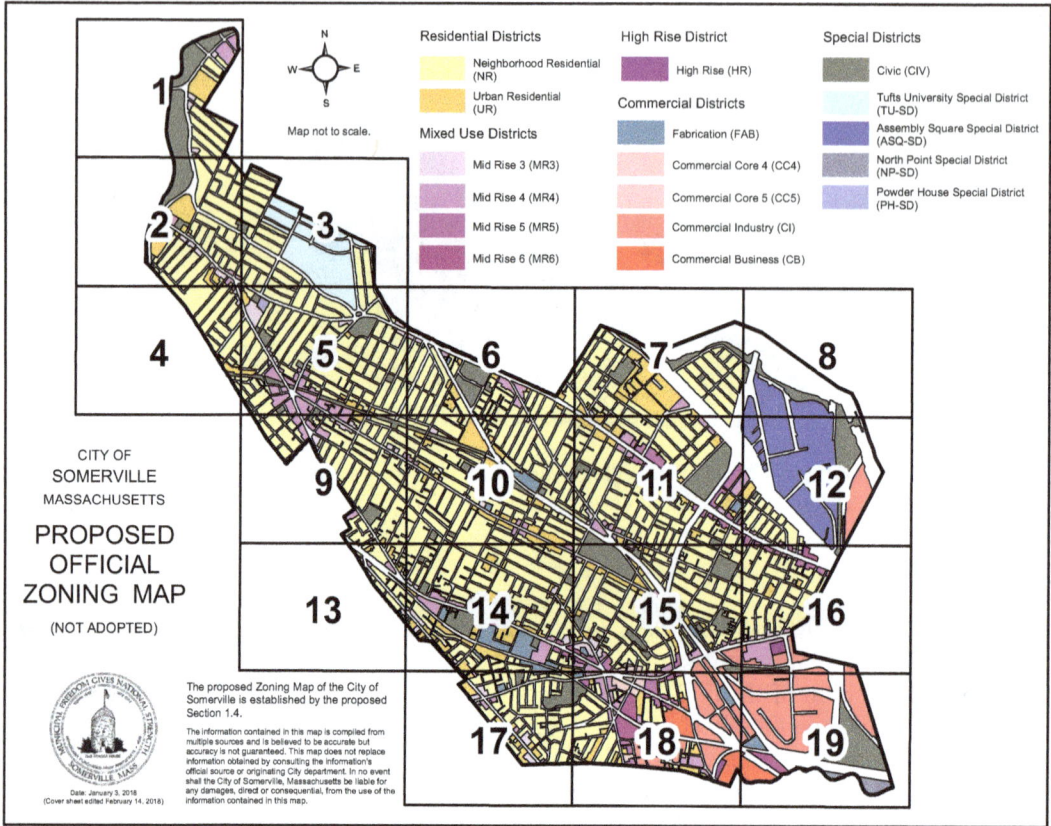

Figure 10.10 Proposed zoning map for Somerville, Massachusetts showing the new Fabrication zones in blue and the fine-grain potential for rezoning for mixed use.

office see potential for new light manufacturing because in that city region the reverse has occurred—land is more expensive on nearby suburban greenfield sites—making exurban industrial development tougher. The Industrial Land Transformation Task Force developed a plan in 2013 to analyze the area, recommending increased industrial use such as light manufacturing, alcoholic beverage and food production, arts, and sustainable businesses—to diversify local job opportunities. The city is also investigating ways to improve services in the area through mixed-use projects. The city uses the mechanism of the Planned Unit Development (PUD) as part of the evaluation process for a case-by-case-basis project review that could have advantages for industrial development. This would preference projects that diverge from the standard zoning code, such as taller factories that could be approved if they are seen as valuable assets to the local economy.

Land Banking

Another instrument to stabilize industry at the district scale is land banking. Used primarily for housing that has been foreclosed or abandoned, which is thus owned by the local government,

Figure 10.11 The mixed industrial waterfront of Brussels with planning underway to maintain industry.

land banks are non-governmental organizations that have a legal statute to assemble properties with community oversight through a board of directors. The land bank receives land or property from donations, or purchases vacant sites at low-cost public auctions; after gaining the rights to the properties it can maintain, rent, sell, or develop them. The land bank's income often comes from government or private foundation grants as well as rent paid by new or existing developments. Rather than sell a property to the highest bidder, the property under the management of the community organization focuses on what is best for local economic sustainability. As a fairly new land-use policy tool, land banking can direct the development of sites, especially in "shrinking cities" where jobs and population have decreased, while the land continues to exist and needs a forward direction to be productive, rather than to languish. In the US, land banks are being used in cities such as St. Louis, Atlanta, and Flint, Michigan, focusing on affordable housing. In Cleveland, one model project is a case in which an industrial-commercial land bank acquired 100 brownfield sites, allowing 30 acres to be reactivated for industry.

Antwerp, Belgium is also directing a new policy by means of a land bank to develop underutilized industrial sites in the neglected district of Hoboken. To develop more industry there, the city planning department organized a coalition of landowners and companies with joint interests in an industrial zone with many brownfield sites and abandoned housing. Using a land bank the owners are coordinating the undeveloped sites or in-between spaces beyond their own borders, to revalue them and propose future developments as a cooperative.[18] While the city will not own the properties, it will guide a master plan framework so that social and design quality will be achieved in any redevelopment. Nine out of ten landowners have signed a Declaration of Engagement for a fair distribution of the value of the future development; as a flexible document, it allows owners to sign on only to those parts to which they agree. Included in the plan are new industrial spaces for low-skilled employment, parks and open space, and new public transit. The coalition and the city would like to encourage mixed-use living and working so that companies can stay and grow but also be integrated into a mixed-use neighborhood.

Beyond Industrial Retention: Mixed-Use

Planning for and promoting a mix of uses in a district are valuable ways to encourage diversity and vibrancy where spaces for working and living are in proximity, leading to neighborhoods that are dynamic around the clock. Often stymied by prescriptive and outdated zoning policies, these vibrant, diverse districts can be encouraged through new tools such as land banking, performance-based zoning, "mixed-use" or "MX" zones, and air rights transfer mechanisms—tools that can shift the balance from typical development patterns toward industrial growth and a mix of uses. If we consider, as did British architect Cedric Price, that a city is a scrambled egg, where everyone and everything mixes, zoning restrictions need to be unraveled for urban life that is truly mixed. Other situations require that new zoning regulations be established as part of a district- or citywide zoning plan that relaxes the regulations and thus entices experimentation. A twentieth-century zoning ordinance focused on strictly segregating uses will never be able to achieve the urban typologies that will define the twenty-first-century city. Other scenarios for mixing uses both nationally and internationally illustrate the potential of this approach.

Mixed-Use Zoning

One mechanism is that of mixed-use zoning districts. As Jenifer Becker and Adam Friedman discuss (Chapter 11), a mix of commercial and industrial uses are possible where industrial has to be enforced more strongly. However, when a district allows commercial, residential, and industrial all within its confines, residential and commercial uses are economically the "highest and best use of the land" and under normal market conditions always win out in development scenarios. Such "MX" zones in New York City are one example where the zoning's traction for encouraging or protecting industrial uses is fragile at best. For instance, one recent transitional project is the Brooklyn Generator developed by Toby Moscovits of Heritage Equity Partners and located at 25 Kent Street in an industrial zone in Williamsburg, Brooklyn. The new eight-story, 480,000-square-foot building designed by HWKA with Gensler includes office space with light-industrial uses.

Figure 10.12 Williamsburg Generator, rendering by HWKA with Gensler, Williamsburg, Brooklyn, New York City, 2016.

As part of an overall fourteen-block rezoning plan, industrial advocates have argued that the project, as a precedent, will have a negative impact on other industrial parcels as it only contains 17 percent industrial space, which is being considered as a bonus in exchange for more commercial space. Instead, what would happen if the building could have a higher percentage of industrial than office space and augment the loss of industrial space in the community? As Philadelphia learned in 2012, the planning department's IRMX (industrial residential mixed-use district) was too broad and flexible; as a result, residential uses seeped into the industrial sites, requiring an amendment three years later mandating that industrial use account for at least 50 percent of the ground floor and allowing both industrial and retail uses to be located on any floor of any building in the district. Globe Dye Works, a large brick, multistoried former thread-dying factory in North Philadelphia, has added work-live units in a lower-rise section of the complex within a side alley, realizing the intended mixed-use concept. Variances can also assist industries, as Beth Bingham and John Shapiro discuss (Chapter 11), where they explore the potential transfer of development rights (TDRs) as a way to set aside and incentivize space for industry when the highest and best use of the land is residential.

Following upon the ideas for mixed-use vertical urban factories, New York City's Economic Development Corporation began a project to support a change in zoning in Long Island City's Hunter's Point South to allow for a 1.5-million-square-foot development, one-fifth of which was to be allocated to light manufacturing.

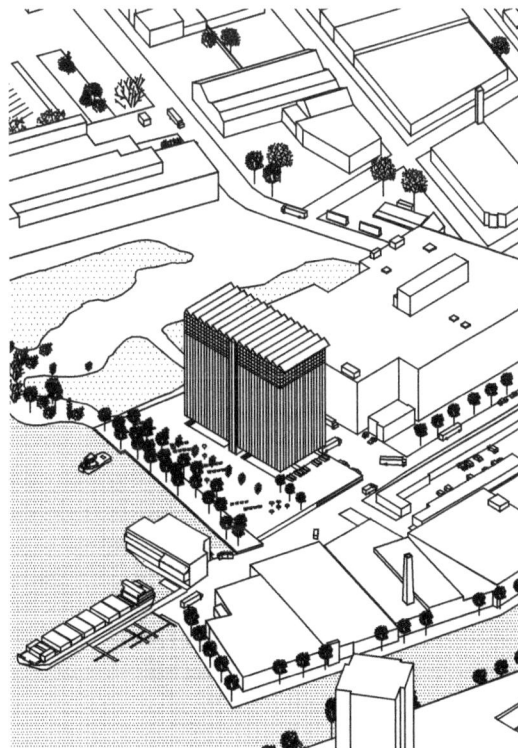

Figure 10.13 Project from Summer Studio 2016 with the University of KU Leuven; rendering of building design to include mixed uses on Long Island City's waterfront.

In an RFP that was awarded in 2017 to TF Cornerstone properties, towers were to contain market-rate affordable housing, retail space, office space, and community amenities. Of particular interest is that the Greenpoint Manufacturing and Design Center was to manage new light-manufacturing spaces as a nonprofit developer. However, in 2018, Amazon was negotiating with the city to obtain the site for their new headquarters. But with lack of community support for their project, they pulled out, and the city is back to square one. As of 2019, the site is being reevaluted by city planning for a fresh start.

Many existing and well-appointed factory buildings, now too large for one company, are perfect to lease to numerous tenants in a "flexible" factory. Andrew Kimball describes this scenario below (p. 230) in writing about Industry City in Sunset Park, Brooklyn, where the owners are seeking zoning changes to allow for a flexible, innovative approach. The mix becomes an essential way to merge innovative new industries and technologies with production in a synergistic industrial space.

Mixed-use districts are also evolving in Belgium, where the city planning departments are creating a new equilibrium as they integrate industries into new urban amalgamations. "Zones of Enterprises" were established in the Brussels Canal Area to stimulate developers to build projects in the midst of abandoned factories. The linear canal with numerous heavy-industrial uses along its shores, and where goods are still transported by barge, operates as a link between urban regions. The city's policy goal is to maintain industrial space for blue-collar jobs while also allowing for new housing that will be limited in size and cost. In terms of economic incentives, new grants and low-interest loans are being provided to stimulate business development. The area is also filled with more informal auto repair and shipping industries that are finally being recognized as legitimate businesses because of the entrepreneurship involved. In order to both identify and achieve this mix, the city departments are collaborating on both building-by-building and site-by-site bases so that the projects comply with noise, pollution, and traffic requirements to allow for the cohabitation of working and living.

Antwerp's Labo XX study, aimed at developing strategies for urban renewal, addresses the city's interest in developing strong industrial and logistics sectors.[19] The guidelines support the use of multistoried buildings, collective amenities, and flexible buildings for industry. While interweaving commercial with other building functions is often not possible—or only achievable on a limited scale—the Belgian economists feel that the inclusion of housing in the area could open up other space for manufacturing and logistics facilities. They also believe in dedicating some specific zones to industries that are harsher on the environment, and plan to remediate brownfields and undeveloped and difficult-to-access sites, such as those "landlocked" between highways. Working in cooperation with the spatial planning department, the economic development office is assisting with policy implementation through an advisory role in granting permits for economic activity. As head of the department, Bart de Greef notes, "the remarks given by the community are actually taken into account and can determine the outcome of the process."[20] This cooperation takes many forms: providing input and study material; participating in juries for awarding studies; and collaborating in work groups for policy paper development. Current projects include the Blue Gate Antwerp, a brownfield where they are targeting sustainable industries in a public–private partnership for new industrial growth. North of the city, in an investment zone, larger multinational companies are engaging in environmental cleanup projects and enlarging their waterfront sites while receiving tax benefits. The synergy between economic development, industrial growth, and new forms of land use is an active policy proposition around which the different government agencies are aligned in their support for urban manufacturing. The idea of creating a new mixed-industrial city within the urban fabric reinforces the potential for working and living as a means of enriching urban life. As Jane Jacobs observed, "To understand cities, we have to deal outright with combinations or mixtures of uses, not separate uses, as the essential phenomena."[21] Thus it is worthwhile to maintain a complexly networked and layered urbanism that resonates in its multifunctionality.

Performance Zoning for a Remix

One strategy to promote mixed use is to regulate uses not on the basis of prescribed lists of specific activities—which is especially problematic for the rapidly evolving manufacturing sector—but on the basis of performance: the effect of a facility on a site and adjacent sites in terms of its impacts. These may be environmental, such as noise and odors, which cannot be quantified, or operational, such as hours of delivery; or, when more broadly conceived, performance can include the impact on long-term policy objectives such as effect on the overall character of the district. Performance zoning, which is more prevalent in Europe than in the US, may not address a building's design, which is accounted for through building codes, but it does encourage elasticity and adaptability for uses that would otherwise be considered incompatible, such as a much-needed supermarket in a primarily residential area or, more to the point, a clean manufacturer in an urban neighborhood. For example, in Chicago negative industrial performance is limited to heavy-industry zones, whereas lighter industries without much output can be included in a light-industry zone. However, if the company meets all of the performance zoning requirements it could actually be built in any number of districts within the city.

Performance zoning would thus allow for the "pig to be in the parlor" after all, if the pig is a clean one. Furthermore, the performance basis actually could incentivize a company to build a more sustainable factory because the industrial building has to perform more efficiently than one sequestered in an industrial district. A shift to performance zoning would encourage increasingly mixed-use areas in cities in a proactive engagement. However, this would require a significant commitment on the part of the city as well as the capacity to monitor and enforce the performance standards.

Conclusion

If we can focus on ways to return manufacturing to cities through land use and economic policies, a potential exists to redefine the urban factory at a crucial time in history when rapid technological advances are catalyzing cross-fertilization, tech innovation, and job development. This opportunity demands new architectural and urban design typologies that activate the open and cosmopolitan city with visual textures and activity. Land use and economic initiatives that guide the future of the new economy's productive city must influence the provision of flexible industrial space that is able to adapt—free of onerous and outdated regulations—to meet the challenges of financial and spatial pressures. While the "diverse city" is an oft-lauded part of today's zeitgeist, it is a fragile ideal that is often lost because politicians too often tilt the balance to the highest bidder; this has led to today's urban homogeneity. It is hoped that the concepts presented here can inspire policies that connect public to private, federal to state, city to neighborhood, and community to household, and have the potential to provide ample space and incentives for manufacturing in cities, ultimately providing places for jobs providing sustainable livelihoods. However, the overall question remains: who will take up the task of reforming these policies and zoning laws, and who can be trusted to monitor and maintain them?

While the monotonous industrial districts of the global supply chain are important for intensive industries of mass production and for clustering innovation, as noted in chapters earlier in this book, the changing nature of industrial technology and the needs of sustainable cities will allow manufacturing to be increasingly dispersed within (no longer simply outside of) the city. Perhaps then people will be making or assembling goods in small batches within residential areas rather than industrial ones. This "neo-cottage" scenario is local, sustainable, and adaptable, although it still needs to be monitored for safety, job equity, and fair labor regulations. And what if industrial zoning restrictions are lifted altogether? Is there still a need for the separation of uses at all, especially given other regulations on pollution and public health? Producers in the new economy would be able to freely make things in their own "cottages" as they did in the nineteenth century. From 3D printing to robotics, new technologies are making it possible to manufacture not just crafts in the home, but bicycles, fashion, furniture, and even engine parts. Urban manufacturing is undergoing a radical transformation; it is nonpolluting, lighter, smaller, and smarter—and with future transportation modes such as drones, goods are already flying into the locally based marketplace. If we intelligently support it, industry can be as ubiquitous as other urban infrastructures and can benefit society by throwing open pathways to increasing prosperity, a higher quality of life, ever-greater sustainability, and social and socioeconomic equity.

Notes

1 See Nina Rappaport, *Vertical Urban Factory*, (Barcelona: Actar, 2015).
2 Henri Lefebvre, *Production of Space*, trans. D. Nicholson-Smith, (1974; Cambridge, MA: Blackwell Publishing, 1991).
3 Nina Rappaport, *Vertical Urban Factory*, 62.
4 Keller Easterling, Naomi Klein, and others discuss this topic in depth.
5 Robert Neuwirth, *The Global Rise of the Informal Economy*, (New York, NY: Pantheon Books, 2011).
6 OECD 2009 study, and GDP World Bank, (2013), www.world.bank.org.
7 Study by Hannah Le Roux, senior lecturer at Johannesburg University of Witwatersrand, South Africa, 2010.
8 The Congres Internationaux d'Architecture Moderne (CIAM) developed separate functions for living in their 1928 Sarraz Declaration that they used to guide city design. They described this further in their 1933 Charter of Athens with the division of housing, work, recreation, and traffic. See Ulrich Conrads, *Programs and Manifestoes on 20th-Century Architecture*, (Cambridge, MA: The MIT Press, 1964).
9 Leonardo Benevolo, *The Origins of Modern Town Planning* (Cambridge, MA: The MIT Press, 1971).
10 See Nina Rappaport, *Vertical Urban Factory*, describing this building type.
11 *Ibid.*; also see new projects for Boyce Electronics in Long Island City, Queens, built in 2017 as a three-story factory.
12 www.paris.fr/pro/2d3es-hebergement-d-entreprises/poles-d-entreprises/rub_9529_stand_22927_port_23414.
13 JTC Corporation Annual Report 2014, Singapore.
14 Inclusionary Manufacturing is a concept that developed as part of the "vertical urban factory," to require manufacturing as part of developments.
15 Study conducted for Vertical Urban Factory, 2016.
16 See Nina Rappaport, *Vertical Urban Factory* and testimony at New York City Council Land Use Committee Hearing in May 2015.
17 Discussion with Nizjoni Granville, January 2018.
18 As in a cooperative model the landowners will be the corporation stakeholders. The intent to form this corporation will be formalized in a letter of intent between the owners.
19 *Lab XX*, study by the City of Antwerp, April 2016.
20 Discussion between Nina Rappaport and Bart De Greef, May 2016.
21 Jane Jacobs, *Death and Life of Great American Cities*, (New York, NY: Random House, 1961).

11 Land Use Regulation for Manufacturing

Beth Bingham and John Shapiro

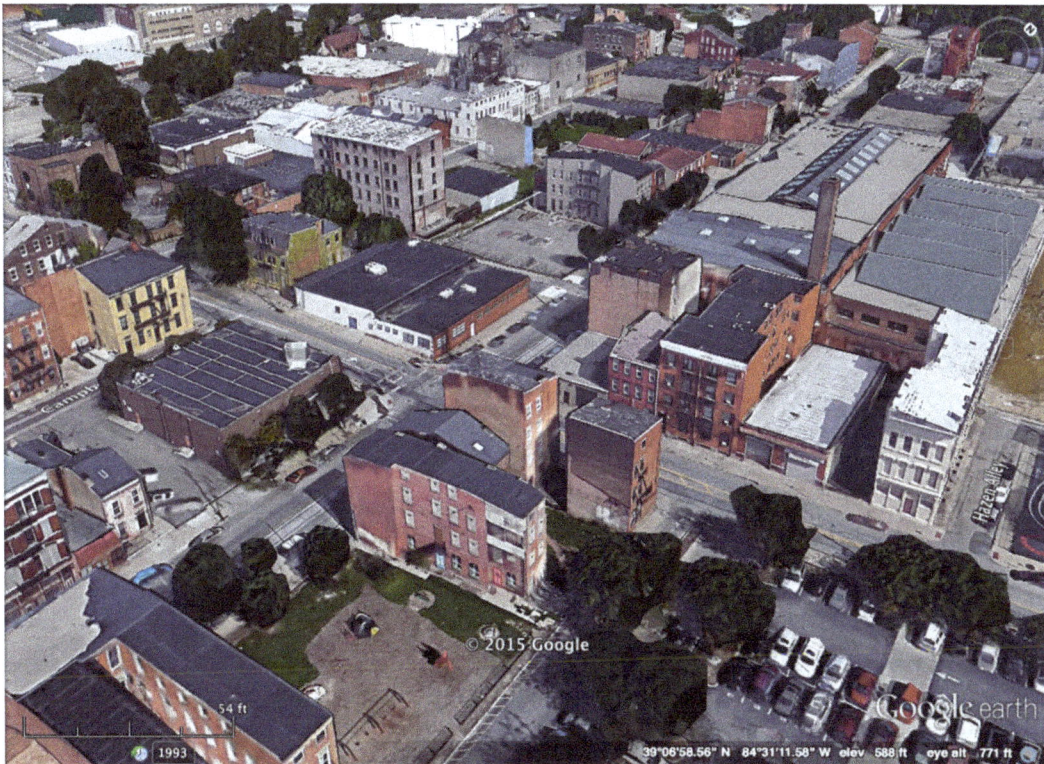

Figure 11.1 Mixed industrial neighborhoods are flexible but raise a host of challenges for regulators.

Google Earth

Industrial Precincts: Protective but Inflexible

The most direct way to protect industry is defensive: prohibit all other uses in a district, as done by cities as different as Baltimore and Berkeley. The original and still largely valid assumption is that manufacturing's negative impacts on other uses means it should be isolated. Speculators are held at bay and property owners lease space for longer periods, allowing industrial tenants to invest in their physical plants and equipment.

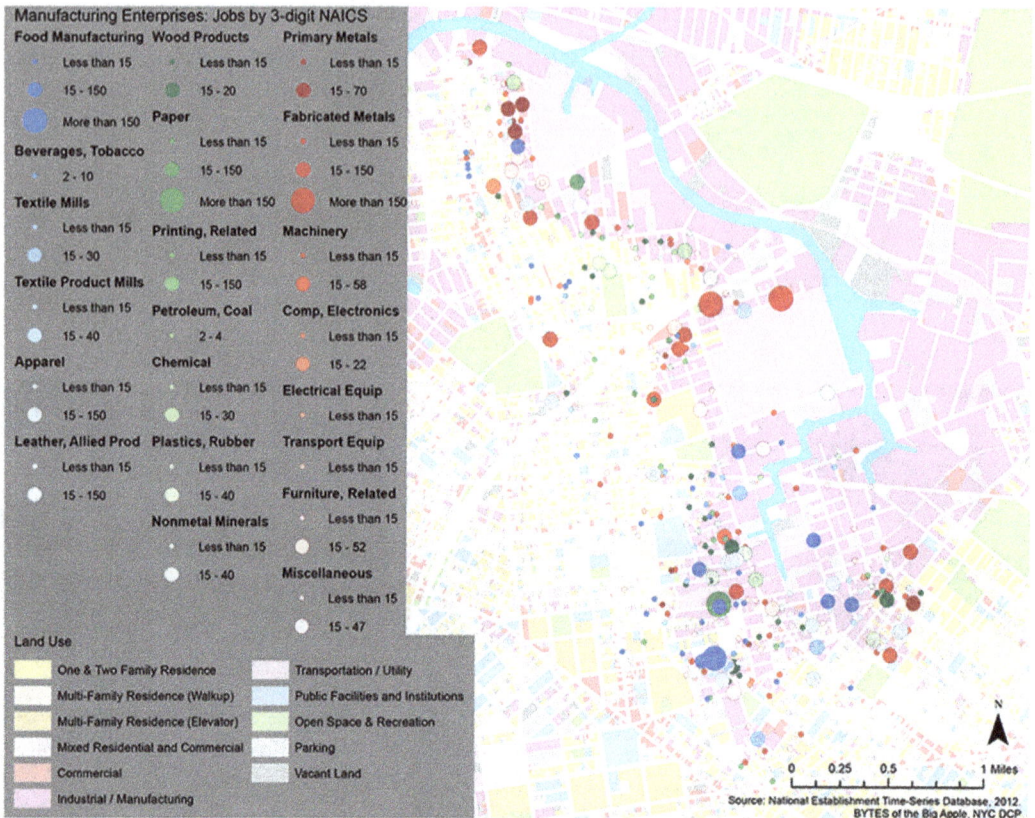

Manufacturing Enterprises: Jobs by 3-digit NAICS

Food Manufacturing	Wood Products	Primary Metals
Less than 15	Less than 15	Less than 15
15 - 150	15 - 20	15 - 70
More than 150	Paper	Fabricated Metals
Beverages, Tobacco	Less than 15	Less than 15
2 - 10	15 - 150	15 - 150
Textile Mills	More than 150	More than 150
Less than 15	Printing, Related	Machinery
15 - 30	Less than 15	Less than 15
Textile Product Mills	15 - 150	15 - 58
Less than 15	Petroleum, Coal	Comp, Electronics
15 - 40	2 - 4	Less than 15
Apparel	Chemical	15 - 22
Less than 15	Less than 15	Electrical Equip
15 - 150	15 - 30	Less than 15
Leather, Allied Prod	Plastics, Rubber	Transport Equip
Less than 15	Less than 15	Less than 15
15 - 150	15 - 40	Furniture, Related
	Nonmetal Minerals	Less than 15
	Less than 15	15 - 52
	15 - 40	Miscellaneous
		Less than 15
		15 - 47

Land Use

One & Two Family Residence Transportation / Utility
Multi-Family Residence (Walkup) Public Facilities and Institutions
Multi-Family Residence (Elevator) Open Space & Recreation
Mixed Residential and Commercial Parking
Commercial Vacant Land
Industrial / Manufacturing

0   0.25   0.5   1 Miles

Source: National Establishment Time-Series Database, 2012.
BYTES of the Big Apple, NYC DCP

Figure 11.2 Exclusive precincts for manufacturing are often confounded by persistent mixed-use patterns. In East Williamsburg, Brooklyn, manufacturing uses represented here by the colored dots, infiltrate the adjacent residential zones.

Segregated precincts for "heavy" or "medium" industrial uses, sometimes also called Intensive High Impact (Cleveland) or General Manufacturing industries, will always be needed. Every city makes this distinction in one way or another. But the precinct approach raises at least three challenges. First, making a definitive list of what should be allowed or prohibited in a more mixed light-manufacturing district is not so easy. The definitions for manufacturing uses are rooted in the local economy and reflect local administrative practices with regards to prescription or discretion. Further, the nature of manufacturing changes so that the use lists become outdated. Some cities, such as Portland, Oregon, have expanded their lists of manufacturing activities to include new forms of production such as media, computer/electronic equipment, and software and web development.

Second, all cities allow for ancillary or accessory uses in light-industrial districts, acknowledging that there is a larger ecology of production, design, and consumption in an urban manufacturing district. In its Central East Side industrial district, Portland identified specific accessory uses that should be permitted to support "target industries" in two new categories:

industrial-serving (engineering, occupational health facilities, construction, and maintenance) and industrial-like (film/video/photography, studio art, and computer-based media).

Mixed Use: Beware of Unintended Consequences

City planners are turning to mixed-use zoning, believing that single-use zoning is not sustainable given that industry is often not able to compete financially or politically with alternative land uses, and hoping that the higher market value of the alternative uses can provide cross-subsidies for industry (see Rappaport, Chapter 5, p. 119).

Mixed use comes in two forms. The first is horizontal mixed use, where industry exists side-by-side with other uses such as housing, as is common in older cities. In north Brooklyn in the 1970s, mixed-use (MX) zoning was mapped to reflect a century-old reality, making the residences in a previously industrial zone fully legal rather than a grandfathered preexisting condition.[1] Also in the 1970s, a vertical mixed-use precedent emerged in some buildings as "loft conversions." The uses were initially quasi-industrial, with artists working in sculpture, painting, and other mediums, and the impacts of those activities, including deliveries, noise, and noxious odors, were akin to those of conventional industry. Manhattan's SoHo neighborhood was the trendsetter.[2] Generally, cities adopted regulations that overlaid mixed-use zoning regulations on top of preexisting industrial base zones.

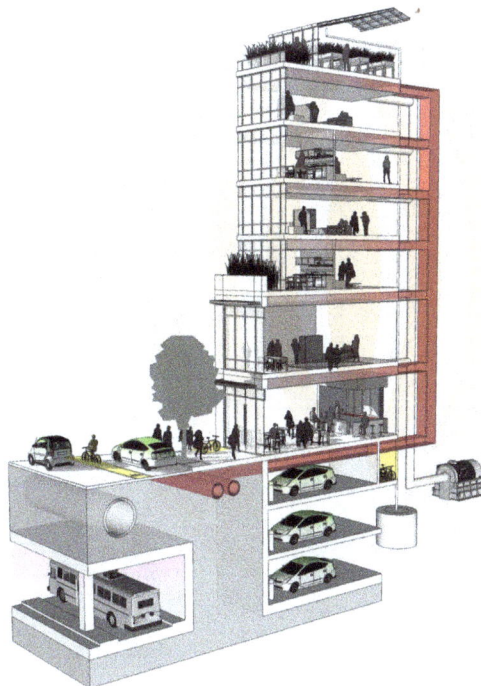

Figure 11.3 Vertical industrial mixed-use buildings enable single owners to cross-subsidize manufacturing.

These mixed-use approaches can have unintended consequences. Zoning ordinances typically itemize uses that are grouped, mindful of their impacts. Housing, offices, and retail are predictable and stable in their impacts. Industry's impacts can fluctuate due to changing technologies (as happened with printing), business practices (as with the amount of deliveries), site conditions (as with sites subject to flooding), security concerns (as with technology firms), and constituent sympathies (as with the popularity of artist studios). Cities vary widely in how they handle definitions and use groups, typically drawing on unique experiences that are hyperlocal and snapshots in time. Perhaps one solution is for an entity such as the American Planning Association to produce, define, and regularly update a model array of industrial uses including characterizations of their impacts. Another solution is to employ "performance" standards in lieu of use groups and definitions (see Rappaport, Chapter 10, p. 201). The two might be combined, with performance standards employed when special permits and exceptions are granted.

In a mixed-use district, the first generation of residential and commercial users may be more tolerant of the noxiousness of their industrial neighbors. The gritty environment may even be enjoyed as authentic and a "cool factor." Not so with later generations of residents—leading to a steady drumbeat for the removal of industry. Regarding the Arts District in Los Angeles: the illegal conversions of the 1970s were retroactively legalized with the 1981 Artist in Residence

Figure 11.4 In the long term, manufacturers and residents may have trouble remaining happy as neighbors, Berkeley, California.

(AIR) regulations; later, conventional residential developments were allowed following the 2001 Adaptive Reuse Ordinance; the industrial district was eventually obliterated. One mitigation might be to have zoning favor unit typologies (lofts, smaller apartments) that skew the market toward alternative lifestyles and transience rather than families with children.

Where there is mixed use on the same site, landlords (whether developers or condo associations) may subvert the intention of the regulations by only renting to quasi-industrial tenants (such as artists and artisans); by designing new buildings and spaces in ways that are problematic for most industry (with low ceilings, supporting pillars, small footprints, and no loading docks); or by cynically leaving the space empty (claiming that tenants cannot be found). One counter-intuitive policy option is to be resigned to this phenomenon, as such space absorbs a source of demand that would otherwise supplant conventional industries elsewhere. Another policy is to increase the amount of industrial space, for instance, requiring two stories of industry for vertical mixed use, or by requiring vertical mixed use in suitable areas that are now single-purpose residential or commercial (such as where industry is the preexisting, nonconforming use) (see Rappaport, Chapter 10, p. 192). A further option is to require deed restrictions or deeding to a nonprofit dedicated to industry (see Becker and Friedman, Chapter 12, p. 214).

A final unintended consequence of mixed use is that there is now greater opportunity for variances. As described below, variances are already significantly undermining the industrial integrity of many districts, and will be more so when it can be argued that nonindustrial development has been allowed and therefore is no longer contrary to neighborhood character.

Variances: Death by a Thousand Cuts

Variances refer to waivers from zoning rules granted by municipal zoning entities when the full enforcement of the ordinance will result in a hardship for the owner. Land-use changes granted by variances differ from those allowable with special permits, which are subject to meeting special conditions and/or accomplishing determined public interests. "Area" variances may be granted for built forms and site plans. Typically the property owner must only show that the area zoning restrictions are unreasonable about the permitted uses of the district. "Use" variances are harder to obtain, and are generally contingent on demonstrating economic hardship on the part of the property owner, and that the project is not a detriment to the immediate area and the public good.

Area variances—and under some circumstances use variances—may benefit industry. Chicago allows area variances to reduce requirements for parking, accessory buildings, curb cuts, building heights, and use of undersized lots. Cincinnati also does this for building placement, yard dimensions, storage containers, and parking lot location and landscaping. A use variance could be about accessory uses such as ancillary retail, offices, showrooms, or outdoor storage.

In many cities sympathetic boards of appeal skew in favor of the applicants. This is often the case when municipal leaders are sympathetic to the applicant's intentions, have negotiated popular features (such as waterfront parks), have put forward the proposal themselves, or are unsympathetic to the underlying zoning but unprepared to go through the time and controversy associated with area-wide rezoning. These circumstances have been evident over decades with regard to New York City's mixed-use and waterfront industrial districts.

New York State requires that proofs be met before the Board of Standards and Appeals (BSA) may grant a use variance. The first is that the owner cannot make "a sufficient return" on investment for each use permitted; the proof is not satisfied by the proposed use simply being more

Figure 11.5 The proposed form-based code for Cincinnati includes design guidelines for industrial mixed use.

profitable than the prescribed use. The second proof is that the site itself presents "unique" circumstances not prevalent in the neighborhood; to do otherwise would lead to the equivalent of a legislative act as other properties seek the same—now precedented—variance. For both proofs neither the hardship nor the unique site condition can be self-created, e.g., the result of paying too much for the property or creating a brownfield condition to be remediated. The third proof is that the proposed use will not alter the "essential" character of the neighborhood; this includes setting in motion other actions that would alter the neighborhood's essence. Note that there is considerable room for interpretation in the words "sufficient," "unique," and "essential."

In the Greenpoint-Williamsburg waterfront neighborhood, the BSA granted more than eighty variances between 1995 and 2002 to applicants seeking to create loft apartments in industrial buildings or to build new housing on land zoned for manufacturing.[3] Meanwhile there has been a steady process of rezoning from industry to mixed use and from industry and mixed use to residential.

One idea might be to have a special permit for mixed use that can only be triggered once the need for a use variance is determined, allowing the planning board to weigh in about mitigation and other considerations. A further idea is to require that the alternative program represent the least deviation from the underlining zoning and existing neighborhood character. Generally the norm about multistory industrial buildings is to allow outright residential conversion. A new variance law could specify that the proposal must minimize the loss of industrial space to achieve "sufficient" project viability.

Performance Broadly Conceived

The requirement cited above to maintain the "essential character" of the district suggests the opportunity to expand the concept of "performance" to address not only environmental standards for things like noise and dust but to capture broader policy objectives relevant to the entire district. Cleveland considers whether the hardship is significant (e.g., rises to bordering on or equal to "a taking") and whether the new development would be consistent with not only the prevailing land use, but also the built conditions of the district. Cincinnati considers whether the new development would introduce land-use conflicts and nuisance complaints. Boston calls for design review. In Chicago's Planned Manufacturing Districts, the evaluation considerations include the area's importance to the city's industrial base; evidence of conflict with or encroachment on industrial uses by nonindustrial uses; the demand for zoning changes or use conversions that may be incompatible with the character of the manufacturing district; the continuing industrial viability of the area; whether the property owner made efforts to market the property for industrial use; and the impact on the number and types of jobs in the district.

Taken together, these softer "performance objectives" constitute a kind of discretionary regime that enables cities to curate the uses in the district. In San Francisco the property owner of Production, Distribution, and Repair (PDR) district projects needs to submit an annual report to the Planning Department describing progress on its PDR Business Plan. In Chicago the Plan Commission monitors the effectiveness of planned manufacturing districts in achieving their stated purposes. However, few cities track performance over time.

TDR: Turning it Upside-Down

Several tools have been developed that can address the market pressures from higher-value land uses, including the Transfer of Development Rights (TDR), in which excess development rights associated with industrial sites can be transferred to other noncontiguous sites.

Success is contingent on three factors. First, there needs to be a "seller's market," otherwise there is no benefit to the owner of the "sending site." In the case of industry the most likely way to achieve this entails a shift to a more lucrative use, such as housing, on the "receiving site." Note that this requires intermittent recalibrations reflecting changing market values. Also the transfer need not be one-to-one. For instance, two square feet of industrial development rights might be convertible to one square foot of housing on another site.

Second, there needs to be a nearby place where the change of use and/or higher density is acceptable. With greater distance it is less likely that the TDR can be legally or politically justified on the basis that the impacts of the development are being realized in the same area. For these reasons TDR may also be tied to major public improvements proximate to the receiving site in addition to preserving industry. This could be accomplished by supplementing the TDR with impact fees and/or incentive zoning requirements. TDR is a key feature of the recent rezoning of East Midtown, Manhattan, where designated landmarks can transfer their unused development rights anywhere in the district—only for commercial development—and subject to an exaction for public realm improvements (set as the higher of either 20 percent of the value of the transaction or a set per-square-foot dollar figure subject to update).

Third, there is a recognizable marketplace for the TDR that absorbs the transaction costs that would otherwise constrain the use of the tool. This is best achieved through a TDR bank, typically the municipality acting as an intermediary, buying development rights, and then selling them; this is usually contingent on a large cash infusion such as that used to create a land trust.

TDR can easily lead to the preservation of a building, but may not preserve a use. This is where TDR might be "turned upside-down." Instead of transferring development rights, it may be possible to transfer *obligations* with a default position that is proscriptive (e.g., revocation of the certificate of occupancy for the sending site), thereby preserving both

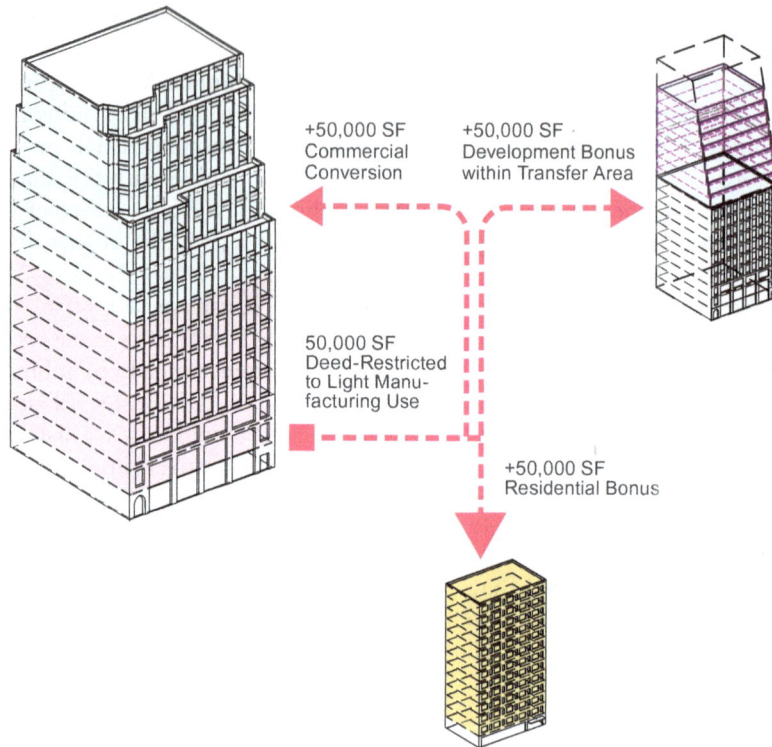

+50,000 SF
Commercial
Conversion

+50,000 SF
Development Bonus
within Transfer Area

50,000 SF
Deed-Restricted
to Light Manu-
facturing Use

+50,000 SF
Residential Bonus

Figure 11.6 Transferring development rights provides another market-based way to cross-subsidize
industrial retention.

the building and the intended uses. A particularly effective option would be to combine
TDR with the earlier recommendation about deed restrictions and/or employing the services of a nonprofit or agency dedicated to industry. As in one scenario, the sending site
may send development rights and at the same time absorb the obligation of the receiving
site to otherwise provide industry on-site, yielding a larger industrial building on one
parcel and a purely residential building on the other—to the market and compatibility
advantages of both.

Provocation

The key issues addressed above are how to create a flexible regulatory regime that can better
manage the complex and changing ecology of a manufacturing district. The proposals indicate how to do it where industrial land is the most accessible and affordable opportunity
for both major and incremental commercial and housing development, as well as parks and
other amenities. All the suggestions entail added regulatory complexity and enforcement
obligations, presenting trade-offs, especially for smaller cities and towns. A suburban or

Figure 11.7 An industrial mixed-use street.

exurban town may find that only one or two of these tools are warranted. New York City's five counties encompass, by contrast, virtually every urban land use and density and would do well to consider all the policies proposed. Most North American cities fall within a range between the two.

The zoning policies and tools described above rely on a longstanding, concerted political and popular promise to preserve industry against other uses that are more profitable, at least in the short term. In the 1964 movie, Mary Poppins says, "That's a pie crust promise. Easily made, easily broken." The regulatory tools are not sufficient in and of themselves; they work in concert with the other strategies presented in this book. Along with the most innovative land use policies, such as TDR, performance zoning, and design guidelines, they are not more restrictive but more proactive.

Notes

1 Laura Wolf-Powers, "Up-Zoning New York City's Mixed Use Neighborhoods: Property-Led Economic Development and the Anatomy of a Planning Dilemma," *Journal of Planning, Education and Research*, vol. 24, no. 4 (June 2005): 379–393.
2 Sharon Zukin, *Loft Living: Culture and Capital in Urban Change* (New Brunswick, NJ: Rutgers University Press, 1982).
3 Laura Wolf-Powers, "Up-Zoning New York City's Mixed Use Neighborhoods: Property-Led Economic Development and the Anatomy of a Planning Dilemma" (2005). Departmental Papers (City and Regional Planning), 17. http://repository.upenn.edu/cplan_papers/45.

12 Mixed-Use Neighborhoods
A Challenging Strategy for Maintaining Industry

Jenifer Becker and Adam Friedman

Introduction

Across the country, cities are seeking to designate existing industrial areas as "innovation districts" that cluster a mix of production, design, and other uses to stimulate creativity and economic activity. However, without careful planning and oversight, the "creative uses" that can typically afford higher rents push out the manufacturers, artisans, and artists who can typically only afford relatively lower rents, thereby undermining both the original policy rationale and attractiveness of the district. While a healthy mix of these uses can initially form organically, it is very difficult to maintain a balance of uses over the long term without a comprehensive set of public interventions. In this chapter we look at some illustrative efforts to create mixed industrial/commercial districts using an array of tools, with particular emphasis on the role that mission-driven organizations can play in managing the gap between the mixed-use vision and the realities of the real-estate market. While this chapter examines policies needed to create mixed industrial/commercial zones, many of the same challenges and tools would apply to a mixed industrial/residential district as well.

Until recently, environmental incompatibility—dust, noise, truck traffic—has dominated the discussion on challenges presented by mixed-use districts. While new technologies, materials, and regulations have alleviated some of the environmental challenges, the economic incompatibility posed by industrial/commercial activities in mixed-use neighborhoods remains largely unresolved. Creating an area that allows for a diversity of uses with different levels of land costs can quickly lead to homogeneity as the higher-land-cost uses push out the lower-land-cost uses. Some city planners may refer to this result as the inevitable and even desirable "highest and best use," a widely used real-estate notion suggesting that the market is the best arbiter for determining what uses should occupy a given area, as opposed to public policy objectives.

However, the market does not exist in a vacuum. It is guided by a variety of interventions including zoning, real estate, and other taxes and marketing to promote a development strategy and policy objectives such as "Silicon Alley" or the "Tech Triangle." The further the public policy objectives divert from the market, the greater the need for public interventions and the more costly and robust the interventions will have to be. In strong market cities like New York, San Francisco, and Los Angeles, it will take deployment of a full array of public policy interventions including zoning, financial incentives (and disincentives), urban design, and strong, consistent communications to influence property owners to resist market forces and preserve mixed use.

Figure 12.1 Mixed uses in Portland, Oregon, 2016.

Figure 12.2 Aerial view of the Brooklyn Navy Yard, New York.

It also takes a local, nonprofit, mission-driven development and management entity (mission-driven manager or MDM) to coordinate the formulation and implementation of these interventions—e.g., to help fine-tune the zoning and deploy building inspectors to enforce it; to be the eyes and ears that serve both as an early warning system against displacement and an area losing its character and to spot opportunities for economic growth; to resolve conflicts between the uses; and to broadcast the mixed-use message to existing and future stakeholders.

Fostering Mixed Use: Important Illustrative Efforts

While the technical and operational challenges of mixed-use districts have been discussed elsewhere in this collection, a different set of political and economic challenges need to be addressed: how can a property owner in a mixed-use district be induced to maintain production uses and therefore accept an apparently lower return on his property? The answer lies in a combination of interventions, which are equitable, consistent, and effective, and in the long-term best interest of the stakeholders.

New York's Garment Center is in many ways the original mixed-use "innovation district" where apparel designers and showrooms, textile and equipment wholesalers, and cutters and sewers have worked in tight proximity—sometimes on one floor, sometimes in one building, but always within a couple of city blocks. In 1985, the Department of City Planning created a special district to preserve these diverse uses in the face of real-estate pressures anticipated from the redevelopment of Times Square immediately to the north of the Garment Center. The Special District provided that a building owner could convert industrial space to offices only if he or she dedicated an equal amount of industrial space within the building to manufacturing, a strategy clearly intended to allow change but also preserve some original uses. While this strategy would limit the return on some properties, the district overall would benefit, particularly the owners of the showroom buildings, who often received higher rents for showrooms than office users while at the same time depending on the nearby low-rent manufacturing buildings to serve the showrooms' tenant designers.

The Mayor's Office of Midtown Enforcement (OME), created in 1976, was originally tasked with dispatching building and fire inspectors to the Garment Center to monitor conversions. In 1993, the Fashion Center Business Improvement District (BID) was formed to promote the area and to provide enhanced security, sanitation, and marketing services for potential fashion buyers. After a few years, in the face of protests from property owners OME severely cut back inspections during a budget crisis and the City refused to enforce the law. In 2001, a report by the New York Industrial Retention Network found that the law had been widely flouted; there had been 202 conversions since the creation of the Special District: two legal and 200 illegal conversions. In addition, as the market dynamics changed and office rents rose above showroom rents, major property owners who controlled the Fashion Center BID began to advocate for changes to the zoning to eliminate the provisions protecting the production space and for an overall repositioning of the area to be less focused on fashion and more open to other economic sectors. The messaging put out by the City and the Fashion Center BID undermined the legitimacy of the zoning, and the owners (correctly) perceived that they could convert their spaces with impunity.

In contrast to the more highly regulated strategy pursued in the Garment Center in the 1980s, both New York and Los Angeles have recently experimented with very flexible mixed-use zoning that allow residential, industrial, and many types of commercial development

Figure 12.3 Garment District in New York City, 2015.

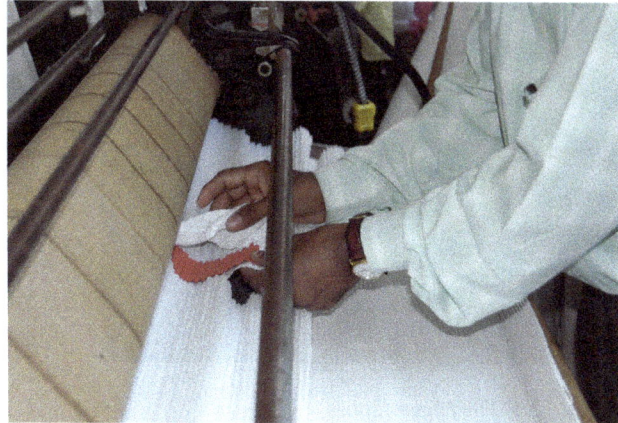

Figure 12.4 Workers in New York City's Garment District, 2010.

"as-of-right," as long as certain environmental standards are met. Despite the city's provision of economic development services to help industrial businesses in these areas, this permissive zoning has almost always resulted in the conversion of the area to residential. In May 2015, the Pratt Center for Community Development released *Making Room For Housing And Jobs*, a report that showed that fourteen of the fifteen mixed-use (MX) zones created by New York City had experienced significant increases in residential and commercial uses at the expense of industrial. Industrial and manufacturing lot square footage had decreased by 41 percent, a loss of over 4.2 million square feet, while residential lot square footage, including mixed residential and commercial land use, had increased by 71 percent.[1] Similarly, Los Angeles's Arts District, which permits a blend of residential, heavy and light industry, high technology, and arts-related uses, is experiencing rapid change whereby the same flexibility that gave birth to the district is giving way to the swift conversion of industrial buildings to high-end residential and retail developments.

A more successful hybrid strategy may be unfolding in San Francisco, where very strict zoning normally prevents the development of residential, office, and large-scale retail in its Production, Distribution, and Repair (PDR) districts. The City Council recently approved zoning that allows developers to build new office space in a select number of PDR sites if they offset their impacts through the development of new industrial space. The zoning was passed with the explicit intent of leveraging the value locked up by the strict zoning and using the office development to cross-subsidize the PDR development. The first project developed under this zoning was 100 Hooper, a mixed commercial/industrial campus that will have approximately 285,000 square feet of office space and 143,000 square feet of production space, half of which will be owned by PlaceMade, a nonprofit organization created to provide affordable space for San Francisco's manufacturing sector. "By being surgical in identifying sites for nonindustrial development, by balancing any negative impacts through nonprofit industrial development, and by integrating the development with SFMade's economic development services, the City can foster a mix of uses," said Kate Sofis, Director of SFMade, PlaceMade's nonprofit corporate parent in a discussion in 2017.

Figure 12.5 The edge of innovation.

Figure 12.6 SF PlaceMade campus model.

Moving Forward: Using Nonprofit Developer-Managers to Achieve More Equitable and Sustainable Mixed-Use Districts

Nonprofit developer-managers have a critical role to play if zoning and financial incentives are to be used effectively to achieve not only real-estate stability in mixed-use districts but to achieve the type of equitable economic growth sought at the policy level for supporting mixed-use districts. The first challenge a city confronts in striving toward these aims is closing the various financial gaps. In many areas of the country, industrial development is not itself profitable, creating the first gap. The second stems from the different returns on investment, which are much greater for residential and commercial development than for industrial.

Direct Subsidies

There are two ways in which cities could directly subsidize industrial uses. One would be to supply vouchers to companies similar to the public subsidies provided for affordable housing. This strategy, however, would no doubt raise red flags about the selection process, the sustainability of such a system as city budgets ebb and flow, and whether or not it would work at all if landlords simply increase rents. Another approach would be to subsidize the acquisition or renovation costs for industrial space, making the return on industrial development more competitive for private investors. However, if the restrictions expire as they typically do, the owner would be once again left with market forces driving conversion to other uses. In addition, enforcing use restrictions is often extremely difficult because penalties are small, inspections sporadic (if they take place at all), and outcomes might result in the eviction of otherwise legal but non-industrial tenants.

But if the funding is directed to an MDM whose mission is to strengthen the industrial sector and to create blue-collar jobs like the Greenpoint Manufacturing and Design Center in New York or PlaceMade in San Francisco, the industrial uses will outlive the funding restrictions.[2] In addition, an MDM might accept a lower return than a private developer, helping to close the gap. Exactly because it is a mission-driven entity, the MDM's investment and tenant selection decisions are likely to incorporate policy objectives beyond just finding industrial users, such as selecting tenants who provide better-quality jobs, work with organizations to hire local residents and those with barriers to employment, and pursue sustainable business practices.[3] In summary, using an MDM provides a level of control far beyond what zoning and even public subsidies can achieve.

A potential revenue source for these funds would be a development or conversion fee to be paid by the nonindustrial developers in the innovation district to recapture some of the benefits they obtain from the creation of the mixed-use district. A conversion fee would advance the equity objective through an internal cross-subsidy, and put modest brakes on the speculative forces in the market. An early model for this was the formerly operational NYC Industrial Relocation Grant Program, which collected a per-square-foot "conversion contribution" from developers who converted space from manufacturing uses to residential uses in certain areas of Manhattan, Queens, and Brooklyn.

Market-Based Mechanisms

Another approach would be to create a market for buying and selling the right to convert space. A typical mixed-use zoning strategy might be to require some production space in every building, as was the case in the Garment Center, but this obligation could be satisfied on-site or through another property within the mixed-use district. A developer who wants to build an office or residential building could pay another owner in the district to satisfy his obligation to build industrial space.

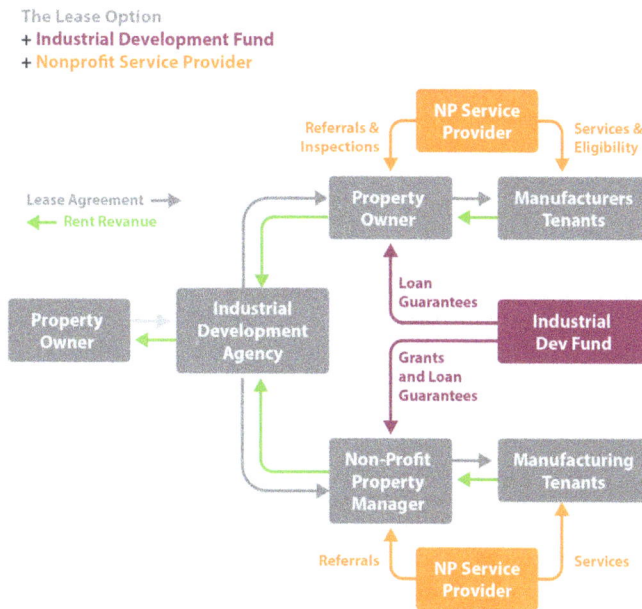

Figure 12.7 Diagram for lease options.

Figure 12.8 Mixed-use street in North East Philadelphia.

There are two roles that an MDM might play in this "Transfer of Development Rights" district scenario. First, a nonindustrial developer might pay the MDM to satisfy his obligation to develop industrial space, similar to the subsidy models discussed above. This dynamic is common in the affordable housing sector, where a market-rate developer pays a nonprofit developer to build affordable housing so that the market-rate developer can use tax-exempt financing. Second, the MDM can be the "market maker," matching buyers and sellers of development rights. In an area with many small property owners an MDM could build the requisite network of relationships with existing property and business owners plus bring insight into where the owner and the business are in their evolution: start-up versus retiring, expanding versus contracting, etc.

Enforcement is the Achilles' heel of complex zoning regulations typical of mixed-use districts. Land use violations are often hard to detect. While manufacturing activities on the first floor are generally visible from the street, upper-floor activities are easy to conceal. When such violations are discovered, evicting tenants—especially residents, even if they are illegal occupants—is often not politically viable and extremely difficult if the errant landlord is siding with the tenants.

An MDM could greatly enhance enforcement in two ways. Its staff could be additional "eyes and ears" and may have some deterrent value. Second, the MDM could be an outpost for building and fire inspectors (similar to the NYC Mayor's Office of Special Enforcement). Dedicating enforcement resources by decentralizing them would allow a city to capitalize on the MDM network's knowledge of trouble spots or illegal conversions and allow it to intervene earlier in the conversion process before tenants move in.

Conclusion

The type of organization that could pull together all of these necessary interventions—real estate development, market making, zoning enforcement—does not exist. Neither the business improvement district, which tends to be governed by the property owners, nor the local development corporation (LDC), which represents business interests, nor the community development corporation (CDC) or block association or community board (if largely resident-oriented) have the independence to balance the interests and broker the compromises outlined above.

A new type of district-management or governance organization whose mission would be to preserve the mixed-use nature of an area is needed to truly create a long-lasting innovation district where a variety of uses with the ability to pay a range of rents can all thrive. Such an organization would combine the best features of existing models such as a BID's power to impose a special assessment and make capital improvements to reflect industrial urban design with an LDC's expertise in business services with a CDC's resident employment services.[4]

Creating a sustainable mixed-use innovation district requires a new type of public intervention. This will require owner buy-in to not view mixed use as a transitional phase to a more profitable residential or office district, but as an adequate and equitable return on investment. With this buy-in, the MDM can develop mechanisms such as conversion fees to support mission-driven developers to own and manage space, preserve the industrial commons, and foster the long-term mix of uses, which drives creativity and innovation.

Notes

1 In the Greenpoint/Williamsburg, Flushing/Bedford, and Hudson Square MX districts—very desirable areas with strong real estate markets—industrial-lot square footage decreased by over 60 percent.
2 Many nonprofits are also using public and philanthropic funding as their equity in industrial real estate projects, including the Greenpoint Manufacturing and Design Center and Evergreen in Brooklyn, New York, and Rukus, a subsidiary of the Riley Area Development Corporation in Indianapolis, Indiana.
3 For a lengthy discussion of the advantages of nonprofit industrial development, see Pratt Center For Community Development (February 2013), "Brooklyn Navy Yard," which analyzes the economic impact and lessons learned through the development of this 300-acre, city-owned industrial park managed by a nonprofit development corporation: http://prattcenter.net/research/brooklyn-navy-yard.
4 Many NYC BIDs, such as the Times Square BID, 34th Street Partnership, Bryant Park Corporation, Downtown Alliance, and Grand Central Partnership, have used their BID assessments to support their own urban design capital projects that included street lighting, information and retail kiosks, and wayfinding signage.

13 The Federal Policy Context for Urban Manufacturing

Laura Wolf-Powers

Manufacturing is enjoying a policy and public relations renaissance in the United States. Renewed interest in the sector at the federal level, after decades of passive tolerance for deindustrialization, is connected with debates about the sources of economic resilience, the nature of the innovation process, and the future of work and earning in a society where economic inequality and the shrinking middle class have become major preoccupations. Drawing on research findings that argue for the importance of production activities to the commercialization of scientific discovery and the application of technological innovation, the administration of Barack Obama aggressively pursued a national advanced manufacturing agenda, creating an Advanced Manufacturing Partnership (AMP) and a network of Manufacturing Innovation Institutes. Through its Office of Science and Technology Policy, the administration also sponsored White House Maker Faire events in 2014, 2015, and 2016, helping to focus greater attention on the potential of technologies such as 3D printing, desktop machine tools, and customizable open-source design software to democratize access to production and help would-be entrepreneurs start firms.[1] Donald Trump, inaugurated as president in 2017, has also made manufacturing a touchstone of his economic growth strategy, though his focus has been on tax and regulatory relief and the formulation of trade policy aimed at boosting the relative price competitiveness of US-made goods.

Despite the federal government's renewed attention to manufacturing in general, the implications of federal policy efforts for *urban manufacturing* have been less clear. It is true that cities, with their extraordinary density of talent, their ability to promote the circulation and absorption of ideas, and their role as test markets for new products, are potentially key sites for the reactivation of dormant manufacturing capacity and for the development of new ventures. A recent report by the American Planning Association[2] cites dozens of examples of cities taking on urban industrial development and retention initiatives, using land-use policy to safeguard industrial property from residential and commercial conversion, and investing in infrastructure (both hard and soft) that is essential to existing manufacturers' survival as well as to new firms' emergence. However, at the federal level, the impulse to view manufacturing policy as science and technology policy rather than policy for places, together with a profound disengagement from urban property market challenges, have kept federal policy weakly aligned with what is occurring on the ground in cities.

This essay argues for a more energetic federal commitment to manufacturing policy as policy for specific geographies, including urban ones. Firms are, of course, the most important actors in urban manufacturing districts, and there is a longstanding aversion to the idea that government at any level should "pick winners." However, small urban producers, in particular, rely on thick local networks of institutions that create supportive, generative environments from which winners are more likely to emerge.[3] These institutions include maker and hacker spaces, market aggregators, technical assistance providers, and advocacy organizations that are often more robust and effective with government support. The capacity of such institutions to thrive within urban industry clusters may make the difference between manufacturing firms' success and failure in cities. As designers bear in mind the need to accommodate this social infrastructure in the urban manufacturing environment, they should also support efforts to garner federal and state resources that keep this infrastructure healthy. To increase such support would require re-orientation in the federal government's approach to manufacturing policy.

Technology over Place

The first factor inhibiting national manufacturing policy from strengthening emergent urban-based manufacturing agglomerations is that policy's historical focus on high-level scientific discovery has largely been linked to national defense. Wary of explicitly extending government support to industry in ways it feared would be seen as anti-competitive, the US government has consistently pursued a "shadow industrial policy" under the guise of military procurement strategy.[4] Lasers, semi-conductors, super-computing, and satellite technology all owe their origins to investment risks taken by defense officials who dispensed billions of research-and-development dollars to private firms. These technologies are of course now in widespread commercial use. While military investment had significant geographical effects, it has (particularly since World War II) tended to favor the Sun Belt over the Rust Belt and suburban over urban locations, for both political and strategic reasons. Moreover, the goal of place development has been absent from the policy, meaning that the pursuit of innovation has remained divorced from questions of place-specific economic well-being. Barack Obama's signature manufacturing initiative, the National Network of Manufacturing Institutes,[5] involved the Departments of Energy and Commerce as well as the Department of Defense; however, the multiparty public–private consortia formed to administer the federal dollars have engaged little with economic development goals or priorities of the cities and regions in which they are located. While hailed in some cases as engines of local development,[6] they have stressed technology transfer and deployment, commercialization, and productivity enhancement over place-based employment or development outcomes.

Other Obama-era federal manufacturing initiatives were more place-focused. The Investing in Manufacturing Communities Partnership (IMCP), which was announced by the Economic Development Administration in the Department of Commerce in April 2013, emphasized that physical and human infrastructure invested in places—and available to all firms that locate in those places—can offer a return superior to that of conventional firm-oriented subsidy or "smokestack-chasing."

> Through the IMCP, the President is directing Federal agencies to provide coordinated assistance to manufacturing communities through a new partnership that will align Federal economic development resources and help U.S. localities make coordinated, long-term investments in their public goods in partnership with universities and industry. These investments will ultimately help regions become more attractive for manufacturers and supply chains.[7]

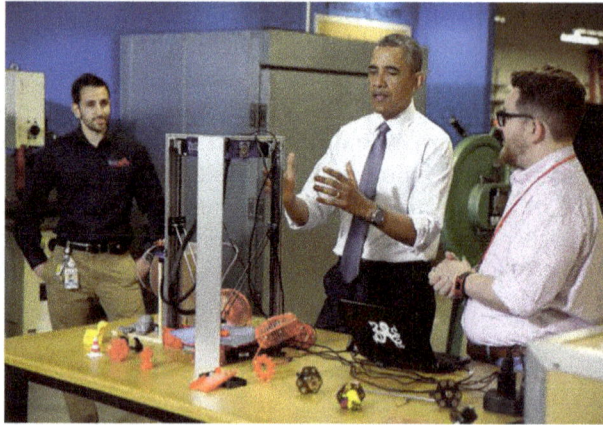

Figure 13.1 White House Maker Faire, 2015.

In contrast with the National Manufacturing Innovation Institutes, however, IMCP was subject to a resource scarcity dilemma common to urban and place-based programs. The Economic Development Administration designated twenty-four IMCP communities in 2014 and 2015, ranging from the Greater Pittsburgh Metals Manufacturing Community to the Central Valley AgPLUS Food and Beverage Manufacturing Consortium in Fresno and Sacramento, California. However, the designation qualified them only for "elevated consideration for … federal dollars and assistance from eleven cabinet departments/agencies."[8] Designees were offered a Financing Guide to help them raise funds for city- and region-based initiatives, but no federal funding was authorized.

A second place-based strategy was the Nation of Makers initiative operating out of the White House Office of Science and Technology Policy (OSTP). This initiative was charged with helping cities tap into the emergent Maker Movement, which officials defined as a set of technologies and institutions that enable learners and entrepreneurs to design and build new products.[9] A group called the Manufacturing Alliance of Communities, with the help of OSTP, coordinated and communicated the activities of city and county governments, universities and school districts to support maker-entrepreneurs and create learning and business development opportunities around the advanced technology associated with the maker movement. Again, however, while they gained from the exposure and technical assistance they received through OSTP, cities associated with the White House Maker effort received no funding to implement projects.

Disengagement from Urban Property Market Challenges

A second factor inhibiting the alignment of federal with urban manufacturing policy is a lack of engagement with the practical challenges most pressing for urban officials, particularly those in cities whose industrial built form was established in the nineteenth and early twentieth centuries. Academic studies have documented the competitive benefits that accrue when innovation and design functions (including manufacturing process design) are located in close proximity to production.[10] This has led to a push at the policy level for increased co-location (or, in many cases, the restored co-location) of production and design activities. This can be seen in the "just-in-time" supply chain dynamics and synergies that characterize, for example, the fashion and electronics industries in New York, Los Angeles, and San Francisco; biopharmaceutical and textile manufacturing in Raleigh, North Carolina; or the artisanal food sector in Portland, Oregon. However, as discussed elsewhere in this volume, many cities attempting to design for manufacturing confront high real estate and operating cost barriers facing local firms. Sites of sufficient size for modern, large-floor-plate industrial facilities with sufficient parking and loading capacity are difficult both to assemble (due to tangled title issues and absentee ownership of small sites) and to remediate (due to environmental contamination from former, "dirty" uses). Market rents for existing industrial space, along with labor and regulatory costs, are incompatible with the profitability of firms whose founders would otherwise wish to establish themselves or to remain and expand in cities. Competition for land and buildings from residential and commercial developers drives up rents and leads to the conversion (both sanctioned and speculative) of buildings suitable for small-batch industrial production. Appetite for

Figure 13.2 Top-of-the-line high-tech fabrication machinery at the Chicago DM11, Chicago, Illinois, 2016.

residential and, more recently, office and studio environments adapted from factory spaces makes maintaining industrial use in legacy industrial buildings an unattractive economic proposition for their owners.

Industry advocates assert that the non-monetized benefits of local production to the environment (in terms of fewer vehicle miles traveled), to the local workforce (in terms of relatively well-paying jobs), and to the innovative milieu are good reason to plan for and in some cases subsidize urban manufacturing.[11] All too often, however, cost considerations overcome the advantages conferred by proximity in urban settings, particularly once firms scale production past a small-batch level. A number of electronics firms founded in New York City in the early 2000s, for example, have kept their research-and-development functions urban and onshore while moving production elsewhere.[12]

The national government's main policy focus—the integration of new technologies into manufacturing process so as to increase productivity—often seems distant to local-level officials preoccupied with these more granular challenges. A 2013 Brookings Institution study of Newark, New Jersey's manufacturing sector is illustrative in that the majority of interventions recommended to city government and regional stakeholders involve market development, workforce development, and the seeding of advanced manufacturing capacity through university partnerships.[13] While these are important opportunities, the tools that local actors in Newark perceive as being available to affect the trajectory of manufacturing development in the city chiefly involve land-use policy and project finance. Newark officials are trying to make parcels suitable for industrial infill development in a city characterized by environmental contamination, multiple industrial landowners, and difficult-to-adapt buildings. In sum, the Brookings report downplays the issues that are of the greatest concern to those seeking manufacturing revitalization in the city.[14]

Aligning Federal Policy with an Urban Manufacturing Agenda: The Role of Local Industrial Ecosystems

Recent studies of America's new production economy acknowledge that manufacturing—the production process itself—plays a large role in stimulating, accelerating, and sustaining the economic innovation that builds national competitive advantage.[15] Scholars also assert that institutions make a critical contribution to both product design and process innovation in manufacturing. Still, their accounts privilege national policies and institutions and, at the local level, research universities. In contrast, Jennifer Clark places more grassroots manufacturing support institutions at the center of her analysis. Clark argues that to participate effectively in current debates about the future of American manufacturing, policy makers must take into account a "regionally varied and industrial system organizing labor markets, supply chains and innovation."[16]

Of key interest are place-bound institutions (common spaces for idea generation and prototyping, technical assistance providers, and brokers of "maker-to-market" and workforce development connections) that make it possible for incumbent and newcomer manufacturing firms to prosper. These institutions are not typically targeted by national-level initiatives in support of advanced manufacturing, nor do they tend to officially partner with universities. However, these institutional participants in local and regional industrial ecosystems have an especially important impact in the urban context. The Columbus Idea Foundry in Columbus, Ohio, a

Figure 13.3 Idea Foundry, Columbus, Ohio, 2018.

65,000-square-foot "maker space" in a former shoe factory, offers serious entrepreneurs (as well as curious civilians) the opportunity to experiment with wood- and metalworking tools, sewing machines, and 3D printers.

Evergreen, in East Brooklyn, New York, helps industrial businesses navigate government incentives and private financing opportunities and champions their interests with city departments to resolve problems around transportation, sanitation, and utilities. SFMade in San Francisco sponsors exhibitions, showcases, and pop-up shows featuring San Francisco-made products, completing the circuit between producers and consumers eager to enact a "buy-local" ethos. Cleveland-based WIRE-Net does something similar in a single-sector context by brokering connections between wind-power equipment producers and clusters of component suppliers in the Great Lakes region. The North Carolina Biotechnology Center in Durham helps homegrown bioscience research firms develop in-house manufacturing capabilities and has, in partnership with the state's community college system, created workforce development programs that serve the industry's needs while helping employ local blue-collar workers in a high-tech sector.[17]

Integrating the diverse institutional actors of the local industrial ecosystem into the design and built form of urban manufacturing districts is not the same project in every city. SFMade, until recently, was housed in the heart of San Francisco in a multitenant building owned by TechShop, the membership-based technology workshop and makerspace. In contrast, the North Carolina Biotechnology Center acts as a manufacturing facilitator and advocate from a freestanding building that conforms to the context it occupies: a suburban-style office park within Durham city limits. As urban manufacturing districts take diverse forms and typologies, so will the physical presence of the embedded organizations that enable them to function.

Architects, planners, and adaptive re-users of urban manufacturing land and buildings should ensure that suitable physical space for critical ecosystem components gets "baked in" to the design of urban manufacturing districts. Beyond local-level design and planning, however,

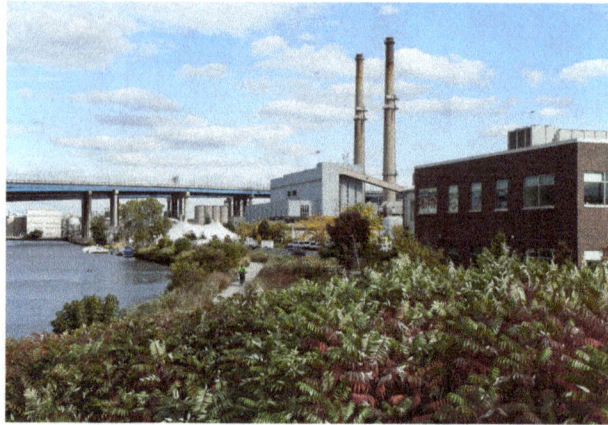

Figure 13.4 In Milwaukee, Wisconsin, local industrial redevelopment includes this greenway through the Menomonee Valley Industrial Center.

Figure 13.5 Fabric Discovery Center at the University of Massachusetts, 110 Canal, Lowell, Massachusetts; renovation designed by Icon Architects, 2017.

resources are required from higher levels of government to keep local ecosystems healthy. This is not to argue that firms themselves (both manufacturers and specialized producer services firms) are not the primary constituents of urban industrial ecosystems. Research findings specific to urban maker communities indicate that firms overwhelmingly look to other for-profit entrepreneurs to help them build their businesses.[18]

Nevertheless, public-sector organizations, and nonprofit groups supported with public dollars, remain important resources for fledgling urban manufacturing enterprises. They provide information, advice, connections, and (critical in hot real-estate markets) affordable production space. The unsuitability of market mechanisms alone to ensure that urban manufacturing entrepreneurs are able to form and scale businesses is demonstrated in the

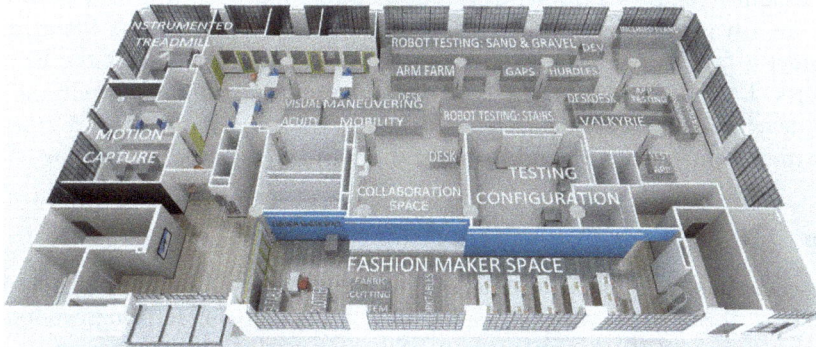

Figure 13.6 Fabric Discovery Center at the University of Massachusetts, Lowell, funded in part by the National Manufacturing Innovation Institutes; rendering by Icon Architects, 2017.

Figure 13.7 A rendering of the Fabric Discovery Center at the University of Massachusetts, Lowell, funded in part by the National Manufacturing Innovation Institutes; rendering by Icon Architects, 2017.

recent bankruptcy filing by TechShop, whose for-profit, venture-investor-driven model for makerspaces has, at least for the time being, proved untenable. Hackerspaces and incubators whose missions are uncomplicated by the imperative to generate competitive investor return are often better equipped to promote the capacity and economic well-being of particular cities and neighborhoods. Yet to do this they may need noncommercial sources of revenue, and the potential of the federal government to play a role here remains untapped. On the ground, local organizations have made strategic use of federal policy tools such as historic preservation tax credits. In other cases state-level agencies have been able to create place-focused programs that complement and build on federal technology investment. The State of Massachusetts, for example, has leveraged the opportunities presented by federal funding for an advanced-fabrics initiative housed at the Massachusetts Institute of Technology to start a fabrics research lab, incubator, and training center at the University of Massachusetts, Lowell. While the focus of federal policy remains squarely on advanced technology development, Massachusetts is using its own funds to connect research with support for micro-entrepreneurs and for education and workforce development.[19]

Conclusion

Even at its most robust, US federal commitment to the growth and strength of American manufacturing has weakly aligned with the aspirations of urban manufacturing proponents. This chiefly stems, as I argue, from a prevalent view of manufacturing policy as science and technology policy rather than policy for places.

A re-orientation in the federal government's approach to manufacturing policy could contribute to urban industrial clusters' potential as forces for placemaking and job generation. This would, however, require institutional cultures focused on advanced technology (in the Departments of Defense, Energy, and to a lesser extent Commerce) to adopt a more diverse set of priorities. Place policy and manufacturing policy can coalesce, but only with conscious leadership from policy makers attuned to the material and social conditions and possibilities present in cities.

Notes

1 The White House events also focused on making as a way of stimulating young people's interest in the STEM fields.
2 Nancey Green Leigh, Nathanael Hoelzel, Benjamin Kraft, and Christopher Dempwolf, *Sustainable Urban Industrial Development* (Chicago, IL: American Planning Association Planning Advisory Service Report, 2014), www.planning.org/publications/report/9026900/.
3 David Bailey, Keith Cowling, and Philip Tomlinson, *New Perspectives on Industrial Policy for a Modern Britain* (Oxford: Oxford University Press, 2015).
4 Gregory Hooks, "The Rise of the Pentagon and U.S. State Building: The Defense Program as Industrial Policy," *American Journal of Sociology* vol. 96, no. 2 (September 1990): 358–404.
5 The Institutes, which continue to exist, focus on the integration and uptake—largely by multinational firms—of cutting-edge technologies such as advanced sensing and control, digital visualization and simulation, advanced materials, and intelligent machines.
6 For example, see Justin Murphy, "Jubilant Reaction in Rochester to Photonics News," *Rochester Democrat and Chronicle*, July 28, 2015. www.democratandchronicle.com/story/money/2015/07/22/photonics-rochester-reaction-schumer/30526593/.
7 US Department of Commerce, Office of Public Affairs, "Fact Sheet: The Investing in Manufacturing Communities Partnership," April 17, 2013,. www.commerce.gov/news/fact-sheets/2013/04/fact-sheet-investing-manufacturing-communities-partnership.
8 US Economic Development Administration. "Place-Based Playbook for the Investing in Manufacturing Communities Partnership," 2015. www.manufacturingcommunities.org/playbook.html.
9 White House Office of Science and Technology Policy, "The Maker Movement," 2015. www.whitehouse.gov/nation-of-makers.
10 Suzanne Berger, *Making in America: From Innovation to Market* (Cambridge, MA: MIT Press, 2013); Gary P. Pisano and Willie C. Shih, *Producing Prosperity: Why America Needs a Manufacturing Renaissance* (Boston, MA: Harvard Business Press, 2012).

11 Karen Chapple, "The Highest and Best Use? Urban Industrial Land and Job Creation," *Economic Development Quarterly* vol. 28, no. 4 (2014): 300–313.

12 In cities with weak real-estate markets and legacy infrastructure, the dynamic is distinct but equally problematic. In those cases, prospective returns on investment may simply be insufficient to draw private investors who wish to acquire, renovate, and manage older industrial buildings and properties; Joan Byron and Nisha Mistry, *The Federal Role in Supporting Urban Manufacturing* (Washington, DC: Brookings Institution, 2011), 44.

13 Nisha Mistry, "Newark's Manufacturing Competitiveness: Findings and Strategies," *Brookings Metropolitan Policy Program*, May 28, 2013, www.brookings.edu/research/reports/2013/05/28-newark-manufacturing-mistry-vey-shearer.

14 Laura Wolf-Powers, "National Manufacturing Policy, Local Real Estate Markets, and the Missing Region: Prospects for Urban Industrial Development in the U.S.," in *Handbook of Manufacturing Industries in the World Economy*, eds J. Bryson, J. Clark, and V. Vanchan, (Cheltenham: Edward Elgar Publishing Limited, 2015), 409–424.

15 Richard M. Locke and Rachel L. Wellhausen, eds., *Production in the Innovation Economy* (Cambridge, MA: MIT Press, 2014).

16 Jennifer Clark, "Manufacturing by Design: The Rise of Regional Intermediaries and the Re-emergence of Collective Action," *Cambridge Journal of Regions, Economy and Society* vol. 7, no. 3 (2014): 433–448, 434.

17 Nichola Lowe, "Job Creation and the Knowledge Economy: Lessons from North Carolina's Life Science Manufacturing Initiative," *Economic Development Quarterly* vol. 21, no. 4 (2007): 339–353; Nichola Lowe and Laura Wolf-Powers, "Who Works in a Working Region? Inclusive Innovation in the New Manufacturing Economy," *Regional Studies*, advance online publication (2017). http://dx.doi.org/10.1080/00343404.2016.1263386.

18 Laura Wolf-Powers, Marc Doussard, Greg Schrock, Charles Heying, Max Eisenburger, and Stephen Marotta, "The Maker Movement and Urban Economic Development," *Journal of the American Planning Association* vol. 83, no. 4 (2017). http://dx.doi.org/10.1080/01944363.2017.1360787.

19 Zeninjior Emwemeka, "Downloaded Designs? UMass Lowell to Open Fabric Innovation Center," *Bostonomix—WBUR*, May 31, 2017, www.wbur.org/bostonomix/2017/05/31/umass-lowell-fabric-institute.

14 Making Urban Manufacturing Pay

Developers and the Innovation Economy

Andrew Kimball

It's a typical morning in 1940 on the Brooklyn waterfront and over 125,000 New Yorkers stream to work at three massive industrial complexes: the Brooklyn Navy Yard ("the Navy Yard"), the Brooklyn Army Terminal ("the Army Terminal"), and Bush Terminal (now called "Industry City"). It is manufacturing jobs that will lift these workers, many of them first- or second-generation migrants, into the middle class. Fast-forward to the early 1990s and the days of the smokestacks are long gone. The buildings on these massive industrial campuses are decaying after fifty years of little or no investment and now are home to fewer than 5,000 jobs. Fast forward again, now to 2019. Once again, public and private resources are flowing into these campuses as a result of leasing and redevelopment strategies that recognize that the nature of manufacturing has changed and now includes a blend of technology, art, fashion, design, and engineering. The innovation economy has taken hold and the Navy Yard, the Army Terminal, and now Industry City are once again thriving hubs for local job creation, with over 20,000 jobs and another 30,000 in the pipeline.

The Navy Yard and Army Terminal redevelopments have been fueled by massive public investments in the basic infrastructure of city-owned assets that leveraged private investment and thousands of new jobs. Industry City, on the other hand, is a privately owned facility where, for the first time at this scale, the private sector is undertaking a massive industrial adaptive reuse project with no direct public capital support and with no housing to fuel the economics of the project. Since the redevelopment began in 2013, Industry City ownership has invested over $400 million to breathe new life into the decrepit infrastructure attracting over 400 new businesses and creating 6,000 new jobs. But the redevelopment is only halfway complete. To drive continued private investment, Industry City is seeking a different form of public support—a rezoning to create an innovation district with a commercial-industrial-retail-academic mixed use that will provide the economic return necessary for the private sector to continue to fund the infrastructure investments paid for by the public sector at the Navy Yard and the Army Terminal. This essay explores what forces drove the turnaround at these iconic facilities and how the introduction of a mixed-use innovation economy district at Industry City can create a model for private investment in modern manufacturing and the innovation economy.

At the core of this success story is the fact that it is simply cool to make things again. The stewards of the Navy Yard, the Army Terminal, and Industry City recognized the shifting nature of manufacturing toward technology and innovation and that creating a community of young entrepreneurs drawn to modern making would be critical to their leasing success. New technologies like 3D printing and laser cutters have allowed for production to occur in minutes and hours for projects and products that used to take days and months to develop. Unlike the

Figure 14.1 Sparks fly with light-duty metalwork at Industry City, 2013.

cavernous factories of our parents' and grandparents' eras, today's entrepreneurs can start a "factory" in spaces not much bigger than a bedroom (as discussed in Chapter 10). Old definitions of workplace—office or factory—have become less relevant as today's manufacturer may produce entirely through digital means or have the ability to print products or prototypes on machines that are clean and quiet. Many of the city's contemporary manufacturing success

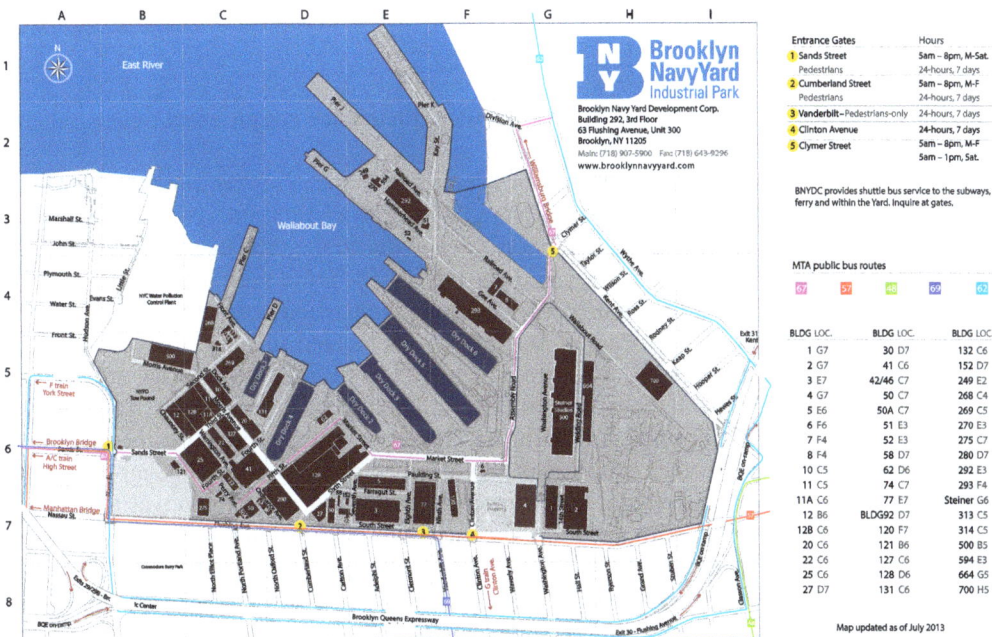

Figure 14.2 Map of the Brooklyn Navy Yard, New York, 2017.

Figure 14.3 Building 77 at the Brooklyn Navy Yard prior to redevelopment, 2016.

stories are companies that started in what many would consider design office space but then decided to bring manufacturing in-house.

Demand for personalization and customization have driven niche maker markets. A growing consumer consciousness of buying local, understanding supply chains, and creating well-paying local jobs has also fed this making phenomenon. Online marketing and sales technologies are bringing the maker closer to the consumer and cutting out the retail middleman.

Young entrepreneurs are flooding to urban areas, drawn, in particular, to areas like the Brooklyn waterfront with low-density residential neighborhoods located in close proximity to large multi-story industrial buildings on the waterfronts where their businesses can grow and thrive in closer proximity and often in collaboration with like-minded creative companies. The buildings at the Navy Yard, the Army Terminal, and Industry City are perfectly suited for these entrepreneurs who have disrupted another traditional manufacturing paradigm (see Chapter 5)—the ground-floor factory.[1] The new breed of contemporary manufacturers and innovators prefer to be on upper floors and are willing to pay more for the light and views as long as there are good freight elevators and easily accessible loading docks. These massive industrial buildings also speak to today's makers, with their rich history and authenticity providing the opportunity to be part of a new era of manufacturing and innovation.

New manufacturers locating in these former large-scale manufacturing spaces include the following:

Figure 14.4 A camera company at Industry City, 2017.

Crye Precision. Crye started as a small design office at the Navy Yard with two young entrepreneurs from Cooper Union committed to designing advanced equipment and technology for the military. Over the last ten years the company has expanded repeatedly, brought manufacturing in-house, and recently opened an 80,000-square-foot manufacturing facility with over 200 employees, who primarily live in the surrounding communities. Among them are a substantial number of Asian Americans who live in Sunset Park, Brooklyn.

UncommonGoods. Founded in 1999 by David Bolotsky, an entrepreneur with the vision of facilitating connections between designers and makers of locally made and sustainable products through an online marketplace, UncommonGoods has experienced continual growth at the Army Terminal. In 2007, the company became a Certified B Corp, meaning it had undergone and passed a comprehensive screening process that evaluates areas including company governance, environmental practices, and impacts on the local community, becoming one of just 1,000 companies to achieve that status.

MFactory. Since arriving as a start-up eyeglasses manufacturer at Industry City in October 2016, MFactory has more than tripled its square footage to 20,000 square feet and added more than fifty employees to become Brooklyn's largest eyeglass manufacturer. At Industry City, MFactory is surrounded by a vibrant ecosystem of fashion companies and manufacturers, including footwear design and production company *ESTAS BRANDS*, swimwear label and manufacturer Malia Mills, fashion jewelry company and producer Alexis Bittar, lighting manufacturers Roll & Hill, Juniper, and Rich Brilliant Willing.

So why hasn't some of this good news been able to stem the tide of dismal reports on manufacturing in New York City? The Center for an Urban Future, one of the city's most respected public policy think tanks, recently reported that the thirty-year downward trend of manufacturing jobs had stabilized and that the overall number may have even grown by a few hundred.[2] A sign of hope?... not really, when you consider that manufacturing jobs make up approximately 2 percent of the private-sector jobs in the city. Unfortunately, economists undertaking these studies rely on the North American Industry Classification System codes (NAICS), a federal classification system used to define business sectors. As a result, manufacturing classifications remain essentially the same in 2015 as they were in 1940.

The NAICS codes fail to pick up media, technology, design, art, architecture, and engineering firms that may have a component of manufacturing. A stark example lies with the city's film and television production sector. Policy makers and industrial advocates broadly accept that this is a contemporary manufacturing sub-sector—think of the "making" that goes into the sets, wardrobes, cameras, and post-production work. This industry employs over 100,000 in full-time equivalent jobs, many of them union jobs, at studios such as Kaufman Astoria and Silvercup in Queens and Broadway Stages and Steiner in Brooklyn. A recent study by the Boston Consulting Group on behalf of the mayor's office showed that the annual impact of the film and television industry on New York City's economy is $8.7 billion. Yet the NAICS codes don't classify film and TV production as manufacturing.

Modern manufacturing is in fact integral to the city's fastest-growing sector: the innovation economy (it goes without saying that the innovation economy is not an official category in the NAICS system). The most accurate definition of the innovation economy is that it represents the broad range of making a physical, digital, or engineered product. From 2007 to 2012, jobs in the innovation economy grew 12 percent, far outpacing sectors such as financial services that have long been counted on for the economic health of the city. In a recent report on urban manufacturing, the Pratt Center for Community Development captures this changing landscape well.

> Manufacturing is at the core of a burgeoning "innovation economy" characterized by specialized markets, flexible business models, cross-sectoral linkages and an emphasis on creativity. While economists regularly report on the demise of manufacturing in NYC, and at the same time trumpet the growth of tech, design, entertainment and media, and arts and culture, the fact is that many of the companies in these sectors are doing some manufacturing.[3]

The Center for the Urban Future recently published the most definitive study to date on the innovation economy's impact on Brooklyn: "Brooklyn's Growing Innovation Economy." The CUF study found that Brooklyn has emerged as one of the nation's leaders in the innovation economy, with the borough's growth in tech start-ups, creative companies, and innovative manufacturers significantly outpacing Manhattan and other leading cities. Employment in Brooklyn's creative industries is up by 155 percent over the past decade, nearly ten times the growth rate of Manhattan. And in eight different creative industries—including film/TV, graphic design, architecture, industrial design, and publishing—Brooklyn was first or second among the nation's twenty-five largest counties in employment growth over the past decade. Additionally, Brooklyn's manufacturing sector has significantly outperformed the city as a whole since the Great Recession, with much of the growth coming from a new generation of companies at the intersection of manufacturing, technology, and design. According to the report, manufacturing jobs declined by seven percent citywide, but were up by one percent in Brooklyn.

Stewards of the Navy Yard, the Army Terminal, and Industry City all recognized the emerging leasing opportunity created by the innovation economy. Yet each faced massive deferred maintenance challenges created by decades of neglect—upwards of $1 billion spread across the three campuses in windows, roofs, electrical systems, and elevators to be replaced as well as subsurface utilities, roads, and bulkheads—all of this made even more expensive as a result of Hurricane Sandy and rising sea levels. By the mid-1990s, many of the approximately sixty-five buildings on these campuses were vacant or partially utilized often with low-cost, low-employment storage.

Beginning in the early 2000s, the leadership at the Navy Yard convinced successive mayors that investment in basic infrastructure would generate substantial private investment and local job creation. Without this public investment, the rents from innovation economy and modern manufacturing businesses simply were not high enough to finance the deferred maintenance. Over the next decade, $250 million in public investment leveraged over $1 billion in private investment with the creation of 5,000 new jobs and another 5,000 in the pipeline. Now that much of the basic infrastructure at the Yard has been modernized, the leverage ratio of one public dollar to four private dollars will only improve over time. More than any other example in the country—with the possible exception of the Philadelphia Navy Yard—the Brooklyn Navy Yard is the model for public investment that leverages modern manufacturing and innovation economy job creation.

The Brooklyn Army Terminal has followed a similar strategy of relying on public support for basic infrastructure improvements in order to leverage private investment. Both the Navy Yard and the Army Terminal are now essentially fully leased. As a result, the city has made another round of major infrastructure investment in both facilities as well as the city-owned Bush Terminal, further leveraging private investment and millions of square feet of renovation of previously vacant buildings as well as new ground-up construction over the next two years.

The redevelopment of Industry City is the private sector's first attempt to redevelop a massive industrial complex without looking to convert a portion to higher-return housing. For decades following the collapse of large-scale manufacturing in Brooklyn, there was a simple reason that the word "storage" appeared on the outside of many multi-story industrial buildings along the Brooklyn Queens Expressway, from Sunset Park to Long Island City: the economics just didn't work for the owners to invest in their renovation so they took the only path they saw: low-investment, low- or no-job static storage. Particularly pervasive has been the explosion of self-storage for the home. While the marketplace demands this kind of use in a dense urban area, the relentless need for storage for the home has cannibalized just the kinds of pre-World War II multistory industrial buildings that are so attractive to modern manufacturers and innovation-economy businesses. Consequently, up and down the BQE, buildings that could be full of jobs have been full of storage. Up until the rebirth of Industry City, the rare exceptions have been where the private sector has been allowed to convert these type of buildings to residential uses, such as in Dumbo, or where the public sector has subsidized the creation of manufacturing jobs, such as at the Navy Yard and Army Terminal.

What had happened at Industry City during its thirty-year decline is case in point. At the time the new ownership of Industry City was formed in 2013, the 6 million-square-foot property spread over sixteen buildings was 30 percent vacant and 40 percent low-employment storage warehousing and faced $350 million of deferred maintenance expenses—17,000 windows to replace, 144 elevators to modernize, a new electrical infrastructure, and the list goes on.

Figure 14.5 Overview of Industry City, 2017.

Figure 14.6 Tenant mixer in courtyard 3–4, 2017.

The Industry City team determined that a full revitalization of the property was possible without introducing housing but only with public support for a rezoning allowing for a commercial-industrial-retail-academic mixed-use district. In the spring of 2014, Industry City announced that it would seek a rezoning to allow it to change its zoning from M3 (heavy manufacturing) to M2 (light manufacturing) with a special Innovation Economy District. In its simplest form, this rezoning allowed for a significant portion of the first and second floors of its buildings to be used for retail, thus cross-leveraging the investment in the entirety of the buildings and allowing for the redevelopment to proceed over a ten-year period (rather than twenty-five to thirty years without the higher return brought by broadened retail and academic uses). Essentially, the $400 million+ each that the city poured into Navy Yard and Army Terminal is replaced by the retail and academic leasing opportunity to induce private developers at

Figure 14.7 Greenspace in newly renovated courtyard 5–6, 2017.

Industry City to undertake such a massive redevelopment. Industry City's Innovation Economy District would include the following elements.

a. Up to 14 percent of the property can be retail, providing higher rents. The three major groups of retail are: a) maker-retail companies where small, artisanal manufacturing includes a retail component; b) mid-size design and home-goods compatible retail that are connected to tenant designers and manufacturers; c) mid-size community-oriented retail and large-format retail that meet the needs of the local and surrounding communities. These retail uses not only cross-leverage the deferred maintenance investments but create an amenity for the innovation economy companies moving into the complex.

b. Up to 12 percent could be used for academic partnerships that support and leverage innovation, entrepreneurship, and local job creation. Successful innovation districts across the world all have academic institutions embedded.

c. Up to 5 percent could be two hotels supporting the 1,000+ businesses and 20,000 jobs Industry City projects to create within ten years with the new zoning. The business-oriented hotels would also support the additional 20,000 jobs that should be coming to Sunset Park over the next ten years through the Liberty View redevelopment, the City's continued investment in the Army Terminal and the expansion of NYU Langone Medical Center.

d.   The balance of the space—approximately 70 percent—would be filled with innovation-economy modern manufacturing businesses, a dramatic turnaround for a site that in 2013 was 70 percent underutilized—30 percent vacant and 40 percent storage with few jobs.

In the first six years of the new Industry City partnership, $400 million of private funding has been invested: $250 million in deferred maintenance, $100 million in tenant build-outs and $50 million in "place-making" initiatives including new outdoor amenities in the complex's dramatic court-yards and raised sidewalks for improved loading and pedestrian safety. Large spaces were divided into Creative Workshops where an artist, designer, tech start-up, artisan manufacturer, and architect might be located side-by-side. Sector-based events like Design Week and American Field show-cased local manufacturers and brought people to Industry City for the first time. A lounge and meet-up space was created to bring tenants together and encourage business-to-business activity. A unique workforce development center called the Innovation Lab was established to support small business development as well as train and place local residents in jobs at Industry City.

During the new ownership's first four years, over 3 million square feet of space was leased. The number of businesses grew from 150 to 550 and jobs from 1,900 to 7,500. With the rezoning moving toward a "certification" or official kick-off in 2019, some have asked why it is needed with so much success during the first four years. The answer is simple: this initial investment and early success were about proof of concept. If Industry City's beautiful buildings were partially redeveloped, would innovation economy tenants move there? The answer is a resounding "Yes." However, without the rezoning, the pace of private investment will slow significantly, resulting in the twenty-five to thirty-year redevelopment scenario with far fewer jobs, limited academic collaborations, and no hotels to serve the rapidly growing business community in Sunset Park. Without the rezoning, ownership will likely have to turn away from the mixed-use innovation economy and manufacturing approach to focus solely on office uses, the highest-return use that is "as-of-right" under M3 zoning. The irony of the 2018 Amazon debacle in Long Island City is that their entire HQ2 office complex could have come to Industry City as-of-right, with no community input.

Figure 14.8 "Innovation Alley" connecting the Industry City campus, 2017.

Figure 14.9 "Salsa Sunday" in courtyard 1–2, 2017.

Figure 14.10 Food trucks in the early days of redevelopment, 2015.

Figure 14.11 "Lunch and Learn" programs in the tenant lounge, 2015.

Passions run high when discussing traditional manufacturing in part because these jobs have long represented the pathway to the middle class. A close look, however, at the kinds of jobs being created at the Navy Yard, the Army Terminal, and Industry City suggest that the innovation economy can play a strong role in filling the void. Over 40 percent of the jobs at these complexes are held by workers with less than a bachelor's degree. They have become a tremendous source for local employment with entry-level jobs paying significantly more than those in the service sector. Nearly 40 percent of the workers at Industry City reside in the surrounding neighborhoods, including Sunset Park, Red Hook, Park Slope, and Bay Ridge.

Cities like New York will always need the services provided by manufacturers: the wood- or metalworker, the food producer and clothing maker. Fortunately, more and more consumers are demanding locally made products and in many cases are willing to pay a premium to buy local. However, without a full embrace of today's modern manufacturing and innovation economy we will continue to wring our hands over the collapse of this once-mighty sector. The Mayor and the City Council have each called for common-sense protections of traditional manufacturers while opening up the door to initiatives ranging from zoning changes to capital infrastructure investment that can fuel the city's emerging innovation economy. While much more can be done to align our educational system, "pre-K to gray", with the skill set needed in the rapidly evolving economy, a positive step forward is embedding universities and colleges with links to vocational high schools in innovation districts alongside growing clusters of innovation economy businesses.

Today approximately 20,000 men and women, many of them walking from nearby homes and many of them immigrants or New Yorkers facing challenging economic conditions, arrive at well-paying jobs in Brooklyn's waterfront industrial campuses. It is critical for the growth of the city's economy and to make the city more equitable that we abandon our reliance on outdated views of manufacturing and our overreliance on obsolete job classifications. We must focus on supporting what is working on the ground, like at the Navy Yard and the Army Terminal, while incentivizing private-sector investment through the creation of commercial mixed-use districts like the one proposed for Industry City. With the right set of public and private investments and with updated zoning that recognizes the sectors of today rather than 1950, jobs at these revitalized industrial campuses should grow to 50,000 over the next ten years.

Notes

1　Nina Rappaport, *Vertical Urban Factory* (Barcelona: Actar, 2016).
2　See report Charles Euchner, *Making it Here: The Future of Manufacturing in New York City* (New York, NY: Center for Urban Future, July 2016), https://nycfuture.org/pdf/Making_It_Here_July_2016.pdf.
3　From report by the Pratt Center for Community Development: http://prattcenter.net/issues-expertise/urban-manufacturing.

Part IV

Atlas

Places of Production and Design Strategies

Places of Production and Design Strategies

Purposes

This atlas is a survey of selected industrial districts, primarily in North America, where cities are actively engaged in defining the changing role that manufacturing can play in the urban economy. While the Atlas focuses on physical planning and design, it also touches on architecture and policy, to create a bridge across the three sections of this book. Following the atlas, there is a brief survey of the edges, streets, and public spaces found in the case studies, as well as some representations of the buildings.

How the Case Studies were Selected

The survey is not meant to be comprehensive, but representative of a range of conditions across a range of cities. The case study search started with an extensive review of current publications and materials from organizations that have been focusing on this issue. Of particular value was Nancey Greene Leigh's American Planning Association Planning Advisory Report 577, Sustainable Urban Industrial Development, which identified what she dubbed "manufacturing-aware cities," or MACs. Member organizations of the Urban Manufacturing Alliance

(then chaired by Adam Friedman, one of the authors in this volume) suggested additional cities.

Other organizations with valuable resources include the Urban Land Institute, the Brookings Institution, and the National Association of Industrial and Office Parks. We also interviewed authors of various publications. The cities were ultimately selected through policy and zoning document review and interviews with key representatives of these cities. The final selection of the eighteen case studies was driven by two primary criteria.

- Is there a commitment to maintaining or growing manufacturing in some form, as opposed to enabling a transition away from manufacturing?
- Is there some attempt to implement new and/or innovative forms of district design and planning?

Thus, the case studies tend to be mixed-use areas where there is still a concentration of small- and medium-sized manufacturers who take advantage of the so-called "agglomeration economies" of an urban location: access to the creative design professions and speed to market. These are the contested places of production, where cities are experimenting as they navigate between transition, stabilization, and expansion.

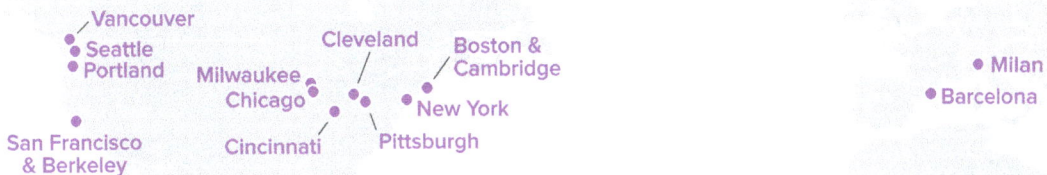

Vancouver
Seattle
Portland
Milwaukee
Cleveland
Boston & Cambridge
Milan
Barcelona
Chicago
New York
San Francisco & Berkeley
Cincinnati
Pittsburgh

Findings: Policy

Because the case-study cities are all "manufacturing-aware cities," the policy documents lead with a strong defense of urban production. Many cities pair this defensive posture of trying to hold on to what exists, with more aspirational language around the transition into higher-value-added, innovation-driven businesses. Not surprisingly, in strong market cities like San Francisco and Chicago, protection of the exiting industrial businesses—not innovation—is the priority. In Europe, where industry is often directly supported by the state, manufacturing innovation is a more explicit objective (see Fossa, Chapter 3). While there are a few districts in North America where manufacturing innovation is a policy objective, such as Kendall/MIT, these places are evolving more like mixed-use urban office parks where the role of production is not robust or well defined (see Corneil, Chapter 2).

Findings: Regulation

In keeping with the mixed land use patterns, most zoning ordinances enable commercial/industrial mixed use although there are usually some restrictions: prohibiting some uses that are perceived to be "invasive," such as hotels, and limiting the maximum size of others. For example, in Cincinnati, food markets must be less than 3,000 square feet, and meeting facilities less than 5,000 square feet. Several cities are contemplating residential/industrial mixed use, such as Pittsburgh's NDI (Neighborhood Industrial zone) and Cincinnati's IX (Mixed Industrial zone). Aware of the challenges of industrial/residential mixed use (see Part III), these codes restrict residential uses in various ways, limiting the size, number, and location of units and even requiring prospective buyers to sign an agreement acknowledging manufacturing activities and essentially waiving their right to complain about nuisances. As discussed in Chapters 11 and 12, it is not clear if even these provisions can stop displacement.

For administrative ease, control is primarily through the conventional strategy of listing uses that are either permitted, prohibited, or conditional, although cities vary in terms of how detailed and place-specific the lists of permitted uses are. There is also considerable variation in the degree of discretion that the reviewing entities allow themselves: special permit and conditional permit processes vary from city to city in terms of the application of more qualitative, performance-based language. For example, Berkeley requires a finding by the planning office that a proposed non-manufacturing use will nevertheless "support the light-industrial character" of the district.

Some measure of curating occurs through the conditional approvals process and the zoning appeals process. Criteria for review can include "softer" criteria about overall impact on the character of the area, for example, in Chicago and Cleveland (see below). In Chicago, zoning requires the Board of Zoning Appeals (BZA) to consider additional factors to grant variances in Planned Manufacturing Districts. The BZA must consider a proposal's potential for land-use conflicts and nuisance complaints, the property owners' efforts to market the property for industrial use, and the number and types of jobs in the district. These guidelines ensure that variances are consistent with zoning codes and protect industrial uses.

Acknowledgments

This Atlas and the research that supports it was created with the help of several people. Most of the GIS-based land-use mapping was done by Ellis Calvin. Anna Ousler did the initial rounds of exploratory interviews and the preliminary assessment of the zoning and policy documents used to select the case study cities and sites. The maps were refined by Manuela Uribe. Minkyung Song and Ruixue Jie developed the layout for the Atlas with the help of Manuela Powidayko Souza, Claire Mardian, and Ben Oldenburg. Additional image research was done by Jessica Laurel Arias. Additional site photos were provided by: Emily Roach, Matthew Coburn, Ekaterina Trosman, Nahal Mohatashemi, Amber Ford, Mesa Sherrif, Patrick Slevin, Jennifer Gonzalez, and Urantsetseg Munkhbayer.

Legacy industrial buildings in Cleveland, Ohio.

CITY-WIDE CONTEXT

Barcelona

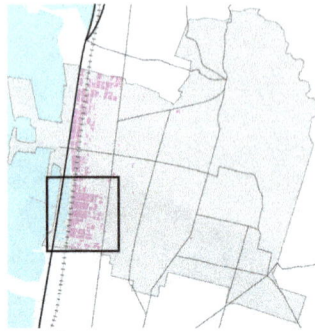

Berkeley

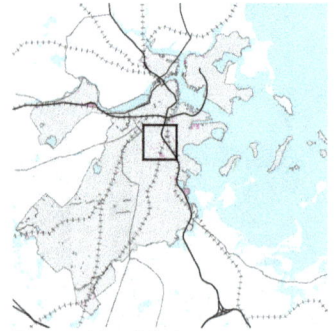

Boston, New Market

Cleveland

Milan Breda

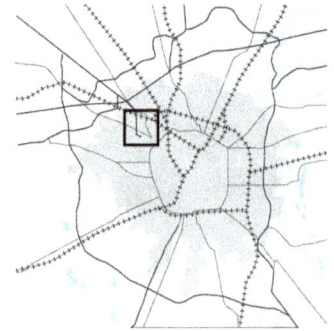

Milan Certosa

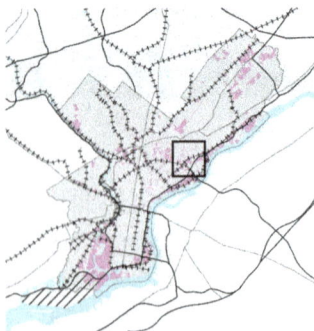

Philadelphia

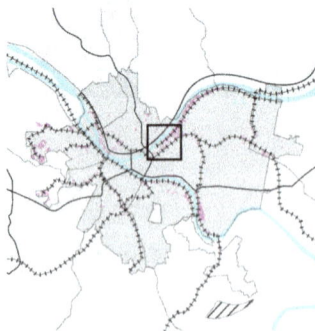

Pittsburgh

Portland

Relationship to the Central Business District (CBD)

Most of the places where cities are wrestling with how to manage urban production are on the edges of the central businesses districts, places that represent the equilibrium—and tension—between excessive real-estate pressure and the benefits of agglomeration such as proximity to their suppliers, customers, designers, researchers, and marketers. A few are farther away (Milwaukee 30th Street corridor, Georgetown district in Seattle, Aramingo district in Philadelphia) and a few are right in the heart of the CBD (LA's Fashion District, Manhattan's Garment Center, the Dog

Patch and Mission districts in San Francisco, Berkeley's industrial west side). Interestingly, the two "Innovation Districts" discussed by Janne Corneil are both center-city locations, as is the Certosa case study in Milan. While most of the case study districts are within a mile or less of the CBD, there is often some clear threshold between the core and the district. Sometimes the barrier is a natural feature like a river (Portland's Central East Side, New York City's North Williamsburg, Chicago's Goose Island). In other cases, highway or rail infrastructure creates the edge (Dogpatch in San Francisco, "the Strip" in Pittsburgh). In all cases, regardless of how mixed the uses are in the district itself, they are all are surrounded by mixed-use neighborhoods.

CITY-WIDE CONTEXT

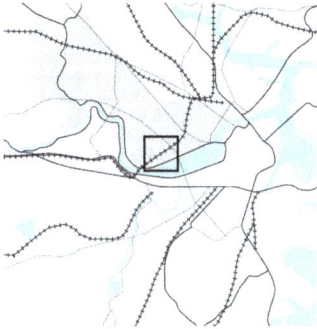

Cambridge, Kendall / MIT

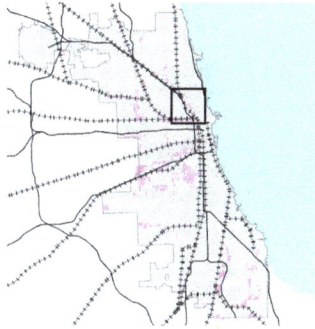

Chicago, Goose Island

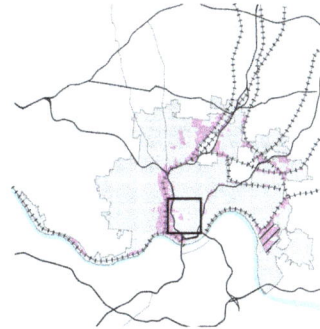

Cincinatti Over the Rhine

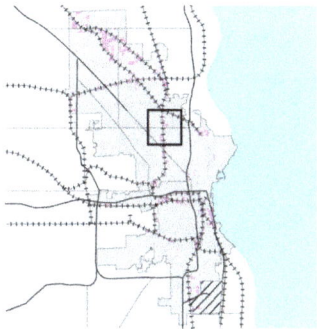

Milwaukee

New York, Garment District

New York, North Williamsburg

San Francisco

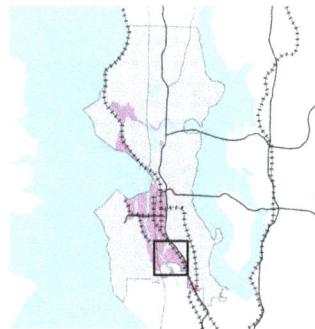

Seattle

Vancouver

Relationship to Major Infrastructure

With a few exceptions (Milwaukee 30th Street corridor, Kendal/MIT), the case study districts have excellent highway access, reflecting the primacy of truck-based goods movement. Neither the Breda (Milan) or 22@ (Barcelona) districts are adjacent to a major highway, but major roads are not far away. Surprisingly, many of the North American case studies have rail access, a legacy of an earlier era. Often, there is still some intermittent service, keeping open the possibility of a less truck-dependent future.

While many of the districts are not far from water, only a few are near active waterfronts (Chicago,

Pittsburgh, Seattle, North Williamsburg, San Francisco, Vancouver). Others, such as Portland and Berkeley, are near recreational waterfronts. As with rail, there is renewed interest in using waterways for goods movement, which, as demonstrated in some European cities, can be reconciled with public access (see Conway, Chapter 4, this volume).

In terms of transit, all of the districts are connected by bus and some by rail and bus, although transit within the districts themselves may be limited. In these cases, pedestrian and bike mobility needs to be reconciled with truck access.

BUILT PATTERN

Barcelona

Berkeley

Boston, New Market

Cleveland

Milan Breda

Milan Certosa

Philadelphia

Pittsburgh

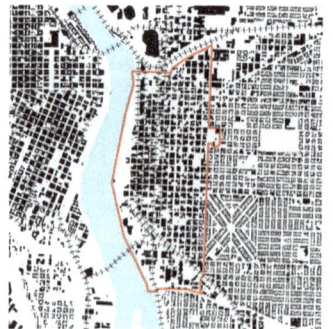
Portland

As the figure and ground diagrams show, built patterns are very diverse, a result of the wide variety of building types and configurations. At one extreme, there are districts where the built pattern is very dense, with factory buildings covering most of their sites, such as the Garment Center in New York and the 22@ Innovation District in Barcelona. At the other extreme are urban industrial parks where single-story "flex" buildings cover half or less of their sites, such as the Georgetown district in Seattle. While building types

are diverse, most of the case study districts have variations on this urban industrial park model—low-rise factories organized around loading and storage areas. However, even in these low-rise districts, there may be a flagship vertical mixed-use building that helps create the identity for the district, such as the Globe Dye Works building in the Aramingo case study (Philadelphia) and the Greenpoint Manufacturing and Design Center in the North Williamsburg (New York City) case study.

BUILT PATTERN

Cambridge, Kendall / MIT

Chicago, Goose Island

Cincinatti Over the Rhine

Milwaukee

New York, Garment District

New York, North Williamsburg

San Francisco

Seattle

Vancouver

Note: All images are the same scale.

LAND USE

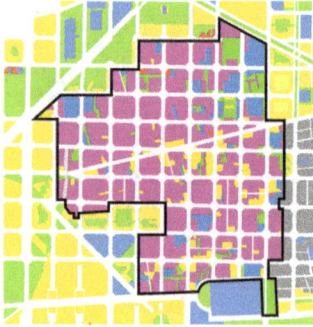

Barcelona

Berkeley

Boston, New Market

Cleveland

Milan Breda

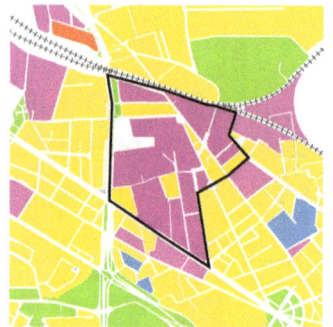

Milan Certosa

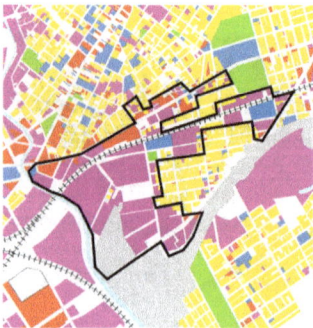

Philadelphia

Pittsburgh

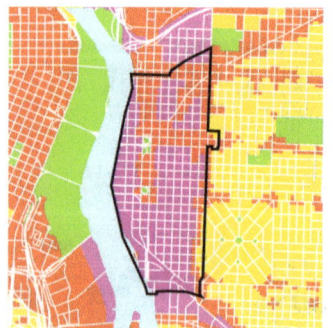

Portland

Land use patterns are diverse. In some cases, such as North Williamsburg (Brooklyn, New York), Georgetown (Seattle), and the Near East Side (Portland), there is a diverse but consolidated mix of industrial uses. More typically there is a mix of commercial and industrial activities, such as the Barcelona and Philadelphia case studies. In about half of the cases studies, there are mixed-use blocks at the edges of the districts, the zone of transition between the district and the neighborhood, including residential uses. Berkeley, Newmarket (Boston), and Over-the-Rhine (Cincinnati) are representative. A few of the European case studies, such as 22@ (Barcelona) and the Certosa district in Milan, fully embrace mixed uses, including social housing.

LAND USE

Cambridge, Kendall / MIT

Chicago, Goose Island

Cincinatti Over the Rhine

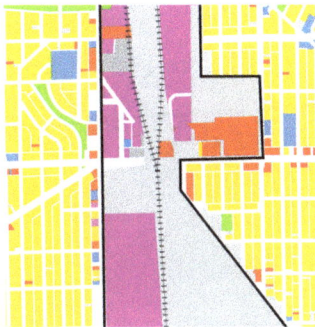

Milwaukee

New York, Garment District

New York, North Williamsburg

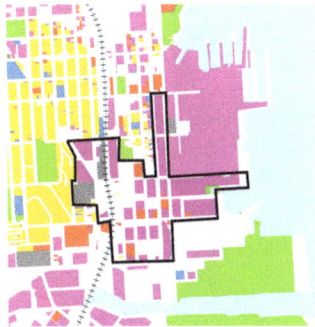

San Francisco

Seattle

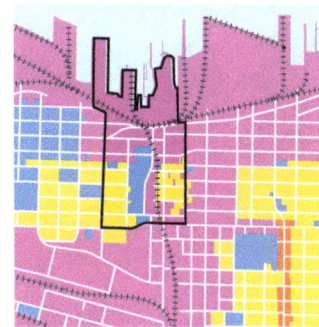

Vancouver

Note: All images are the same scale.

Residential
Commercial
Industrial
Institutional
Vacant
Open Space
Water

STREET AND BLOCK NETWORK

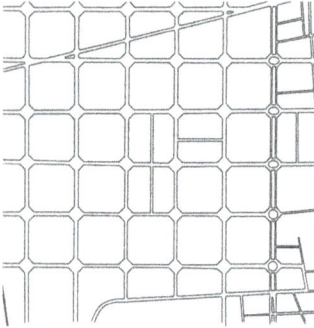
Barcelona

Berkeley

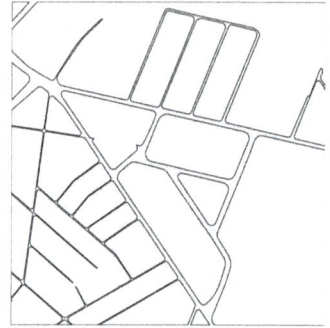
Boston, New Market

Cleveland

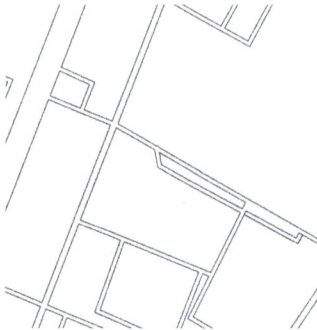
Milan Breda

Milan Certosa

Philadelphia

Pittsburgh

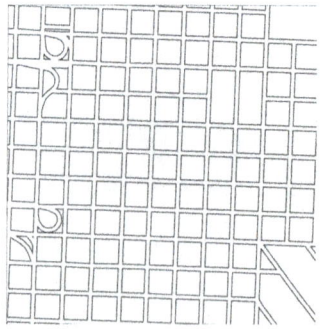
Portland

Many industrial districts have street and block patterns that are extensions of the surrounding neighborhoods. Portland's Near East Side, Manhattan's Garment District, and Barcelona's 22@ are the purest examples, demonstrating that a healthy industrial district can flourish even where the edge is completely permeable and that most contemporary manufacturing can be accommodated in the city fabric. A similar but less pure condition is West Berkeley, where most of the blocks are standard in size, but where in parts of the district discontinuous streets create superblocks.

In as many cases, the regular street and block pattern gives way to over-sized and irregular blocks, a legacy of former large-scale factories and rights-of-way for infrastructure such as canals, highways, and rail lines, some of which are now underutilized. While these irregular blocks sometimes reduce connectivity, they also help create the type of diverse and adaptable fabric that supports urban manufacturing, and the discontinuity with the surrounding neighborhoods can help define the edge of the district, as in the Newmarket (Boston) case.

STREET AND BLOCK NETWORK

Cambridge, Kendall / MIT

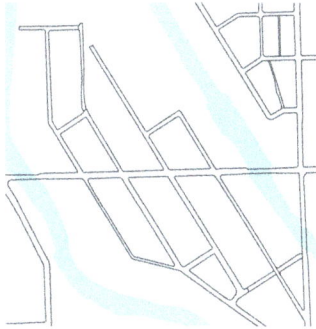

Chicago, Goose Island

Cincinatti Over the Rhine

Milwaukee

New York, Garment District

New York, North Williamsburg

San Francisco

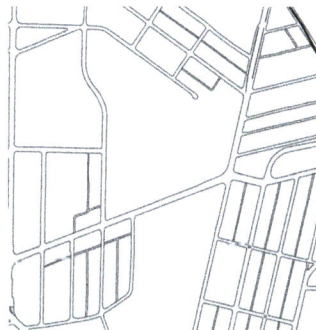

Seattle

Vancouver

Note: All images are the same scale.

At Kendall/MIT the large blocks create an environment more akin to an office campus than a production district.

Larger complexes that were once stand-alone facilities, and that are now managed by public or private mission-driven entities, like Breda in Milan, the Brooklyn Navy Yard, and Industry City, have their own idiosyncratic campus structure.

OBLIQUE AERIALS

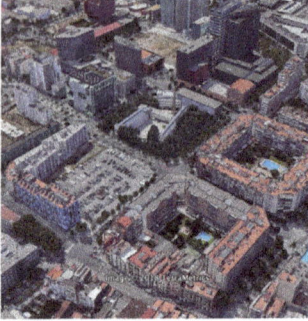

Barcelona
● Loft
● Neighborhood
○ Industrial Park

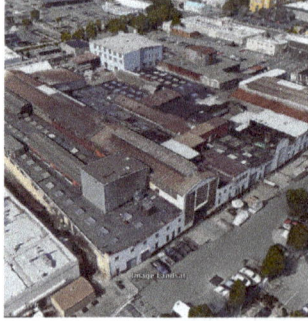

Berkeley
○ Loft
◐ Neighborhood
● Industrial Park

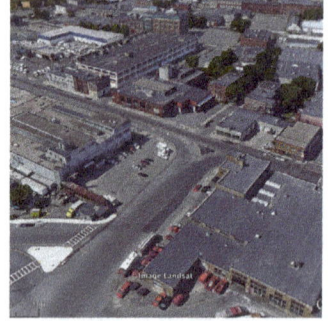

Boston, New Market
○ Loft
◐ Neighborhood
◐ Industrial Park

Cleveland
◐ Loft
◐ Neighborhood
  Industrial Park

Milan Breda
◐ Loft
○ Neighborhood
● Industrial Park

Milan Certosa
◐ Loft
● Neighborhood
○ Industrial Park

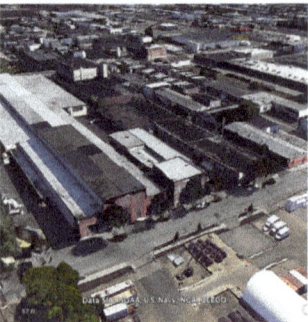

Philadelphia
○ Loft
○ Neighborhood
● Industrial Park

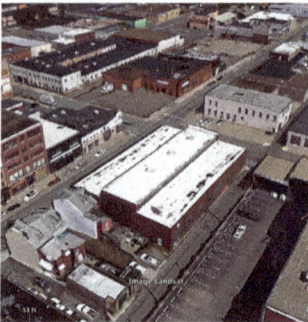

Pittsburgh
○ Loft
◐ Neighborhood
◐ Industrial Park

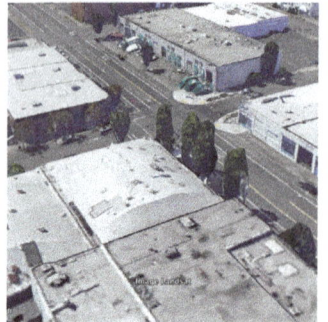

Portland
○ Loft
○ Neighborhood
● Industrial Park

All images courtesy of Google Earth.

Google Earth

OBLIQUE AERIALS

Cambridge, Kendall MIT
● Loft
○ Neighborhood
○ Industrial Park

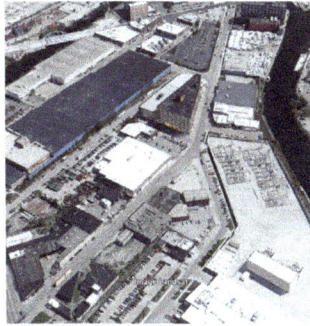

Chicago, Goose Island
○ Loft
○ Neighborhood
○ Industrial Park

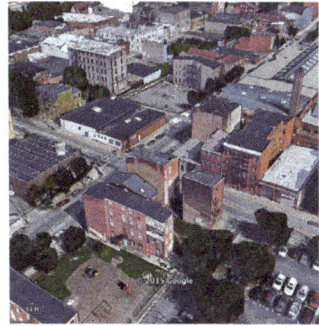

Cincinatti Over the Rhine
○ Loft
● Neighborhood
○ Industrial Park

Milwaukee
○ Loft
○ Neighborhood
● Industrial Park

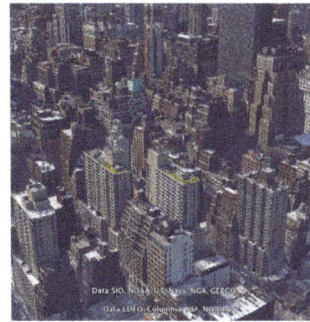

New York, Garment District
● Loft
○ Neighborhood
○ Industrial Park

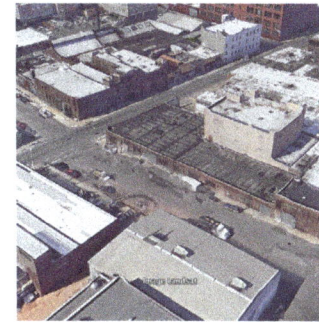

New York, North Williamsburg
○ Loft
◑ Neighborhood
● Industrial Park

San Francisco
○ Loft
● Neighborhood
◑ Industrial Park

Seattle
○ Loft
◑ Neighborhood
● Industrial Park

Vancouver
○ Loft
○ Neighborhood
● Industrial Park

All images courtesy of Google Earth.

Google Earth

INDUSTRIAL DISTRICT TYPOLOGY

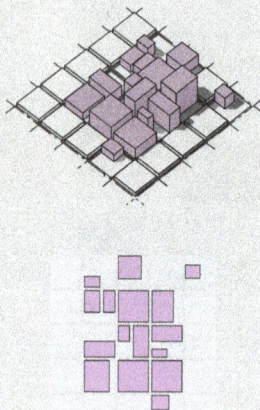

Loft districts. Loft districts are populated primarily by large-footprint, mid-rise (six to twelve stories) factories that are characteristic of the first wave of urban industrialization when vertical integration and gravity-flow production methods dominated (late seventeenth to mid-twentieth centuries). These districts were exclusively industrial at first, but because many of them are closer to the center of the city where real-estate values are highest, new commercial and residential uses have displaced much of the manufacturing, creating more mixed-use districts. These buildings create well-defined and active streets. Some loft districts were designed and planned by a single developer or manufacturer but most were developed organically following the same street and block pattern as the rest of a city and so the edges of the district may be ambiguous.

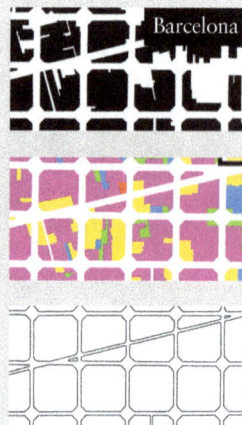
Barcelona

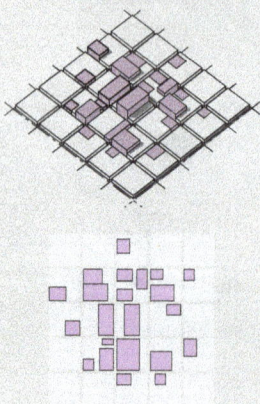

Manufacturing neighborhoods. Manufacturing neighborhoods, as the name suggests, feature a fine-grain mix of activities with production spaces next to or below living spaces. This reflects the organic growth of these places at a time before zoning or urban design sought to separate or rationalize the uses. The edges of the neighborhood may be hard to define because most of the streets extend into the surrounding areas and land uses change gradually. The streets are generally well-defined and active and may have buildings of every scale and type side-by-side, from small walk-up apartment buildings to loft factories, to small one-story sheds with only an entry and roll-down gates along street frontages.

Berkeley

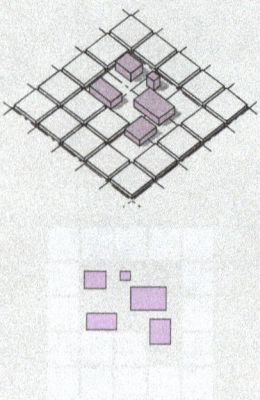

The urban industrial park. The urban industrial park has many of the same features associated with its suburban counterpart: many single-story factories with large expanses of windowless walls; lower-coverage site plans to enable off-street loading, storage, or expansion; and almost exclusively industrial uses. As a result, the edges of the district may be clear but inhospitable to the surrounding neighborhoods; the space of the streets may be well-defined but not well-animated; and there may be fewer land-use conflicts but also fewer amenities for workers including public spaces for interaction.

Seattle

INDUSTRIAL DISTRICT TYPOLOGY

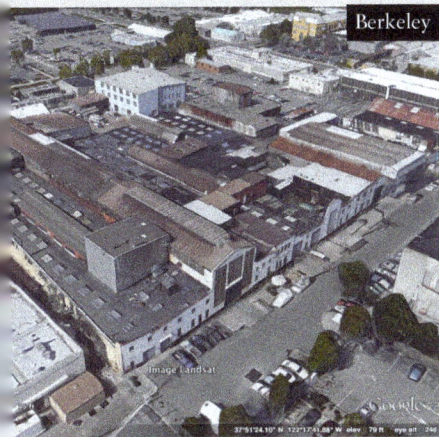

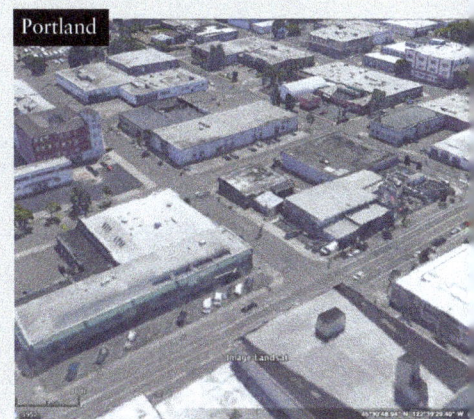

Oblique aerial views courtesy of Google Earth.

Google Earth

EDGE TYPOLOGY

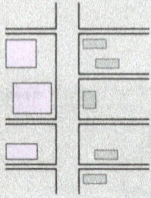

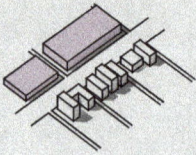

Hard edges. Differences in use, building type, and configuration make the edge of the industrial district extremely clear. While this creates a clear and defensible boundary from both a design and regulatory perspective, stark differences in building scale and character can make for a harsh, unbalanced, and uninviting streetscape.

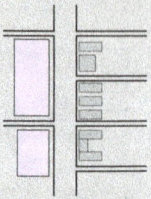

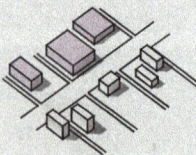

Philadelphia, Aramingo

Soft edges. There is a consistent break between industrial uses and non-industrial neighborhood uses. However, because often there are sparsely developed or vacant parcels, and because buildings do not have a consistent relationship to the street, the boundaries of the district are not well defined and the streetscape is uninviting.

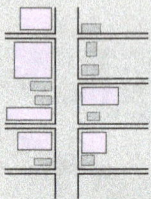

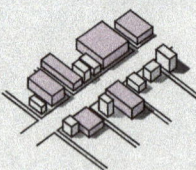

Berkeley, West Side

Mixed edges. There are industrial and non-industrial uses on either side of the industrial district boundary, which has been established for the purposes of policy and regulation. While this condition is often associated with the complex mixed-use patterns of active manufacturing neighborhoods, it is also the most challenging condition to manage. (see Rappaport, Chapter 10.)

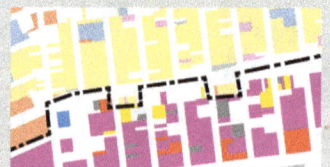

Boston, New Market

EDGE TYPOLOGY

Vancouver, Strathcona

Philadelphia, Aramingo

Berkeley, West Side

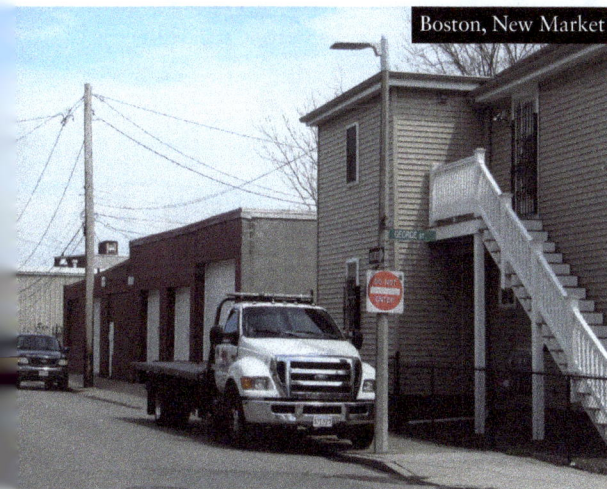

Boston, New Market

Edge Typology

The edge of the industrial district is the frontier where real-estate markets, urban design, and policy intersect. Is it a wall or a filter? There may be "hard edges" where abrupt changes in buildings scale and land use create a clear but intimidating edge; or "soft edges" where building types are mixed, land uses are mixed, and continuous streets make the edge porous and less discrete.

Typically, the districts are bounded by two, sometimes three "hard edges" created by a highway, rail line, or water body and creating some discontinuity in the street pattern. "The Strip" in Pittsburgh, for example, is bounded on three sides—by topography. These edges have helped create a bulwark against displacement.

However, in most cases there are just as many—or more—soft edges. Because a district boundary may run down the middle of the street, the industrial and residential sides of the street are sometimes in uncomfortable opposition.

These edge conditions manifest the dynamic between the need to defend against displacement and the desire to connect to the life of the city.

STREETS

Cleveland: Mixed-use street in the Mid-town industrial district

Barcelona: Mixed-use street in Barcelona's @22 innovation district

Vancouver: Diversity of factory types and sizes along a street in the Strathcona district

Los Angeles: On-street loading and staging at the edge of the Arts District

Boston: Houses and factories side-by-side in the Newmarket innovation district

Los Angeles: Diverse building stock along this street in the Arts District

STREETS

In very dense districts, such as New York's Garment District or Barcelona's 22@, industrial streets are alive not only with production-related activities like loading and delivery, but with all the activities of the city from retail and restaurants to office and hotel lobby entrances. However, these are exceptions, even in Europe where districts are more mixed-use. More representative is the industrial street that is lined with one-story windowless factories, which both make the street spatially well-defined and at the same time inhospitable. Even if this is a representative condition, the case studies reveal many other idiosyncratic conditions; in Portland, even though the one-story factory box is almost universal, many of the streets are interesting and animated because there are openings onto the street. Similar conditions can be found in Los Angeles. In addition, in Portland and Berkeley, some streets are designed to be through-corridors for pedestrian and bicycles as well as trucks. On some mixed-use streets, there can be asymmetrical conditions where, similar to some of the hard-edge conditions, factories and residences are in opposition. This is apparent in Milwaukee, Seattle, and Newmarket (Boston). As the Portland (Oregon) and Certosa (Milan) case studies show, street landscaping can soften the impact of long expanses of blank wall or the opposition of different scale uses.

Portland: Bike routes are accommodated in the streets of the Near East Side

Berkeley: Bayer campus streets were redesigned to link to the rest of the district

N. Williamsburg, NYC: Typical street in a lowrise industrial district has loading and staging activities spill out onto the sidewalk

PUBLIC SPACES

Milan Navigli District: Ansaldo inner courtyard. Laboratory spaces on the right make sets and costumes for La Scala

Milan Navigli District: Via Tortona during Design Week

Berkeley: Service alleys lead to the interior of the block

Beyer campus in Berkeley: What were leftover spaces between production buildings were re-designed as shared amenity spaces

Berkeley: Left-over spaces are fitted out for visitors and workers

Milan: This service area in the Ansaldo district is now landscaped public space

PUBLIC SPACES

Formal public spaces are unusual in the case study industrial districts surveyed here, with a few exceptions in those places like Berkeley, where groups of buildings are managed by a single owner or entity. Other exceptions in Europe are the mid-block spaces like those found in Barcelona's 22@ district or courtyards like those found in the Breda (Milan) case study. Sometimes, as at Over-the-Rhine in Cincinnati, formal open spaces are just outside of the industrial district, but are so proximate and well-connected that they feel like they are part of it.

However, typically, industrial districts are spotted with informal, leftover spaces that can be appropriated for different kinds of production-related uses. These kinds of spaces can be seen at the Newmarket, Dogpatch, and Cleveland case studies. In Barcelona, the chamfered corners of the Cerda blocks are used this way.

Many of the districts have waterfront edges and this creates a conflict between production and public access. In Georgetown (Seattle), there is no access. In North Williamsburg, there is single point of access at the end of a dead-end street. In Portland, however, it is possible to access the waterfront greenway by passing through the Near East Side Industrial Area.

Portland: Loading docks become sites for meals and meet-ups

Industry City, Brooklyn, NY: Courtyards between loft factories are being converted into interactive spaces

ARCHITECTURE

Berkeley: Industrial materials are used on this live-work streetscape

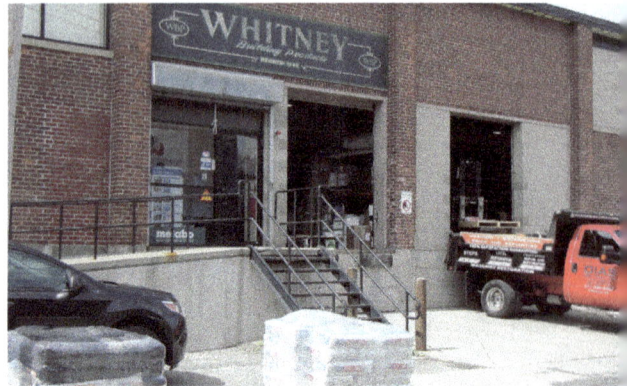

Boston: Loading dock and retail office side-by-side in Newmarket.

Portland: Individual workshop entrances animate streetscape in the Near East Side

Los Angeles: One story factory in the Arts District

Boston: Loading dock for the Markforged factory (see interview, p. 19)

Cleveland: Typical one-story factory shed

ARCHITECTURE

Industrial district architecture is extremely diverse, reflecting successive generations of production methodologies and scales, and each with different programmatic and spatial requirements. The loft districts have largely been converted to non-industrial uses, although, as the Garment Center (NYC) case study shows, there are some exceptions. More typically, these districts are populated with low-rise factories, occasionally covering their entire site but more typically covering anywhere from one-third to two-thirds of the site, with the rest given over to storage or offstreet loading. The Georgetown (Seattle) case study is representative of this condition. However, even where low-rise factories dominate, there is a great deal of variation in the scale and massing of the buildings, reflecting successive generations of modification, replacement, and adaptation, as seen at Dogpatch (San Francisco, California), Cleveland (Ohio), and Berkeley (California). In the "Innovation Districts," such as Breda, Barcelona, and Kendall/MIT, there may be office, lab, and even residential buildings mixed in. These districts are sometimes anchored by a vertical, mixed-industrial building where a single owner has the ability to curate the business mix. Examples include the not-for-profit Greenpoint Manufacturing and Design Center in North Williamsburg (New York) and Globe Dye Works building in Philadelphia's Aramingo district. In Milan, legacy factories, like those at the Certosa complex, are reused as part of a conscious effort to project the manufacturing culture of the city.

Philadeplhia: Diverse mix of historic low-rose and loft factories in the Aramingo mixed-manufacturing district

MIlan: Sustainable wooden skin on this building by Citterio in the Rova 1920 factory complex, Brianza (courtesy of Rova 1920)

All images courtesy of Google Earth.

Milwaukee: 1-story factory boxes are the most comon factory type in N. American industrial districts

Google Earth

INDUSTRIAL DISTRICT STRATEGIES

Manufacturing Neighborhoods

- *Edges*. Because these places developed organically in an era before zoning, the edges are often without definition except for those edges defined by some infrastructure element such as a highway or rail line or a natural feature such as a waterfront.

- *Streets*. The space of the street is generally very well-defined by buildings that meet the sidewalk, although a mixed-manufacturing street may have buildings of every scale and character side-by-side, from small walk-up apartment buildings, to loft factories, to small one-story sheds with little more facing the sidewalk than an entry and roll-down gate. Narrow streets struggle to accommodate pedestrians, bicycles, cars, trucks, and off-loading operations.

- *Public spaces*. Because these places are true neighborhoods, there are often parks, playgrounds, and other kinds of formal open spaces in addition to the various informal open spaces that tend to be found in industrial districts.

Loft Districts

- *Edges*. Because the older loft buildings are similar in scale and character to other buildings in the core, and because the street grid is continuous, the edges of loft districts are almost indiscernible unless there is some large infrastructure element present such as a waterway, highway, or rail line.

- *Streets*. The space of the street is well defined and animated by the loft buildings that may have entries and activities facing the sidewalk. In still-active production areas like the Garment Center in New York City, goods movement will compete for street and sidewalk space.

- *Public spaces*. More so than elsewhere in the core, open spaces are scarce because these older manufacturing districts were not planned with urban amenities in mind. In some places that are transitioning to a more mixed-use pattern, loading docks are becoming opportunities for pop-up activities.

Urban Industrial Park

- *Edges*. The edges of the urban industrial campus are of all kinds. For an industrial redevelopment project, such as Bathgate or a restored navy yard, the edges may be designed to be very discrete. However, where the industrial park is created by simply superimposing a new jurisdictional boundary over an existing industrial area, the edges are likely to be much less well defined. In this case the edges can vary from being very hard—a highway or rail line—to quite soft—blocks with mixed building types and uses. Here the issue of balancing integration with encroachment comes to the fore. (See Edge Typology, above.)

- *Streets*. Streets in the urban industrial park are of different kinds. There may be mixed-use streets at the edges—a legacy of a former era. However, because the predominant factory type is a low-rise building with open loading and storage areas, the more typical street is one lined with one-story block walls, with or without openings or clerestories, and interrupted by the occasional yard, which may or may not be well screened.

- *Public spaces*. As with other industrial areas, these districts were not planned with urban design and amenity in mind so there are few public spaces. In some cases where these areas are along waterways, there may be some waterfront access points. In addition, open land devoted to off-street loading and storage often serves as informal open space where workers gather to have lunch or other activities.

RECOMMENDATIONS

Form/Strategies Matrix

	Edges	Streets	Public Spaces	Other
Loft Districts	• Create an identity for the district using lighting, signage and other streetscape elements. • Implement design guidelines to create transition in scale from loft buildings to smaller buildings.	• Design streets that accommodate pedestrians but enable flexible goods movement and curb-side loading/un-loading. • Enable selected streets to be programmed for alternative, complementary activities such as trade fairs and exhibitions.	• Enable loading docks and service areas to be used for alternative, complementary uses at different times of the day. • Use residual spaces such as alleys to create alternative means of moving through the district, both for people and goods. • Use building courtyards or block interiors as places for interaction, public communication, programming.	• Allow building on top of larger structures where possible. • Consolidate manufacturing on lower floors to enable vertical mixed use • Identify locations for district freight consolidation and distribution.
Manufacturing Neighborhoods	• Create an identity for the district using lighting, signage and other streetscape elements. • Promote mixeduse infill buildings on gap sites at the edges.	• Create flexible street designs that can accommodate alternative frontage conditions for residential, commercial and industrial uses. • Create and map street typologies calibrated to primary use/character: residential, industrial, mixed.	• Identify neighborhood spaces that can function as centers of interaction, public communication, and complementary programming. • Repurpose underutilized infrastructure rights-of-way, such as rail yards, to create new kinds of public spaces.	• Allow flexible live/work infill buildings.
Urban Industrial Park	• Create district boundaries at the mid-block or at the ends of blocks to avoid streets with opposing residential and industrial uses. • Clearly articulate the boundaries of the district through landscaping, artwork and signage. • Enable mixed-use buildings that create the transition between industrial and non-industrial zones	• Identify strategic corridors connecting the district to the context and design these corridors for multiple users. • Use openings and changes in massing to mitigate unrelieved expanses of blank walls.	• Rationalize/consolidate parking and loading areas to create new open spaces for shared services, interaction, programming • Identify spaces where manufacturing processes can be made visible to the public • Create shared mid-block spaces for production- related activities by limiting through traffic and aggregating street space, offstreet parking and loading areas. ("semi-superblocks"). • Create new rights-of-way through excessively long blocks.	• Enable higher building coverage and space for expansion through flexible parking and off-street loading strategies. • Promote transformation of the "factory shed": create new openings, subdivide for multiples users, attach new structures for new programs
Other/for all	• Repurpose underutilized infrastructure rights-of-way, such as rail yards, to create new kinds of public spaces, green infrastructure opportunities. • Internet access upgrades. • Eco-industrial strategies • District energy strategies. • Linkages to anchor institutions.			

Note: Many strategies apply to more than one district type.

STREET AND BLOCK STRATEGIES

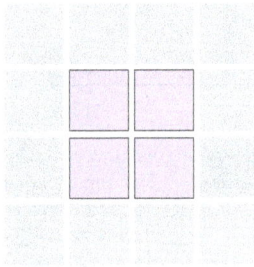

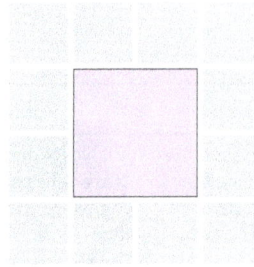

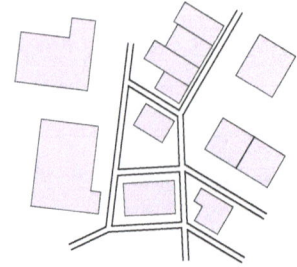

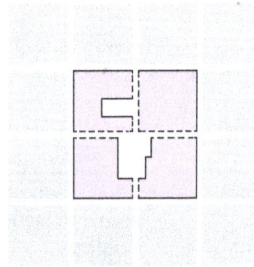

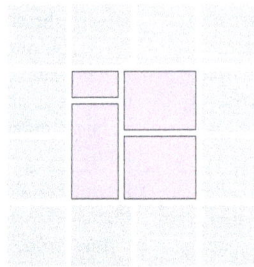

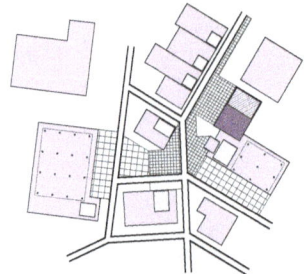

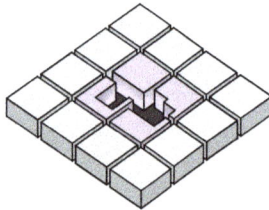

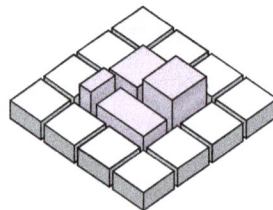

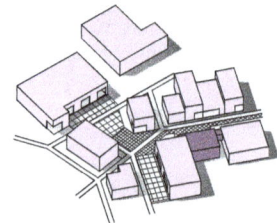

Create "Virtual Superblocks"

Informal and irregular shared spaces promote interaction and the mixing of different kinds of activity at different times of the day. By mapping some streets as dedicated "factory streets," a sort of industrial "superblock" is created that is connected to the surrounding context, but also enables the unfettered movement, interaction, and activity of an industrial park and creates an internal courtyard where manufacturers can share resources, consolidate goods movement and delivery, and host informal amenities such as food trucks.

Create a Diversity of Block Sizes

Large, oversized parcels are common in industrial districts. When introducing new streets into these areas, balance direct extensions of surrounding streets with off-set and discontinuous streets. This will create a diversity of parcel sizes for different production building types and help create the kinds of incidental and informal spaces that promote interaction and different kinds of activity.

Leave the Left-Overs

Street patterns in older industrial districts may be irregular and idiosyncratic, a result of historic factories and the infrastructure that served them. While the standard urban design approach would be to infill these left-over spaces, in fact, these incidental and informal spaces can promote interaction and activity. These spaces should be rationalized and redesigned to promote different kinds of use at different times of day.

STREET AND BLOCK STRATEGIES

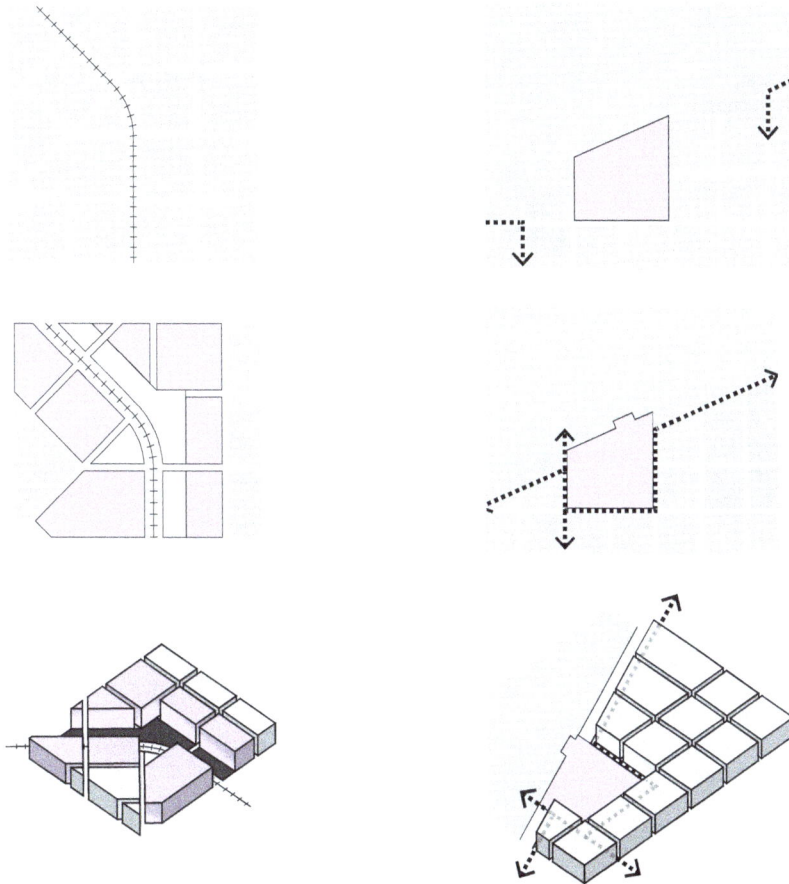

Create Multi-Purpose Infrastructure Corridors

Industrial districts are rich in transportation infrastructure, including active and inactive rail lines. As with stretches of working waterfronts, these rail corridors should be preserved not only in anticipation of future rail-based goods movement, but as corridors for other kinds of in-ground infrastructure such as internet fiber, as movement corridors, and as open-space amenities both within the district and beyond.

Balance Waterfront Access with Goods Movement

Many, if not most, industrial districts are along waterfronts that enable current—or future—opportunities for water-based goods movement. In some cases this creates conflicts with the objective of creating continuous public waterfront access that has become a staple of urban revitalization. While waterfront access is increased by completing and connecting discontinuous streets along the water's edge, this should be balanced with enabling waterfront access for goods movement. Single access points should be created where possible. Waterfront greenways should have clear routes inland and around the working waterfront areas.

EDGE STRATEGIES

Avoid locating district boundaries on street alignments. This often creates "hard-edge" asymmetrical streets where neighborhood scale entrances and activities must face off against industrial-scale buildings with large expanses of blank walls and loading operations. Where land use patterns support it, two alternative configurations are suggested: mid-block alleys and block ends.

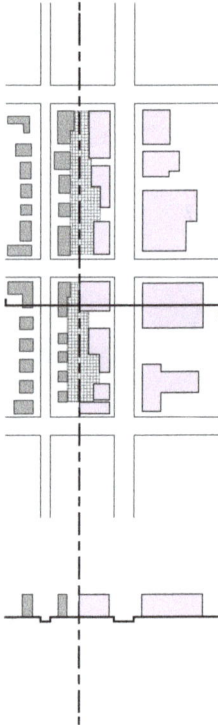

Mid-Block Alleys

Use a midblock laneway or alley as the transition between the backs of the residential properties facing the residential street and the backs of the industrial properties facing the industrial district street. The laneway or alley can become a shared service zone for both the residential and industrial properties. This pattern is observed at the Cleveland and Vancouver case studies. Industrial uses must be compatible in terms of noise, hours of operation, and traffic volumes and building massing needs to allow for transitions in scale between industrial and residential buildings.

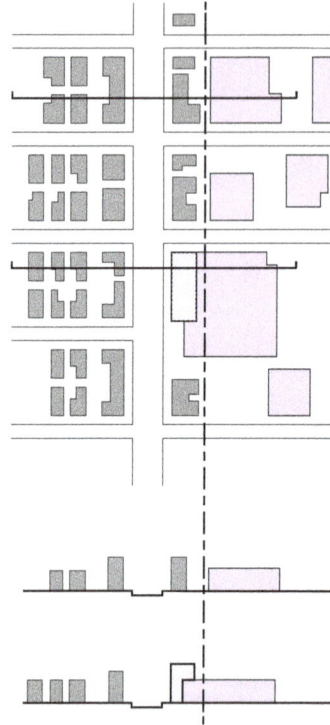

Block Ends

The parcels at the ends of the blocks facing a wide street are often deeper than the side-street parcels and accommodate larger-scale residential or mixed-use buildings. The alignment along the back of these properties can create a clear transition between a residential or mixed-use avenue and the consolidated industrial land uses behind. This pattern is observed at the North Williamsburg case study. Where industrial parcels meet the avenue, hybrid industrial-residential mixed-use building types can be used to complete the avenue while creating the transition to the industrial district uses. (See design studies by Pandolfo, p. 43, and Lane, p. 44).

EDGE STRATEGIES

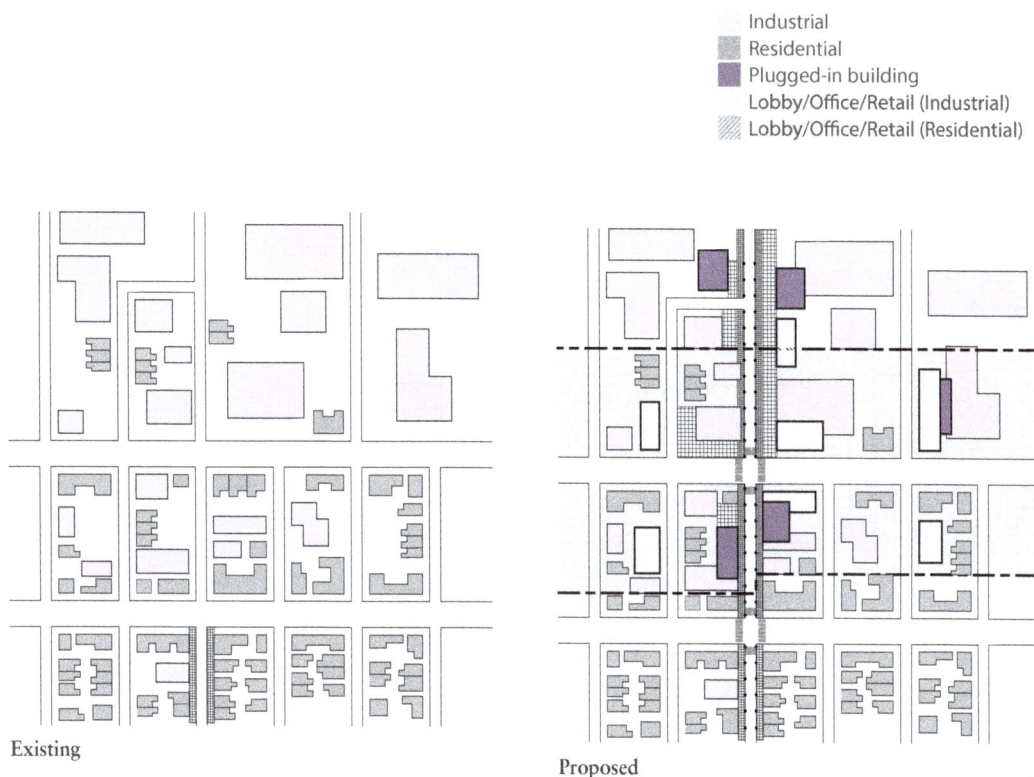

Industrial
Residential
Plugged-in building
Lobby/Office/Retail (Industrial)
Lobby/Office/Retail (Residential)

Existing

Proposed

Mixed-Use Overlay Zones

At mixed-use edges, district boundaries are often gerry-mandered to approximate as best as possible some consolidated land-use patterns. A challenging but dynamic alternative is to create a mixed-use transitional zone between the neighborhood and the industrial district. As with other mixed-use neighborhoods, it is a challenge to resolve conflicts and sustain the mixed-use pattern over the long term.

- Along predominantly residential streets, enable industrial/residential mixed-use building types.
- Soften large expanses of blank factory walls by creating new openings and promoting context-sensitive building artwork.

- Enliven factory elevations along key connecting corridors by promoting visible entrances and by encouraging ground-floor retail outlets or other activities that relate to the street.
- Allow additional floor area so that the "factory box" can be enlivened with additional program elements.

EDGE STRATEGIES

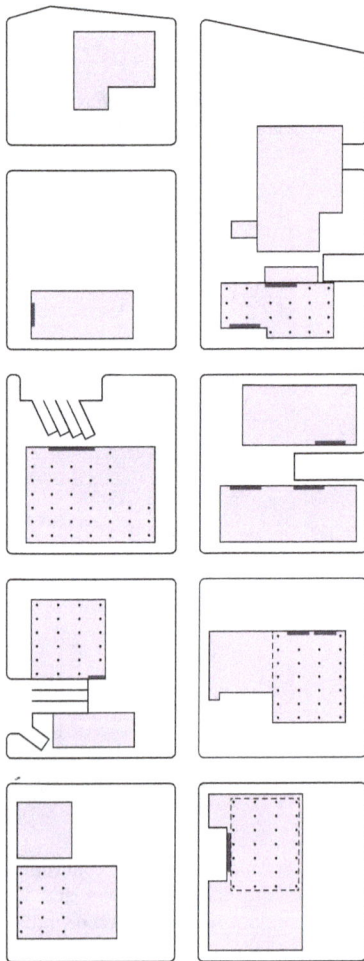

Existing

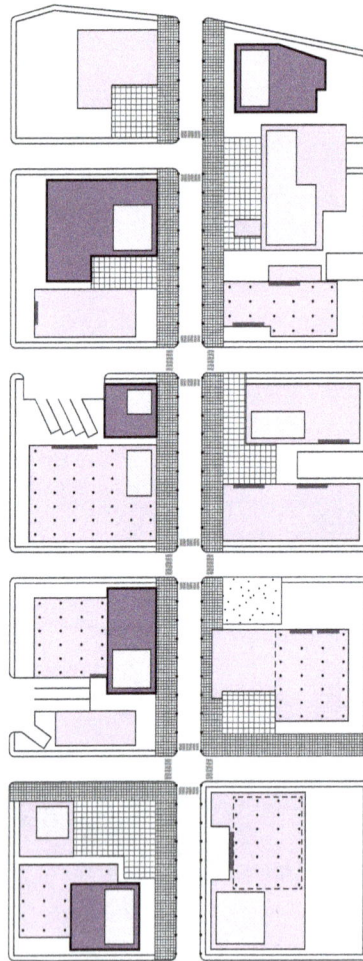

Proposed

Industrial
Residential
Plugged-in building
Lobby/Office/Retail (Industrial)
Lobby/Office/Retail (Residential)

Create New Connecting Corridors

One way to integrate industrial districts with their surrounding context is by identifying roads that can function as mixed-use corridors, linking the district to other destinations. Along the corridor, manufacturers should be encouraged to display their processes and to open offices, showrooms, and outlets. Incidental and left-over spaces along the corridor become places for manufacturers to gather and interact with the public. To keep the adjoining industrial areas intact, mixed-use overlay zoning would be

Vancouver: Diversity of factory types and sizes along these streets in the Strathcona district

confined to the properties immediately abutting the corridor. This strategy is effectively used at the Beyer facility case study in Berkeley and the Certosa case study in Milan. As with the mixed-use overlay zones described above, this strategy is supported by design.

- Enable industrial/residential mixed-use building types (see Part III).
- Soften large expanses of blank factory walls by creating new openings and promoting context-sensitive building artwork.
- Enliven factory elevations along key connecting corridors by promoting visible entrances and by encouraging ground-floor retail outlets or other activities that relate to the street.
- Allow additional floor area so that the "factory box" can be enlivened with additional program elements.
- Provide enough infrastructure to enable left-over spaces along the corridor to be programmed in different ways at different times of the day.
- Link the corridor to destinations just off of the corridor, including spaces in the interiors of the adjoining blocks.

Index

Page references in italics indicate figures

For Product Safety Concerns and Information please contact our EU
representative GPSR@taylorandfrancis.com
Taylor & Francis Verlag GmbH, Kaufingerstraße 24, 80331 München, Germany

www.ingramcontent.com/pod-product-compliance
Lightning Source LLC
Chambersburg PA
CBHW080130270326
41926CB00021B/4423